Strange TV

Recent Titles in
Contributions to the Study of Popular Culture

Strange TV

Innovative Television Series from *The Twilight Zone* to *The X-Files*

M. Keith Booker

Contributions to the Study of Popular Culture, Number 77

GREENWOOD PRESS
Westport, Connecticut • London

Library of Congress Cataloging-in-Publication Data

Booker, M. Keith.
   Strange TV : innovative television series from The Twilight Zone to the X-Files /
M. Keith Booker.
     p. cm.—(Contributions to the study of popular culture, ISSN 0198–9871 ; no. 77)
   Includes bibliographical references and index.
   ISBN 0–313–32373–9 (alk. paper)
    1. Television broadcasting—Social aspects. I. Title. II. Series.
PN1992.6.B656   2002
302.23′45—dc21   2002067826

British Library Cataloguing in Publication Data is available.

Library of Congress Catalog Card Number: 2002067826
ISBN: 0–313–32373–9
ISSN: 0198–9871

First published in 2002

Greenwood Press, 88 Post Road West, Westport, CT 06881
An imprint of Greenwood Publishing Group, Inc.
www.greenwood.com

Printed in the United States of America

∞™

The paper used in this book complies with the
Permanent Paper Standard issued by the National
Information Standards Organization (Z39.48–1984).

10 9 8 7 6 5 4 3 2 1

For Amy

Contents

Introduction:
Television and the Novel

In an engaging discussion of the relationship between television and American fiction in the late twentieth century, David Foster Wallace notes the crucial impact of the former on the latter, warning that American writers, while often drawing images and motifs from television, have not taken television "seriously enough as both a disseminator and a definer of the cultural atmosphere we breathe and process" (27). Indeed, Wallace goes on to conclude that American fiction, especially when it is self-consciously postmodern, is "less a 'response to' television culture than a kind of abiding-in-TV" (34).

The particular convergence of television and fiction discussed by Wallace is a distinctively postmodern phenomenon. However, he himself (citing de Tocqueville's comments on the nineteenth-century American affinity for least-common-denominator mass-market spectacles) notes that television's proclivity for commodified images has roots that go deep into the history of American culture. Indeed, phenomena such as Buffalo Bill Cody's Wild West show demonstrate the extent to which many of the strategies of television programming (and marketing) were already well developed by the end of the nineteenth century.[1] In addition to this suggestion that televisual culture does not represent the sudden historical irruption of totally new tendencies in American culture, I want to argue in this volume that the postmodern convergence of television and the novel is at least partly enabled by the fact that television and the novel have many similarities as genres and that critics who regard them as radically different phenomena (usually to the detriment of televisual culture and the elevation of the written word) are missing the strong historical continuity that connects the two genres.

Among other things, a recognition of this continuity suggests that television programming deserves serious critical attention of the kind that has traditionally been devoted to literature. In the following chap-

ters, I present detailed readings of some of what I regard as the most interesting—and most definitively postmodernist—programming that appeared on American television in the second half of the twentieth century. I argue that, by virtue of the social, historical, and technological positioning of the medium itself, *all* television is postmodern. The medium
of television is, in fact, not only inextricable from the broader cultural
phenomenon of postmodernism, but largely constitutive of that phenomenon. Meanwhile, commercial television programs are commodities
and therefore to a great extent interchangeable. I continue to believe,
however, that there is a limit to this interchangeability and that some
programs are more interesting than others. In particular, I focus in this
study on the ways in which certain television programs produce a kind
of cognitive estrangement that encourages viewers to look at the world in
new and different ways, rather than merely act as passive consumers of
the television signal and the consumerist messages that it inevitably carries.

I call such programs "strange TV," both because they stand out as
unusual when compared with the mass of more ordinary programming
and because they produce this cognitive estrangement. I focus on four
specific series: *The Twilight Zone, The Prisoner, Twin Peaks,* and *The X-Files.*
I hope, through these readings, to illuminate both the specific programs
discussed and the phenomenon of postmodernist television as a whole.
In addition, I hope to contribute to the development of a better methodology for the serious critical treatment of the television series as a cultural text. After all, given the unprecedented size of the audiences involved, I think one might make a very convincing argument that television series are the most important cultural texts we have had in the past
half century—or, perhaps, in all of history. Yet television series have received relatively little critical attention, perhaps because critics have felt
that they lack the richness and complexity that, since the long hegemony
of the New Criticism in the 1950s and 1960s, we have come to regard as
the hallmark of genuine artistic achievement.[2]

I hope to counter this trend. Indeed, I might equally well have called
the programs I discuss "good" TV, because I do feel that the four programs on which I focus have a richness of both style and content that
places them well above ordinary television fare. This is not to say that
television's bad critical reputation is entirely undeserved, or that most
television is not pretty awful by almost any standard, but that is not
really a fair criterion by which to judge the medium. After all, most films
and novels are pretty awful as well, and all culture tends to adhere to the
dictates of Sturgeon's Law of cultural production: "90% of everything is
crap." Here, however, television suffers from its own success. Partly because of its much smaller audience penetration, the novel (and, to a
slightly lesser extent, film) tends to be judged by its greatest achievements, not its typical ones, which receive little or no critical attention and

thus pass quickly away, leaving most readers entirely ignorant of their existence. But television has achieved so much more penetration into the everyday lives of viewers that vast numbers of people are familiar with even the worst that television has to offer, especially as some of the worst television programming (*Three's Company*, *The Dukes of Hazzard*, *The A-Team*) has been among the most popular. And, of course, there is a sense in which television is all of a piece, all flowing into and out of the same box and all to a certain extent jumbled up together, especially in the age of remote controls and channel surfing. As a result, all television programming tends to be tarred with pretty much the same critical brush, despite the obvious fact that some programs are better than others, even if different sets of criteria might yield different judgments in this sense.

I should hasten to point out, however, that this study is not a celebration of the grand achievements of American commercial television. In some ways, in fact, my conclusions are particularly pessimistic, suggesting as they do that many of the worst things that critics (especially on the Left) have had to say about television programming (its status as a commodity, its tendency to inculcate habits of economic consumption and political obedience in audiences) apply to the best programming as well as to the worst. However, I do believe that the best television programming offers important indications of the potential of the medium, suggesting that the current baleful condition of television is inherent, not in the medium, but in the particular system that happens to have control of the medium at this particular juncture in history.

Here, I stand with Raymond Williams, who agrees with so many others that television broadcasting "can be diagnosed as a new and powerful form of social integration and control. Many of its main uses can be seen as socially, commercially and at times politically manipulative" (17). At the same time, Williams repeatedly warns us against the technological determinism of confusing the medium with the message. He insists that television programming developed in the way it did not because of properties inherent in the technology, but in response to certain specific social, economic, and political stimuli. For Williams, then, television retains powerful utopian dimensions: change the stimuli and television itself can change.

In making an argument for the utopian potential of television, I want to suggest numerous points of contact between television programming and its cultural predecessors, especially the novel. In particular, I want to argue that many of the most damning diagnoses of television programming (that it is thoroughly commodified, that it manipulates viewers into acquiescence with the prevailing ideology) apply equally well to the novel (the official genre of emergent capitalism and the first fully commodified cultural form), except that television is simply far more effective and powerful than the novel ever was. Here, I will draw a great deal upon the theoretical work of Mikhail Bakhtin, whose descriptions of the novel as a genre also apply, in many ways (and sometimes even more so), to television. After all, Bakhtin's celebration of the dialogic potential of the novel came largely in response to a critical tradition in which the novel was viewed as a substandard, plebeian genre that lacked the literary grandeur of poetry or drama—much in the way that television today is widely regarded as inferior to the novel. I also draw upon the work of critics such as Lennard Davis, who reminds us of the crucial role played by the novel in the transformation of Western society during the bourgeois revolution of the Enlightenment, noting that the novel as a form is inherently designed to purvey bourgeois ideology and that "novels themselves have entered and changed our culture in ways that in fact may not be salutary" (*Resisting Novels* 2).

The increased effectiveness and power of television certainly make it seem more sinister than the novel as a form of social control, but they also suggest a greater utopian potential. Of course, television, especially American commercial television, has a long way to go before it might become some sort of powerful force for progressive social change. American television is, after all, a "vast wasteland." At least (in what has become perhaps the single most often quoted remark ever made about American television) that was the judgment of Commissioner Newton Minow of the Federal Communications Commission (FCC) in a speech delivered at a 1961 meeting of the National Association of Broadcasters. Minow went on to remark that anyone who watches television all day long, from sign-on to sign-off, will observe a procession of violent, stupid, formulaic programming punctuated by an endless stream of "screaming, cajoling, and offending" commercials (qtd. in Barnouw 300). Minow, of course, had his own agenda (he was hoping to gain increased support for government-funded public television), and he also reminded his listeners of the many impressive achievements of television programming. But his diagnosis of American television as a vast wasteland nevertheless set the tone for much subsequent television criticism. Television has become the medium critics love to hate, and the critical commentary on television is filled with descriptions of programming that is (on the one hand) silly, vapid, insipid, and just plain boring, while (on the other hand) also carrying out, in diabolically clever ways, a thorough interpellation of the American population, converting them into a passive and mindless herd of obedient sheep, driven by an urge to consume and conform.

Thus, numerous social commentators, attempting to diagnose the malaise of contemporary American society, end up pointing their fingers at television, or at least at some broader conception of the "media," of which television is clearly the dominant element. For Christopher Lasch, our modern media culture has led to a degradation of our very identities and to the development of a "minimal self" that has trouble distinguishing between fiction and reality. Indeed, our experience of reality is now so filtered through the media that "reality itself is no longer real" (133). For Neil Postman, meanwhile, the image culture of television has led to an overall degradation in the level of public discourse in America. In particular, Postman argues that the emphasis on quick and easy entertainment (at the expense of profundity, complexity, and thoughtfulness) in television programming has "made entertainment itself the natural format for the representation of experience" (*Amusing Ourselves* 87). For Postman television is producing a mindless and entertainment-drugged America somewhat along the lines of the dystopian society depicted in Aldous Huxley's *Brave New World*.

Mark Crispin Miller, one of television's most bitter detractors, draws upon a similarly dystopian (though less apt) analogy in his condemnation of the negative effects of television on American life. In particular, he likens television's conditioning of its viewers to consume and obey to the mind-numbing machinations of the Party (with its ever-present telescreens) of Orwell's *Nineteen Eighty-four* ("Big Brother.") For Miller, television is the perfect medium for the delivery of the ideology of consumer capitalism. Television, he writes, works to "promote consumption as a way of life," seeming, very much like the consumer capitalist system itself, to offer a vast array of choices, thus enhancing our feeling that we are lucky to live in the prosperity and freedom of contemporary America ("Deride" 223). But, despite (or perhaps because of) this active promotion of consumerism, television is rapidly becoming disengaged from material reality, increasingly referring to nothing but itself: "For all its promises of 'choice,' TV is nearly perfect in its emptiness, all but exhausted by the very irony that it uses to protect itself from hostile scrutiny" ("Deride" 225). In this same essay, Miller compares television to a drug, and it is clear that, for critics such as Postman and Miller, television has become the new opiate of the masses (228). Indeed, for Miller, television is quite literally mind-numbing, its content little more than a "sequence of harsh fragments," most of them violent, though the true violence of television, he argues, lies not in the specifics of individual images, but in "the very density and speed of TV overall, the very multiplicity and pace of stimuli; for it is by overloading, overdriving both itself and us that TV disables us, making it hard to think about or even feel what TV shows us—making it hard, perhaps, to think or feel at all" ("Deride" 224).

There is, of course, no reason why television cannot simultaneously be boringly stupid and simplistic on the one hand and diabolically complex and clever on the other. Capitalism itself is that way, as Marx knew long ago. Indeed, much of Miller's project is to take television's stupidity seriously, reading beyond the surface content to uncover and reveal the commercial forces that lie behind the programming, what Fredric Jameson might call television's political unconscious. Meanwhile, one can, in reading Miller on television, sense constant echoes of the indictment of the Western Culture Industry by Max Horkheimer and Theodor Adorno. Indeed, much sophisticated criticism of television has followed in the footsteps of Adorno and Horkheimer, who, writing before television had become an important element of Western mass culture, already saw that culture as a mind-numbing barrage of banalities designed precisely to keep the brains of audiences occupied with meaningless stimuli, thus rendering audience members incapable of complex, critical thought.

For example, Julian Stallabrass works very much in the tradition of Horkheimer and Adorno in his view of television as part of a larger system of commodified mass culture (he also looks at such diverse phenomena as photography, automobiles, advertising, and the Internet). Thus, Stallabrass begins his discussion with the reminder that he is addressing "a mass-produced culture which is bought and sold. The culture's status as a commodity is the most fundamental fact about it, deeply affecting its form and inherent ideology" (3). For Stallabrass, this commodification has important (and sinister) consequences. He characterizes contemporary mass culture (including television) as an endless stream of "mild, happy brain-fodder." But, for Stallabrass, this weightless culture has heavy consequences, working in direct support of a world economic system that "denies the great majority of people the necessary means to live a decent existence" (11). Stallabrass is absolutely correct, of course, yet his disdain for television prevents him from analyzing actual television programming in any detail, perhaps because he feels that television programming is so thoroughly commodified that one program is as good (or bad) as another.

Similarly, in the most extended published analysis of the actual process through which the culture industry decides which programs to broadcast (and when), Todd Gitlin notes the basic banality of programming, emphasizing the status of television programs as commodities. For Gitlin, all cultural products under modern capitalism tend to become "supermarket goods," but television, with its high cost of production and distribution (and equally high potential profits), is especially prone to a strategy in which it "automatically caters to a hypothetical least common denominator—or dips below it" (28, 30). After all, Gitlin points out, television networks "aim to create not purposeful or coherent or true or beautiful shows, but audiences" (56). If Gitlin sometimes thus seems to tend toward the view that television is insipid and stupid because that is what audiences demand, Stallabrass makes clear his view that television, far from simply responding to the poor tastes of viewers, does a great deal to determine those tastes. Thus, "a vicious circle is established in which broadcasters' falling expectations of people's attention span and general knowledge contribute to their decline" (191).

Interestingly, Gitlin, like Stallabrass, pays relatively little attention to the style or content of actual television programs, concentrating instead on the general principles according to which these programs are conceived and produced. Miller pays a bit more attention to individual programming in some of his work, though he has a tendency to cite examples of television's worst programming in order to prove his point about the sinister emptiness of television. Indeed, Miller seems to find it difficult to imagine that television might be any different than it already is, instead offering as a utopian alternative to contemporary commercial television only a few passing nostalgic references to a "pretelevisual moment" ("Deride" 226). In particular, Miller privileges the written word, though he also finds film and radio preferable to television, largely because he finds those media generically diverse, while in television, all forms have collapsed into a bland homogeneity of spectacle.[3]

James Twitchell agrees almost entirely with Lasch, Postman, Gitlin, and Miller about the emptiness and vulgarity of most television programming. However, he believes that they confuse causes with effects, arguing that the baleful condition of American television is the result, not the cause, of the larger ills of American society. For Twitchell, sounding a bit like a superannuated (but hipper and wittier) Ortega y Gasset, it is not television that critics should be bashing, "but rather the political system that allows such discourse. That system is Democracy, the supposed will of the majority. Show business, like politics, is an expression of that will" (258). Though carefully avoiding Marxist terminology, Twitchell also admits an economic dimension to this rule by the bad taste of the majority, concluding that "the triumph of vulgarity is the application of the marketplace to taste" (269).

Having thus attributed the state of contemporary culture to democracy and capitalism, Twitchell not surprisingly feels that the vulgarity of this culture is hardly unprecedented, even though he does grant that television has a unique and unprecedented power. Pointing, among other things, to a long legacy of concerns about the vulgarity and tastelessness of novels, he thus notes that "the concerns of many television critics today are the same as they were for the Victorian critics of popular print, to wit: the medium corrupts consciousness, the work ethic, natural desires, concentration, and culture itself" (250).

Here Twitchell resembles Davis, who reminds us that the rise of the novel of the seventeenth and eighteenth centuries was the beginning of the movement toward high-tech media of the kind bemoaned by Postman and Lasch, making the novel the beginning of "the process that got us to the world of the 'minimal self' in the first place" (6). After all, Don Quixote and Emma Bovary are the great forerunners of those postmodern subjects who, for Lasch, confuse fiction with reality. Davis, to an extent, focuses on technologies for rapid dissemination of information in seeing the novel as the forerunner of contemporary electronic media. Indeed, Davis, in *Factual Fictions*, argues that a blurring of the boundary between fact and fiction (such as that discussed by Lasch in relation to modern media culture) was crucial to the discourse that gave rise to the novel in the seventeenth and eighteenth centuries. Twitchell, however, focuses on audiences. For him, "the history of all modern media has been similar. As the economies of mass production give greater access to those previously excluded—the young, the unsophisticated, and the aggressive—the stories demanded and produced become progressively more crude and 'vulgar'" (260).

Twitchell, I think, is astute in realizing that contemporary mass culture, particularly television, operates in much the same way as its predecessors throughout the capitalist era. He is also surely right in thereby attributing the real problem to the capitalist system. On the other hand, Twitchell seems disturbingly elitist when he takes it for granted that the masses have bad taste and that any system that lets more people have a say in the nature of cultural production will have a more vulgar culture. Twitchell's argument that the market-driven culture of capitalist democracy responds all too well to mass taste is almost indisputable. However, he is surely wrong in failing to grant the possibility that mass taste is itself largely a product of this same capitalist democratic system and that, in other systems, mass taste might be very different.

Twitchell does, however, grant that someday, in some unspecified way, we might come out the other end of our descent into vulgarity and find that "the untranscendent, banal, sensational, democratic, immediate, trashy, tribalizing, and unifying force of the Vulgar" might ultimately lead to something better than we have any right to expect (274). Many other critics of television and other forms of contemporary mass culture have felt the same, thus aligning themselves less with Horkheimer and Adorno and more with Williams or Walter Benjamin, who saw so much potential in modern mass media technology. However, the attempts of these critics to find promise in contemporary televisual culture, no matter how seemingly bleak the offerings of that culture, typically grant far more intelligence and creativity to television audiences than does Twitchell. Even critics who have attempted to find more positive potential in television have tended to grant that the programming itself is either mindless, or directly aligned with the ideology of official power, or both. Thus, these critics have again avoided extensive critical analysis of specific programs, but have instead concentrated on the ways in which audiences might have opportunities to resist the encoded messages of television programming, reading against the grain to produce subversive readings of even the most insipid (or sinister) programs.

John Fiske, probably the most influential of these audience-response theorists, envisions a utopian situation in which viewers take their principal pleasure from resisting the dominant messages of the programming they watch on television, asserting their own individual identities in opposition to the roles that are thrust upon them by the official messages of the programs. Nobody, Fiske, argues, enjoys being a "cultural dope" (19). Of course, Fiske here assumes (somewhat questionably, I think) that audiences who fantasize about, say, living the glamorous and affluent lives that they typically see on television will realize that they are being dopes and will consequently reject such lifestyles. In any case, Fiske, too, pays relatively little attention to actual programs, locating all of the interesting action in the responses of resisting viewers.

Fiske's approach, in fact, makes the actual content of specific programs almost irrelevant, because his central argument is that, in order to achieve the broad audiences required of commercial television, all programs must be designed to allow a wide variety of interpretive responses, thus opening a space for readings that challenge the "dominant ideology," with which he grants that commercial television programming is principally aligned. Fiske's notion of the potential multivocality of television (reminiscent of Bakhtin's vision of the dialogic multiplicity of the novel) is probably accurate. However, his confidence in the inherently democratic nature of television as a medium may be a bit overly optimistic. Fiske sees multiple viewer (he likes the term "reader") responses to television as arising from the varied social experiences of individual viewers, but pays too little attention to the extent to which that experience consists of watching television, so that responses to television are, in fact, conditioned by television itself.

Further, Fiske makes the common mistake of assuming that the "dominant ideology" is monological and thereby automatically threatened by any sort of multivocality. What he fails to take into account is the fact that in America (or any capitalist society) the dominant bourgeois ideology is itself extremely flexible and multivoiced. Thus, Terry Eagleton points out that it is difficult to see plurality and multivocality as inherently subversive of capitalism, given that "capitalism is the most pluralistic order history has ever known, restlessly transgressing boundaries and dismantling oppositions, pitching together diverse life-forms and continually overflowing the measure" (*Illusions* 133). There is, in short, little reason to believe that television programs are at all subversive of the dominant ideology in America simply because they allow a range of interpretations. Specific interpretations might be potentially subversive, but surely the nature of such interpretations is a function not merely of productive audience response, but also of the form and content of specific programs.

David Buxton, departing from the central tendency in recent television studies, attempts to analyze this form and content. In his notable and extremely useful book-length study, *From* The Avengers *to* Miami Vice, Buxton employs a Marxist interpretive framework (especially influenced by Pierre Macherey) in an attempt to determine the "ideological projects" of various television series. Rejecting the reader-response approach of Fiske, Buxton concentrates on the programs themselves, arguing that television series are typically constructed in ways that disguise and attempt to make invisible their ideological underpinnings—

something that one might, of course, say about all products of bourgeois ideology, which quite universally works by declaring itself as natural, non-ideological, and common-sensical. Buxton attempts to unveil the ideology behind television programming and "to show that the strains and contradictions of a television series can be publicly engaged with at the very level it refuses to acknowledge—its own ideological premises" (19).

In order to do so, Buxton does pay significant attention to individual series and even to readings of individual episodes. However, he is really more interested in a general examination of the series as a form than in the interpretation and analysis of individual series. Moving toward a general taxonomy of the television series (he divides the various series he discusses into "the human nature series," "the pop series," and "the police series"), Buxton ultimately pays relatively little attention to specific programs. Approximately eleven pages of his book are devoted to *The Avengers*, while approximately twenty pages are given to a discussion of *Miami Vice*. Most of the other numerous series discussed by Buxton are treated within four or five pages of text, though he grants that longer treatments would be desirable and bemoans the fact that "the time has not yet come when particular series can be given academic monograph treatment" (16). At the same time, Buxton concludes his study by characterizing *Miami Vice* as a sort of failed last-ditch effort to combine and thus reinvigorate dying forms. Indeed, he sees the fictional television series, in the mid-1980s, as possibly being "a fictional form that has come to the end of the road," soon to be replaced by pure spectacles such as music videos (160).

Several post–*Miami Vice* series, including *Twin Peaks, The X-Files*, and (most recently) *The Sopranos* (not to mention such astonishing achievements as the 1986 British miniseries, *The Singing Detective*, a *Miami Vice* contemporary) have tended to suggest that Buxton's report of the death of television fiction is greatly exaggerated and that the fictional television series is still a form to be reckoned with. Moreover, since the publication of Buxton's book, several series (mostly those, such as *Miami Vice, Twin Peaks, The Simpsons*, and *The X-Files*, that one might consider postmodern) have received a reasonable amount of concentrated critical attention, including the publication of the kind of dedicated academic monographs that Buxton thought impossible. However, critical discussions even of these series remain extremely meager compared, say, to the critical attention given to the postmodernist novels of Salman Rushdie or Thomas Pynchon. I do not, however, think that this lack of attention to critical analysis of individual television series arises from the fact that such series are simply not interesting enough to repay critical attention. In fact, my own experience in preparing this study has been that critical analysis of television series is difficult not because there is nothing to say about them, but because there is far too much. Television series are hard to discuss critically not because they are too simplistic as cultural phenomena, but because they are too complex.

Part of this complexity arises from the fact that the intertextual connection between individual programs and the overall environment of broadcast television is probably more important and extensive than the same dialogue between individual novels and the context of novel publishing. There is, after all, a reason, why so many astute critics have been more interested in television as a general phenomenon than in individual programs. The early-1990s MTV series *Beavis and Butt-head* is an excellent case in point here. Notorious as an example of the stupidity of American commercial television programming, *Beavis and Butt-head* is in fact quite structurally complex and highly dialogic.[4] Crucial to the effect of the program, for example, is its location on MTV, a network that, in its entirety, is quite often cited as the quintessential example of postmodern television.[5] The program consists of two basic types of segments. In one type of segment, the eponymous ill-educated and ill-behaved teenage protagonists pursue various mindless endeavors, typically either in an effort to torment various figures of adult authority by wreaking miscellaneous destruction or in an attempt to "score" and thus lose their troublesome virginity. Actually, however, Beavis and Butt-head seem to spend most of their time on the couch in Butt-head's dilapidated home (there is no sign of parental supervision), watching television. They are, being members of the MTV generation, particularly drawn to music videos, and the second major type of segment in their program consists simply of embedded music videos, accompanied by the irreverent running commentary of the two main characters. Their basic critical strategy is to divide videos into the categories of those that "suck" (usually because they seem to have some intellectual content, including a reliance on "words") and those that are "cool" (usually because they feature images of destructive violence, salacious displays of female flesh, or both).

As Kellner notes, *Beavis and Butt-head* immerses itself in media culture, including an engagement with a number of direct precedents, including perhaps most obviously the "Wayne's World" segments from *Saturday Night Live*, which ultimately became two feature films (*Media Culture* 145). Meanwhile, the commentary of Beavis and Butt-head on the videos they are watching is merely a direct dramatization of the dialogue of the entire program with the genre of the music video, a cultural form essentially invented (and certainly popularized) by MTV, which, in its initial years, used videos as its principal programming. *Beavis and Butt-head* is thus highly intertextual, engaging in an unusually extensive dialogue with its media context. Meanwhile, the program switches from the narrative segments to the video segments without warning, using the style of rapid transition that was first popularized by MTV music videos. Add in the fact that these segments are themselves periodically interrupted (again without warning or gradual transition) by commercials, and the show becomes almost as fragmented and potentially confusing as the avant-garde art of the first half of the twentieth century. Few viewers, however, are likely to be confused, because the MTV audience is accustomed to quick-cut editing and has thus already learned to follow rapid non sequitur transitions without difficulty.

Indeed, one of the most interesting aspects of *Beavis and Butt-head* is the way its protagonists, depicted as mindless and destructive, are nevertheless also ironically presented as representative members of the MTV audience — or at least of that audience as it has been perceived by some critics. The show makes clear, in fact, that the protagonists have been rendered so spectacularly stupid largely by watching programming of precisely the type that is presented on MTV. The point, presumably, is that viewers will laugh because they know very well that watching MTV has not rendered *them* spectacularly stupid. Stallabrass thus evinces *Beavis and Butt-head* as a crucial example of the move toward "reflexive irony" in contemporary television, a move by which television "preempts criticism of itself by using it as an important element of entertainment" (203).[6] In the case of *Beavis and Butt-head*, of course, this self-criticism invites viewers to play along, announcing an awareness that MTV viewers are far too hip and media-savvy to be influenced by television anyway. The actual butt of the joke, then, is naïve critics who would complain about the representation of unacceptable behavior on the series, fearing that it will have a bad influence on young viewers.

The intertextual structure of *Beavis and Butt-head* is particularly postmodern, showing the series as constructed from bits and pieces of popular culture. However, various forms of complex intertextuality are central to the phenomenon of television as a whole. As Fiske notes, television programming has a particularly close relationship with "secondary texts" that comment on it (*TV Guide* would be a prime example) as well as with "tertiary texts" produced through discussions of the medium among audience members (117–27). For Fiske, this intertextuality greatly enhances the polysemy of television, helping to produce meanings that escape control of the text itself. But, even within television programming there are complex forms of intertextuality. For example, episodic series that feature continuing characters and scenarios (and sometimes, continuing plot lines) have their own special complexities in the way individual episodes interact intertextually with other episodes. Indeed, one could argue that the complex interrelationships among different episodes of a given series, combined with the dialogue between any given series and the larger televisual context, is one of the crucial distinguishing features of television as a cultural phenomenon.

Among other things, these complex interrelationships are reminiscent of the vast intricacies of the capitalist system itself, adding another layer to the way in which television culture directly mirrors the system that produces it. In any case, this kind of intertextuality greatly complicates the critical discussion of any individual episode of a television series, forcing the critic to keep in mind, at least to some degree, all of the other episodes as well. Again, however, this situation is not unique to television. One immediately thinks of genre fiction series such as Edgar Rice Burroughs's Tarzan or Martian novels. But the various installments of Honoré de Balzac's mighty novel sequence, *The Human Comedy*, also interact with each other somewhat in the same manner as the episodes of a television series, standing alone but also combining with one another to create an overarching view of the totality of French bourgeois society in the first half of the twentieth century. Indeed, the inherent intertextuality of individual television programs does not make them impervious to analysis any more than the intertextuality of the novel as a genre makes it impossible critically to comment upon individual novels. Thus, critics have had no trouble commenting on the novels of Balzac, even though they engage in extensive dialogues with one another and with their overall cultural context.

The Human Comedy may be a special case in this sense, but Bakhtin has seen the inherent dialogic intertextuality of the novel as one of the defining characteristics of the genre. After all, it was not for nothing that Julia Kristeva, coining the term "intertextuality," attributed to Bakhtin her notion of every text as the absorption and transformation of other texts. For Bakhtin, the novel, more than any other genre, is able to incorporate the heteroglossia of the social world, reflecting the diversity of society through the dialogic versatility of its own style and language. For Bakhtin, "diversity of voices and heteroglossia enter the novel and organize themselves within it into a structured artistic system. This constitutes the distinguishing feature of the novel as a genre" (*Dialogic* 300). But the languages in a novel have specific sociopolitical connotations as well, each language representing an entire worldview. Bakhtin's key concept of heteroglossia refers not just to the words used by different groups in society, but to the entire social, cultural, and ideological context in which those words are used. In the novel, the languages interact in a dynamic way, typically with the development of an opposition between "high" languages and "low." The dialogue in the novel thus dramatizes ideological struggles in the society as a whole.

Bakhtin at times falls into the trap of seeing the novel as inherently antiauthoritarian because of its ability to incorporate a variety of voices and points of view, a vision that might hold in, say, the medieval Europe of Rabelais, but one that certainly does not apply to the complex and multiple ideology of modern bourgeois societies. But Bakhtin also emphasizes that this ability to incorporate various points of view gives the novel an especially close contact with the historical world, contributing to its ability continually to change and grow as a genre, keeping pace with changes in the outside world and maintaining a powerful sense of "contemporaneity," reminiscent of Fiske's discussions of the "nowness" of television (145). For Bakhtin, "The novel comes into contact with the spontaneity of the inconclusive present; this is what keeps the genre from congealing" (27). The novel is therefore "a genre that is ever questing, ever examining itself and subjecting its established forms to review. Such, indeed, is the only possibility open to a genre that structures itself in a zone of direct contact with developing reality" (*Dialogic* 39).[7]

For Bakhtin, the evolving nature of the novel has to do not only with the genre's contact with social reality, but also with its ongoing dialogue with other novels, as well as with other literary and even nonliterary genres. The novel as a genre is "both critical and self-critical, one fated to revise the fundamental concepts of literariness and poeticalness domi-nant at the time" (*Dialogic* 10). For Bakhtin, the novel is able to incorpo-rate other genres and engage in dialogue with them (often through par-ody), while still remaining a novel. "The novel parodies other genres; it exposes the conventionality of their forms and their language; it squeezes out some genres and incorporates others into its own peculiar structure, reformulating and re-accentuating them" (5). Indeed, for Bakhtin, the novel is so flexible and so capable of mutating itself in response to exter-nal historical circumstances that it becomes not so much a traditional genre, with established forms and characteristics, as an ideological ten-dency toward the centrifugal celebration of openness and diversity. In this sense, television might even be called a "novel," or at least a novel-ized form. Indeed, Robert Stam goes so far as to describe television as "an electronic microcosm, a contemporary version of Bakhtin's omnivo-rous 'novel,' which reflects and relays, distorts and amplifies, the ambi-ent heteroglossia" (221).

Meanwhile, Bakhtin's comments about the novel would seem to make it the ideal literary representation of bourgeois ideology, which centrally privileges both diversity and innovation. Indeed, the novel is quite gen-erally accepted (Watt's *The Rise of the Novel* is the classic text here) as the bourgeois genre *par excellence*, having risen to literary dominance in tan-dem with the rise of the bourgeoisie as the new ruling class in Europe from the seventeenth to the nineteenth centuries. Of course, Bakhtin wants to make larger claims for the novel, tracing it back to the ancient Greeks, on the one hand, and insisting on its unlimited potential for fu-ture evolution on the other. In short, Bakhtin wants to argue that the novel transcends bourgeois ideology, thus, among other things, making it a candidate for use as a literary tool in the project of building socialism in the then-new Soviet Union. Even Bakhtin, however, grants that the novel has an especially close connection to the bourgeois cultural revolu-tion of the modern era. For Bakhtin, the novel has experienced several eras of strength (including classical Greece), but he admits that the novel emerges "with special force and clarity in the second half of the eight-eenth century" (5).

The close connection between the novel and bourgeois ideology (a connection explored at length by Davis in *Resisting Novels*) helps to explain the fact that most of Bakhtin's comments about the novel seem to apply so well to television programming, which is the central cultural instantiation of bourgeois ideology in its late capitalist phase. Among other things, the relevance of Bakhtin's work to television suggests not only an underlying continuity between the novel and television, but an even more basic continuity of bourgeois ideology through the various stages of the historical development of capitalism. Little wonder, then, that the novels of Balzac (which Marxist critics from Engels on have regarded as the paradigm of bourgeois literature) have so much in common with television series.

If the inherent intertextuality and variable format of television do not necessarily make it fundamentally different from the novel, it is also the case that the status of television as commodified culture does not make it fundamentally different from predecessors such as the novel and film. As the three dominant media of the capitalist era, the novel, film, and television are all, first and foremost, capitalist enterprises designed to generate profits. As such, all three are commodified, and the characteristics of all three are largely determined by market forces, though these forces themselves have changed considerably over time. For example, it is certainly the case that the late consumer capitalism of the end of the twentieth century differs in many particulars from the emergent capitalism of the eighteenth century, but then consumerism of one kind or another has been crucial to capitalism from the beginning. Indeed, as McKendrick et al. indicate, many of the characteristics of our modern consumer society—characteristics that have obviously conditioned the evolution of television programming—actually arose in the eighteenth century, during the period of the rise of the novel. Indeed, the novel, as the first mass-produced literary genre, was the first genre to be conceived specifically as a commodity. As a result, numerous aspects of the novel (the relatively straightforward prose style, the emphasis on plot and character, the mode of realism itself) evolved largely in response to market forces and to the demands of readers—whose taste was largely determined by reading novels, again creating the vicious circle noted by Stallabrass in relation to television. Ian Watt, for example, notes that the initial ill repute in which the novel was held was closely connected to its perceived status as commodified culture: "The novel was widely regarded as a typical example of the debased kind of writing by which the booksellers pandered to the reading public" (54). Watt goes on to discuss the ways in which various characteristics of the novel (including even such basic attributes as being written in prose rather than verse) were largely driven by market forces, though his major point is more ideological than directly economic: that the novel as a form grew to reflect the point of view of the emergent middle class.

In short, the commodified nature of television programming does not make television fundamentally different from predecessors such as the novel; instead, it merely identifies television as the culmination of a long historical process of the commodification of culture (along with everything else) that began with the novel. Of course, novelists themselves have long complained of the commodification of culture in which their own works participated. By the early nineteenth century, Balzac was able to make the gradual commodification of everything in bourgeois society one of the great themes of his fiction. Indeed, one of his most important works, the three-part *Lost Illusions* (1837–43), focuses specifically on the commodification of literature—with consequences that sound suspiciously similar to the complaints of critics such as Stallabrass, Gitlin, and Miller about television. In the novel, a young and idealistic Lucien Chardon/de Rubempré travels from provincial France to Paris with dreams of being a great poet and producing pure art. Instead, he finds himself caught in a web of market forces in which the job of the artist is not the creation of beauty for the spiritual enrichment humanity, but profits for the economic enrichment of publishers. Under these circumstances, books are "like cotton bonnets to haberdashers, a commodity to be bought cheap and sold dear" (202). What's worse, the quest for quick profits tends to make literary merit a definite liability. To Paris's publishers,

a book is merely a capital risk. The finer it is, the less chance it has of selling. Every exceptional man rises above the masses, and therefore his success is in direct ratio to the time needed for his work to prove its value. No publisher is willing to wait for that. Today's book must be sold out tomorrow. Following that policy, publishers refuse substantial books which can only gradually obtain the serious approval they need. (277)

The similarity here to common complaints about television programming, where sophisticated programs are frowned upon because they might take too long to find an audience, is obvious.

Commodification is also the key motif in *Madame Bovary*, the most important novel of Gustave Flaubert, Balzac's great successor. Here, a young and idealistic Emma Bovary (again, a native of provincial France) finds herself caught in a web of desire (largely produced by her reading of novels) so confusing that she finds it impossible to distinguish between her search for erotic satisfaction through adulterous affairs and her search for material satisfaction through the purchase of commodities on credit. This confusion is, of course, no surprise: commodified desires, like all commodities, are entirely interchangeable. Thus, for Emma, "the desires of the flesh, the longing for money, and the melancholy of passion all blended into one suffering," a suffering that is itself thoroughly commodified (77).

As Jameson has suggested, the novels of Balzac and Flaubert can be taken as signposts along the historical road toward commodification of everything, leading to the work of Theodore Dreiser, whom Jameson describes Dreiser in *The Political Unconscious* as a sort of modern American Balzac whose work differs from that of his French predecessor primarily because in the half century that lies between them "*bovarysme* has fallen, and the congealment of language, fantasy, and desire into Flaubertian *bêtise* and Flaubertian cliché transmutes Balzacian longing into ... tawdriness ... a tawdriness that Dreiser's language ambiguously represents and reflects all at once" (159). One might then add television as a fourth marker along this road, presumably signaling the completion of the process, though it is also the case that Balzac, Flaubert, and Dreiser each in turn had already complained about the thorough commodification saturating their own societies.

According to the narrative, *The Human Comedy* and *The X-Files* are not located in unrelated and incommensurate cultural worlds, but at different points in the same continuous historical process. Balzac writes at a moment when the gradual commodification of every aspect of human existence is only just becoming visible; *The X-Files* appears at a time when this commodification is essentially complete and accepted as a given fact. Georg Lukács, writing in the late 1930s, captured some of this phenomenon in his appreciation of Balzac as a great realist who honestly portrayed the revolutionary victory of the emergent European bourgeoisie over the traditions and values of the *ancien régime*, however horrified Balzac was by the implications of this victory and however much he himself would have liked to return to the prerevolutionary era. For Lukács, the work of Balzac is particularly powerful and dynamic because it captures a historical moment in which the victory of capitalism is not yet total. The ultimate commodification of everything—including humans and human relationships—is not yet complete in Balzac's world and is not yet accepted by his characters as a given fact of modern life. Thus, even in a work such as *Lost Illusions*, that great epic of the commodification of literature itself, "the fact that the spirit has become a commodity to be bought and sold is not yet accepted as a matter of course and the spirit is not yet reduced to the dreary greyness of a machine-made article" (Lukács, *Studies* 59–60). However, Lukács further notes that the opportunity offered by Balzac's particular postrevolutionary historical moment would not last long: "Balzac depicted the original accumulation of capital in the ideological sphere, while his successors, even Flaubert, the greatest of them, already accepted as an accomplished fact that all human values were included in the commodity structure of capitalism" (*Studies* 63).

For Lukács, capitalism had pretty well run its course by the late nineteenth century and was (or so he at least hoped) in its death throes in the Depression years of the 1930s, about to be swept from the historical stage

by worldwide socialist revolution. He could not, of course, have anticipated that capitalism (aided by a world war) was about to mutate itself
into a new form that would make the superficial commodification at
work in French society in the days of Flaubert look like a mere rehearsal
for the more radical and penetrating commodification to come in the
days of post–World War II consumer capitalism. Television, of course,
has been crucial to the latter, but the novel was crucial to the commodification of culture from the seventeenth through the nineteenth centuries,
and nostalgic visions of the good old days when people read books instead of watching television are based on a fundamental blindness to this
basic parallel. Television doesn't do anything fundamentally different
from the what the novel has always done — it just does it more effectively.

If the commercialization of television culture is really not so different
from that of the novel or of film, then it nevertheless remains true that
critical expressions of horror at this commercialization have been particularly vehement in the case of television. Part of this vehemence is no
doubt due simply to the far greater audience penetration of television,
though I would also argue that the low repute in which television has
conventionally been held by critics is closely connected with the fact that
television emerged as an important cultural force at the peak of the Cold
War, that is, at a time when mass culture was particularly suspect because the "masses" were inevitably associated with communism, and
communism was associated with unmitigated evil. This horror of the
masses was so thoroughgoing that it infected even the work of vaguely
left-leaning American critics such as the New York Intellectuals who
voiced a mandarin contempt for all aspects of mass culture while making
a central contribution to the glorification and canonization of modernism.
Meanwhile, the excesses of the new television medium seemed to many
to bear out the most woeful aspects of the "Culture Industry" that had
recently been bemoaned on the Left by Horkheimer and Adorno as one
of the most pernicious products of Western capitalism. Indeed, the explosive growth of television in the 1950s was part of an explosive growth
of consumer capitalism itself, a phenomenon that brought unprecedented
material prosperity to Americans but also led to an unprecedented commodification of virtually every aspect of American life. Any critique of
this commodification from the Left also inevitably included a component
critical of television.

Television thus caught it from both sides; it was perceived as representative of both the debased collectivism of socialism and the dehumanizing commodification of capitalism. Meanwhile, just as leftist critics
have warned of the inherent tendency of television as a medium to produce a passive audience, obedient to authority, critics on the Right have
made the content of television programming a favorite target in their
jeremiads concerning the moral decline and decay of "traditional values"
in American society in the late twentieth century. Such complaints are

dangerous because they divert attention from more genuine social problems (such as the growing economic gap between the rich and the poor). To my mind, these complaints are also patently silly, because they ignore the fact that "American" values have been antitraditional ever since the nation's birth in revolution. Indeed, the values of capitalism itself, with its central emphasis on innovation and change, are antitraditional.

If right-wing complaints about the "immorality" of television programming are thus more properly addressed to capitalism as a system, it is perhaps not surprising that such complaints have also been launched against the novel and film, the other two great capitalist cultural innovations. Complaints about the possible bad effects of the behavior depicted in novels were legion in the eighteenth century, as when no less a cultural authority than Samuel Johnson, who warned in one of his *Rambler* articles (No. 4) that novels, so popular with young readers, were "the entertainment of minds unfurnished with ideas, and therefore easily susceptible of impression" (11). In particular, he warned that this susceptibility might lead readers (especially young ones) to admire (and thus, presumably, emulate) the vices that were depicted in realist novels, which tended, he claimed, to "confound the colours of right and wrong, and instead of helping to settle their boundaries, mix them with so much art, that no common mind is able to disunite them" (14).

Similar criticisms were leveled against film in its early days, especially by elitist observers who were horrified as much by the unwashed working-class audiences of early films as by the films themselves. As Robert Sklar notes, the "protection of American youth" from bad influences was typically cited as the "rationale" behind "dire warnings about the baneful effects of movies" (79). This youth theme echoed Johnson's warnings about the novel in a particularly direct way, though Sklar insists that it was largely a smokescreen designed to obscure the real (class-based) motivation behind such criticisms of the immorality of film, which threatened, in the minds of elitist critics, to overwhelm the Arnoldian legacy of Western High Culture with this new, debased, culture of the masses: "Since the enemies of movies could deal only indirectly or covertly with the issue of class conflict, they made their case on the ground of protecting the young" (123).

Of course, the novel continued its triumphant march to literary hegemony despite Johnson's complaints, just as film charged into its golden age in the 1930s despite the warnings against its bad influences in the teens and twenties. The same was true of television, of course, and the new medium was easily powerful enough to steamroll all criticism leveled against it and to move forward on its inexorable path to global cultural domination. Meanwhile, reminders that various warnings about the bad effects of television echo earlier warnings about the novel reinforce my belief that there is no fundamental reason why television series cannot be approached using many of the same critical tools that have formerly been used for the criticism of novels or of films, as long as one keeps in mind certain basic differences in these various phenomena.

Of course, formalist techniques such as the New Criticism, as well as much poststructuralist criticism, are ill-suited to the discussion of television because of their strong emphasis on language. Of course, such techniques are not well suited to the novel, either, and have always gotten their best results with poetry. Still, despite its supposed demise in recent years, New Criticism still exerts a strong influence in the American academy, where its long years of dominance during the Cold War produced criteria of literary excellence that still tend to be defined in terms of a linguistic richness and complexity that can only be teased out by detailed close reading. The same kind of close reading does not do justice to television for at least two different reasons. For one thing, this close reading focuses on language, while television's richest resource is the image. For another, New Critical close reading of the "words on the page" cannot adequately account for the inherent richness of television intertextuality.

This richness is closely connected to another of the most important obstacles to the detailed critical analysis of television series: the sheer volume of material involved in examining even one series. Indeed, the amount of "text" involved in a series such as *The X-Files* (which comprises more than 200 episodes — plus a related feature film — through nine seasons) is almost mind-boggling, roughly the equivalent of nearly 100 feature-length films or the entire *Human Comedy* of Balzac. Some episodes of *The X-Files* are more interesting than others (just as some of Balzac's novels are more interesting than others), but many of them are worthy of detailed critical discussion. In the early days of television criticism (when many critical trends were established that still have influence today), this complexity was exacerbated by the fact that television programs were fleeting phenomena, broadcast at a certain time, then gone, though perhaps reappearing as a rerun at some unspecified later date. This situation made such programs difficult to study closely and carefully, especially in comparison to other episodes, which could not be consulted at will, as in the case of printed books. In addition, this situation made detailed critical discussion of specific individual programs seem almost pointless because readers of the criticism would be unable to consult the primary texts being discussed.

The widespread availability of relatively inexpensive videocassette recorders by the beginning of the 1980s changed all of this, of course, making the close critical examination of individual television programs much more feasible. Moreover, especially after the popularization of the DVD format (which greatly facilitates the distribution of large volumes of recorded material) in the late 1990s, many prominent television series (especially those with dedicated "cult" audiences) are now becoming commercially available in recorded form, producing a corpus of fixed texts upon which critics can comment with some assurance that audiences will be able to consult the original works being discussed if they so desire. Among other things, this phenomenon, taking television fully into the age of mechanical reproduction in the sense discussed long ago by Walter Benjamin, makes television more like written culture (including the novel) and less like traditional oral culture.[8] In fact, the mechanical reproduction of television texts adds an important new wrinkle to the critical discussion of the opposition between written and oral culture, suggesting that, in many ways, the opposition is really one between the reproducibility of recorded cultural performances and the fleetingness of live, unrecorded culture.

In addition, the development of new recording technologies introduces further complications, allowing television series to be viewed in a number of different ways, calling into question the very definition of the artifact under consideration. My study of *The X-Files* is again a good case in point. While gathering information for this project, I watched every episode of the ninth season as broadcast on the Fox network on Sunday nights. Actually, I picked up this weekly viewing early in the eighth season, though there I began my weekly viewing with the fourth episode, along the way catching up on the first three episodes by borrowing the videotapes made of them by a local X-Phile graduate student.[9] Moreover, I only watched a handful of episodes as they were actually broadcast, switching in February to taping the episodes for later viewing.

This taping allowed me to view the episodes on my own schedule and also more carefully, rewinding where necessary and fast-forwarding through the commercials. Besides, taping *The X-Files* allowed me to watch *The Sopranos* on HBO during the time slot in which *The X-Files* was broadcast from February, 2001, until the end of the season in May. And I typically then watched the taped *X-File* episode immediately after *The Sopranos*, so that the two series are probably forever interlinked in my mind in all sorts of ways. But this fact merely serves to illustrate the complex and fragmented intertextuality of the television viewing process. *The X-Files* (like all programs) never exists in isolation, but as part of a stream of programming on Fox and the other commercial networks, not to mention the dozen, or even hundreds of cable networks now in existence.

Moreover, viewing episodes on tape, complete with rewinding and fast-forwarding, is a qualitatively and quantitatively different experience from viewing a live broadcast. In the meantime, I have watched dozens of episodes from earlier seasons broadcast in syndication on the F/X network during the past few months, some on tape and some as they were actually broadcast. And, during this same period, I watched the first three seasons straight through in sequential order in the sleek new DVD versions (with the commercials entirely removed) that were released as I was working on this project.

Thus, I have viewed the different episodes in a complex and scrambled chronology and in a variety of formats. Further, in terms of sheer volume, I saw, in the course of eighteen months, over 190 different episodes of *The X-Files*, many of them multiple times. Most of these I saw in a period of only eight months. This is surely different from the experience of the presumed "normal" viewer, who sees one episode a week, 25 or so weeks a year and at whom the show was initially directed. Further, I no doubt watched the series in ways that were conditioned by my search for elements that I could comment upon in a critical way, whereas this "normal" viewer presumably watches primarily for entertainment.

Such considerations make television criticism especially problematic, but they do not make it impossible. Nor do they necessarily make television criticism radically different from the criticism of more traditional literary forms, such as the novel. Novels, too, can exist in a variety of formats (such as hardback versus paperback), with different qualities of paper, different typefaces, and so on. Indeed, novels can now be read in either printed or electronic form, and (having recently read *Lost Illusions* and *A Harlot High and Low* on a handheld "Pocket PC" device) I can attest that the experience of reading electronically differs in many ways from the experience of reading a printed book. This phenomenon raises other questions as well, in particular blurring the boundary between written texts and digitally recorded performances. Is a novel, stored as a stream of 1's and 0's on a hard disk or handheld PC, still a "written" text?

In this volume I remain aware of such questions while discussing specific television series using nonformalist critical tools, drawing in particular on the tradition of Marxist critiques of literature (a tradition that has informed the phenomenon of cultural studies from the very beginning), but also drawing extensively on Bakhtin's influential theorization of the novel as a genre. In viewing television as a historically evolving phenomenon, I also draw upon models of cultural history that have been developed primarily from the study of literature and, to an extent, other traditional "arts." For example, as my title indicates, I see television as a crucial factor in the gradual transition, in the second half of the twentieth century, between modernism and postmodernism as dominant modes of aesthetic innovation in American culture. Indeed, television is, I think, the ideal focus for any study of this transition, especially in the United States. American television emerged as a powerful cultural phenomenon in the 1950s, precisely when the American academy was canonizing modernism as the dominant paradigm of high cultural aesthetics, but also precisely when postmodernism was already beginning to emerge as an alternative paradigm. Moreover, this historical confluence was no accident. In addition to being perhaps the quintessential postmodernist cultural form, television was crucial to the canonization of modernism in the 1950s in that many critics who promoted modernism in the decade saw modernist cultural production specifically as a high culture alternative to what they regarded as the debased massification of American culture, of which television was supposedly the central and most horrifying instance.

The concept of postmodernism will, according, be central to my discussion of television in this volume. Indeed, virtually all of the comments made by the critics cited above in their attempts to characterize television closely resembles comments that have been made about postmodernism as a cultural phenomenon. For example, Fiske's insistence on the inherent multivocality of television programming parallels numerous critical discussions of the plurality of postmodern culture. Meanwhile, the view of Stallabrass and Gitlin that television culture is thoroughly commodified and thus directly aligned with the ideology of consumer capitalism recalls Fredric Jameson's influential theorization of postmodernism as the "cultural logic" of late consumer capitalism. Similarly, Lasch's notion of the "minimal self" is reminiscent of Jameson's comments on the postmodern dissolution of the stable bourgeois subject, with a concomitant "waning of affect." Finally, Miller's diagnosis of the collapse of genre boundaries in television programming, accompanied by a retreat into self-referentiality, applies equally well to much postmodern fiction and film.

These parallels are not surprising, given that television is the most important cultural form of the postmodern era. However, my reading of television within the context of postmodernism and my historical placement of television within the transition from modernism to postmodernism does not ignore the fact, pointed out by many critics, that the aesthetics of most television programming remain fundamentally realist. Fiske, for example, continually argues that "the ideologically dominant reading and acting strategies [of television] are those of realism" (169). His resisting readers thus resist interpellation within the dominant ideology by challenging these realist premises, which promote individualism and discourage collective political action, a point that Davis also repeatedly makes about the novel in *Resisting Novels*. Similarly, Douglas Kellner argues that most commercial television is inherently conservative and highly formulaic, employing a simplistic mode of realism largely designed to pacify and reassure audiences, who are being groomed thereby as ideal consumers. However, Kellner also argues that the quest for higher ratings produces innovation and experimentation as programmers continually seek new audiences. Thus, the very need to "sell their artifacts means that the products of the culture must resonate to social experience, must attract large audiences, and must thus offer attractive products, which may shock, break with conventions, contain social critique, or articulate current ideas that may be the product of progressive social movements" (*Media Culture* 16). In particular, Kellner argues that some television programs, which he identifies as postmodernist, achieve

their effects precisely by violating the conventions of mainstream programming. For Kellner, then, postmodernism in TV is "a reaction against
realism and the system of coded genres (sitcom, soaps, ac-
tion/adventure, and so on) that define the system of commercial television in the United States" (*Media Culture* 235).

To an extent, I follow Kellner's lead in my identification of certain
programs as more postmodernist than others. However, I do not believe
that the distinction between realism and postmodernism is a matter of
simple either-or categorization. Indeed, I would argue that realism remains the dominant aesthetic mode of all postmodernist culture, which
consistently violates the conventions of realism, but which thereby depends upon those conventions (and on audience familiarity with and expectation of them) in order to achieve its effects. This is especially the
case with what I am calling "strange" television, which is largely strange
to the extent that it deviates from expectations derived from the conventions of realism.

The ongoing vitality of realism indicates that cultural history (like the
material history that underlies it) is considerably more continuous than
some visions of postmodernism as the sudden emergence of a new post-
Enlightenment stage of history tend to imply. Among other things, the
continuing ideological power of realism provides a framework within
which to understand the continuity in Western culture as it moves
through eras dominated by the novel, film, and television. I address this
model of historical continuity in more detail in the next chapter, which
also seeks to clarify my understanding of the phenomenon of postmodernism and the place of television within that phenomenon.

1

Television and Postmodernism

Any number of commentators have identified television as the quintessential form of postmodernist culture. For example, discussing the historical evolution of the concept of postmodernism, Perry Anderson identifies television as "the development that changed everything" (87). He then goes on to note that the new medium of television brought "a combination of undreamt-of power: the continuous availability of radio with an equivalent of the perceptual monopoly of print, which excludes other forms of attention by the reader. ... If there is any single technological watershed of the postmodern, it lies here" (88). Similarly, Steven Connor notes that TV and video, as examples of technology-driven mass-culture, "seem structurally to embody a surpassing of the modernist narrative of the individual artist struggling to transform a particular physical medium" (182). He then points to TV's capacity for "fragmentation and interruption," which combines with "the growing habit of channel-jumping" and "the intensifying absorption of TV in its own forms and history" to bring us to "a view of TV as constituting the postmodern psycho-cultural condition—a world of simulations detached from reference to the real, which circulate and exchange in ceaseless, centreless flow" (191).

In short, the obvious participation of American commercial television programming in the system of consumer capitalism would seem to be the perfect illustration of the complicity between postmodernism and late capitalism emphasized by theorists such as Fredric Jameson. The history of television supports this view as well. In particular, the rise of commercial television remains perfectly consistent with Jameson's basic proposition that works of postmodernist art express the "cultural logic" of "late capitalism," or capitalism in its post–World War II, global, postimperial phase as described in Ernest Mandel's seminal work, *Late Capitalism*, first published in German in 1972 (and in English translation in 1975).

The collapse of the great European colonial empires and the consequent spread of a more subtle, neocolonial form of global capitalist
domination began immediately upon the end of World War II, as did the
rise of American commercial television. Due to this historical placement,
the phenomena of late capitalism and television are both inextricable
from the phenomenon of the Cold War. In fact, late capitalism took on
many of its characteristics (including decolonization) at least partly as
specific Cold War strategies. For example, presenting itself as the champion of global liberation, the West was forced by its own rhetoric to
withdraw from overt colonial domination of the Third World and to
adopt more subtle cultural and economic forms of domination.

Meanwhile, American television programming began to saturate the
world's airwaves in the early 1950s and quickly became a key ingredient
in the American Cold War propaganda campaign. As Erik Barnouw
notes in his important history of the evolution of American television, the
U.S. Information Agency, the key government organ for propaganda distribution, was by 1954 heavily involved in the production and international distribution of television programming designed principally to
"fight international communism" (218). Television programming also
served to promote international capitalism, as American companies, increasingly involved in international operations, saw the new medium as
a key support for their expanding global businesses, both because of the
advertising opportunities it presented and because of its ability to promote a pro-Western consumerist mentality. As Barnouw puts it, "in the
mid-1950's, television, like missionary expeditions of another era,
seemed to serve as an advance herald of empire. Implicit in its arrival
was a web of relationships involving cultural, economic, and military aspects, and forming the basis for a new kind of empire" (233).

The historical rise of both commercial television and late capitalism
can thus be located in the peak period of the Cold War, in the years
(1946–64) that I have elsewhere called the "long 1950s." On the other
hand, most critics, including Jameson, tend to locate the rise of postmodernist culture in the late 1960s or early 1970s, suggesting (not illogically)
that postmodernism, as the cultural logic of late capitalism, lags behind
late capitalism itself in its historical development. However, I think the
inability of such critics to see the emergence of postmodernist culture in
the 1950s derives largely from their inattention to commercial television,
which was surely the most important postmodernist phenomenon of that
decade. Moreover, I have argued in *Monsters, Mushroom Clouds, and the
Cold War* that the beginnings of postmodernism in American culture can
already be detected in the "Golden Age" science fiction novels and notorious science fiction films of the long 1950s. Further, I have extended this
analysis in *The Post-Utopian Imagination* to demonstrate that postmodernist impulses, particularly as registered in a decline in utopian energies,
are present in the literary fiction, crime fiction, and mainstream films (as

evidenced in the work of Hitchcock and Disney) of that decade. Indeed, I argue that, in the long 1950s, even leftist writers, who continued to produce fiction under the duress of the McCarthyite purges, lack the ability to imagine a genuine utopian future.

By my reading, then, postmodernism begins to arise as a force in American culture immediately after the end of World War II, essentially simultaneously with the rise of late capitalism — and of commercial television in the United States. Barnouw points out that commercial TV was ready to go on line at the beginning of the war, but was put on the back burner during the war years. It was thus poised and ready to leap into operation as soon as the war was over. By 1953 (year of the death of Stalin and of the execution of the Rosenbergs), commercial television was in full swing, and TV had become a genuine mass phenomenon, quickly supplanting the radio industry that had been its progenitor and that had, in fact, supplied the funding for the bulk of TV research and development.

Commercial television developed postmodernist tendencies very early on. For example, the simultaneous broadcast of widely different programs on multiple channels and the frequent interruption of programs by commercials (or, perhaps more to the point, vice versa) can both be cited as examples of postmodernist plurality. And these basic characteristics led naturally to the eventual practice of channel surfing, skipping wildly and discontinuously from one channel (one program, one genre, one mode) to another with remote control in hand, a practice that might be cited as a paradigmatic experience of postmodernist fragmentation. Indeed, Jameson notes that media theorists have often taken channel surfing as "the very epitome of a postmodern attention and perceptual apparatus" (*Postmodernism* 373).

Jameson himself argues that video is "postmodernism's most distinctive new medium" (*Postmodernism* xv). On the other hand, he distinguishes between two basic kinds of video, arguing that the medium needs to be approached via "its twin manifestations as commercial television and experimental video" (*Postmodernism* 69). Interestingly enough, however, Jameson actually discusses only the second of these two phenomena, arguing that our contemporary cultural is so saturated by commercial television that we cannot possibly gain the critical distance necessary to think about it effectively. Instead, he concludes that we need to approach commercial television via experimental video, which will supply the cognitive estrangement necessary to allow us to begin to think critically about the never-ending stream of commercial images that incessantly flows across our television streams. Thus, for Jameson, "thinking anything adequate about commercial television may well involve ignoring it and thinking about ... experimental video," though he acknowledges that MTV music videos might fall in the latter category, however commercial they might be (71).

Jameson's meditations on postmodernism provide the single most important theoretical background to my own understanding of the relationship between television and postmodernism. However, I find his argument that we need to ignore commercial television if we hope to be able to understand it less than convincing. For one thing, the whole argument smacks of elitism and sounds like an excuse for a sophisticated intellectual to concentrate on "high" art while ignoring "mass" culture, even though Jameson himself protests that his point is "not a matter of mass versus elite culture" (71).[1] For another, Jameson's acknowledgment that MTV videos might be regarded as experimental, rather than commercial, television shows just how hard it is to distinguish between the two categories.

Of course, Jameson's decision not to discuss commercial television programming in any detail places him very much in line with much recent television criticism, as I noted in the previous chapter. Indeed, one of the pitfalls of discussing television within the context of postmodernism is that such an approach tends to lead to general discussions of the properties of television as a medium and postmodernism as a cultural phenomenon rather than to detailed analyses of specific programs. For example, Glenn Hendler actually starts out by seeking evidence of postmodernism in the style and content of various individual series, rounding up many of the usual suspects, including MTV, *Seinfeld*, *The Simpsons*, *The Larry Sanders Show*, and (especially) *Miami Vice*. Ultimately, however, Hendler invokes Raymond Williams's hugely influential notion of "flow," whereby Williams argues that, while it is important to examine the content of specific programs, the real object of analysis in television criticism should be the sequence of images that flows across the screen, not just in a given program, but on a continual basis, spanning different programs, as well as advertising and other "interruptions." In particular, Hendler follows Williams in concluding that "television is not really made up of separate texts" and echoes Nick Browne in concluding that what critics really need to consider when discussing television is the giant "supertext" in which individual programs are embedded (182).[2]

That such contextual analyses are needed in order fully to understand television culture is self-evident. However, the need for such analyses does not imply that critics need not pay attention to the actual programs themselves. It merely implies that such analyses of programming are only a partial move toward understanding television as a cultural phenomenon. Meanwhile, modern technology has complicated Williams's concept of flow considerably, remote controls in particular giving individual viewers an opportunity to take an active role in determining the specific flow that comes across their television screens.

Meanwhile, the almost universal availability (in the West) of remote-control channel surfing substantially adds to the plurality and fragmentation that many critics have seen as crucial to the postmodern quality of television. For example, Jim Collins (who makes virtually no distinction between television and postmodernism as cultural phenomena) argues that what makes television truly postmodern is not so much the content of any particular program as the fact that multiple programs are simultaneously available via the same multichannel medium. For Collins, television is thus the central example of the simultaneous presence of multiple styles that for him is characteristic of the "postmodern context."

What differentiates Post-Modernism from earlier periods is that while a specific style may be identifiable, its circulation and popularity do not define what is distinctive about the period. ... Post-Modernism departs from its predecessors in that as a textual practice it actually incorporates the heterogeneity of those conflicting styles, rather than simply asserting itself as the newest radical alternative seeking to render all conflicting modes of representation obsolete. ... *Diva* may be a Post-Modernist text, but the truly Post-Modernist context is one in which Beineix's film plays on Cinemax, while *Murder, She Wrote* and *Mickey Spillane's Mike Hammer* runs [*sic*] on opposite network channels. (114–15)

For Collins, what characterizes postmodern culture is not the dominance of any particular style, but the "recognition that culture has become a multiplicity of competing signs" (115). This emphasis on multiplicity recalls the work of John Fiske, except that Collins locates the multiplicity within television programming, while Fiske concentrates on audience response to that programming. Both views make a positive virtue of plurality; Collins, in particular, thus makes the postmodern world sound like the ultimate instance of the heteroglossia that, for Bakhtin, informs all cultures to a greater or lesser extent, while making the complex interactions among postmodernist texts seem an ultimate example of Bakhtin's concept of dialogism. Indeed, Collins invokes Bakhtin's work several times in his book (as, for that matter, does Fiske), though he wants to argue that the competition among different popular forms and discourses in the postmodern era leads to a centrifugal fragmentation and multiplicity that goes beyond anything envisioned by Bakhtin, who tends to want to locate dialogism in specific genres (especially the novel), or even in specific texts or authors (such as Dostoevsky).[3] For Collins, however, specific popular texts, or even whole popular genres, can be monological and centripetal, yet still contribute to the centrifugal dialogism of postmodern culture through interaction with a diverse array of other texts and genres.

Bakhtin's theoretical work helps Collins to link postmodernism and television, which is something I wish to do as well. However, before reading television as an instance of postmodernist culture, I want to establish a clear initial hypothesis about the nature of postmodernism, especially as I view the phenomenon in a way that makes the term somewhat inappropriate. In particular, I would argue that postmodernity is not a distinctively new period of history, but merely another stage in the long, slow, continual process of modernity, or what Fredric Jameson has referred to in several places as the "bourgeois cultural revolution." This revolution began with the dissolution of the monological world of medieval Europe, moved into high gear from the fifteenth to the nineteenth century as the bourgeoisie gradually supplanted the aristocracy and the Catholic church as the most powerful ruling force in Europe, and continues today, in the era of global consumer capitalism. Much has changed in the course of this process, but all of those changes have been relatively superficial compared to the radical transition from the medieval Catholic hegemony to the emergent capitalism of early modernity. Indeed, Jameson argues that the story of "the transition from feudalism to capitalism is what is secretly (or more deeply) being told in most contemporary historiography, whatever its ostensible content." Further, Jameson points out, this view of history makes the bourgeois cultural revolution "the only true Event of history" (*Signatures* 226–27). In short, history in the modern sense is an invention of the European bourgeoisie, designed to narrate (and justify) the centuries-long cultural revolution through which they rose to hegemony in Europe.

This broader view of the modern is, of course, somewhat similar to both Jürgen Habermas's virtual equation between "modernity" and the Enlightenment and Marshall Berman's characterization, in *All That Is Solid Melts into Air*, of Marx as the greatest modernist. Berman's direct alignment of Marx with the modern insists on the dialectical character of both Marx and modernity and thus anticipates my argument that Jameson's alignment of postmodernism with late capitalism remains dialectical. Berman importantly emphasizes that Marx's dialectical approach to modernity was necessary and appropriate because modernity itself is an inherently dialectical phenomenon. "To be modern," Berman writes, "is to find ourselves in an environment that promises us adventure, power, joy, growth, transformation of ourselves and the world—and, at the same time, that threatens to destroy everything we have, everything we know, everything we are" (15). For Berman, Marx and modernist literature have a great deal in common because they both manage to capture (perhaps because they participate in) the complex doubleness of modernity. Thus, for Berman, it is valuable in general to "read modernism in a Marxist way, to suggest how its characteristic energies, insights and anxieties spring from the drives and strains of modern economic life" (121).

For Berman, the essence of modernity is a permanent sense of impermanence, an expectation of continual and never-ending change as the basic fact of modern life. Of course, a similar sense underlies both realism and modernism, though realism, at its early-nineteenth-century height, was more informed by a confident sense that change was good, history virtually being equated with progress. And it is certainly the case that a similar acceptance of change remains central to the worldview of the capitalist West at the beginning of the twenty-first century, though with much less faith in the inevitability of progress. Moreover, one could argue that the modern world expected more dramatic, sweeping, and fundamental changes than does the postmodern one, where changes tend to be more superficial, less earth-shattering, and (in particular) less threatening to capitalist hegemony, which observers such as Francis Fukuyama have come to see as permanent and unchallengeable in the wake of the collapse of the Soviet bloc at the end of the Cold War.

I do believe that important changes have occurred since World War II in almost every aspect of human endeavor. Nevertheless, capitalism remains the dominant defining force in contemporary society, complete with the requisite bottom-line profit motives and class inequalities. Thus, while also believe that it is useful to distinguish between postmodernism and modernism in the cultural realm, in the larger sense postmodernity is still modern, by my definition, even if it does differ from previous stages of modernity in important ways. By the same token, the realism that preceded modernism was already modern, as I am equating modernity with the bourgeois cultural revolution and its aftermath, i.e., with the era of capitalism. Put differently, the era from the end of the Middle Ages to World War II might be described as "classical" modernity, while the period since World War II might be described as "postmodern" modernity, however clumsy and confusing that terminology may be, and however little it may do to lessen the general confusion about just what postmodernism is or means.

Of course, one solution would be to jettison the term "postmodern" altogether, especially as I am arguing that the postmodern does not lie after the modern, but within it. Unfortunately, the terminology is probably too well entrenched to change now. Meanwhile, such entangled and inaccurate terminology may be one reason commentators have had so much trouble agreeing on the exact nature of postmodernism, though numerous critics have developed accounts of the formal and aesthetic strategies of postmodernist works.[4] While the specifics of these accounts vary, there is a reasonable consensus that postmodernist works tend to be self-conscious, ironic, parodic, and formally fragmented. Terry Eagleton summarizes this consensus as a belief that postmodernist art is a "depthless, decentred, ungrounded, self-reflexive, playful, derivative, eclectic, pluralistic art which blurs the boundaries between 'high' and 'popular' culture, as well as between art and everyday experience" (*Illusions* vii).

In addition, Eagleton notes that this vision of postmodernist art has been closely aligned with the notion that such art arises within the context of fundamental shifts in Western thought that occur in the decades following World War II. This era of "postmodernity" is, in the consensus view, characterized by a style of thought which is suspicious of classical notions of truth, reason, identity and objectivity, of the idea of universal progress or emancipation, of single frameworks, grand narratives or ultimate grounds of explanation. Against these Enlightenment norms, it sees the world as contingent, ungrounded, diverse, unstable, indeterminate, a set of disunified cultures or interpretations which breed a degree of skepticism about the objectivity of truth, history and norms, the givenness of natures and the coherence of identities. This way of seeing, so some would claim, has real material conditions: it springs from an historic shift in the West to a new form of capitalism—to the ephemeral, decentralized world of technology, consumerism and the culture industry, in which the service, finance and information industries triumph over traditional manufacture, and classical class politics yield ground to a diffuse range of "identity politics." (vii)[5]

Despite his title, Eagleton's own concern in *The Illusions of Postmodernism* is not with postmodernist culture, but with postmodernity, with the complex of ideas that have informed postmodern—and, to a large extent, poststructuralist—thought. And his critique of the diffuse, confused, and contradictory nature of those ideas goes a long way toward explaining why it has been so difficult to reach a critical consensus concerning the true nature and historical implications of postmodernism and postmodernity. In any case, however, Eagleton reminds us that postmodern plurality and boundary crossing are hardly subversive of capitalist authority, given that "capitalism is the most pluralistic order history has ever known, restlessly transgressing boundaries and dismantling oppositions, pitching together diverse life-forms and continually overflowing the measure" (*Illusions* 133).

However contradictory, critical attempts to characterize postmodernism have often been tied together by a common attempt to characterize postmodernist works in contrast to modernist ones. Many accounts of postmodernism, in fact, have simply argued that postmodernist works are informed by essentially the same aesthetic impulses as modernist ones, but that these impulses take more radical forms in postmodernism. For example, Brian McHale, in an influential survey of postmodernist fiction, notes the epistemological skepticism that is crucial to both modernism and postmodernism. However, McHale argues that modernist fiction is informed by a belief in the existence of a fundamental reality about which basic truths exist, however difficult those truths might be to determine. Postmodernist fiction, on the other hand, is, for McHale, informed by a basic skepticism toward the very existence of such truths, reality itself being unstable, multiple, and socially determined.

This notion of the skepticism of postmodernism has often translated into a vision of postmodernist works as fundamentally opposed to authoritarian versions of truth and reality, often in contrast to a basic desire for order and authority that informs modernist works. Ihab Hassan, one of the critics most responsible for initially promoting the idea of postmodernism in the 1960s, characterizes postmodernism in a crucial article by listing the major "rubrics" of modernism, then explaining the ways in which postmodernism moves beyond modernism through subversive challenges to modernist ideas of order and authority. For Hassan, "whereas Modernism created its own forms of Authority, precisely because the center no longer held, Postmodernism has tended toward Anarchy, in deeper complicity with things falling apart" (29).

Hassan's quintessentially 1960s view of postmodernism has informed many accounts of the phenomenon, with critics such as Leslie Fiedler and Susan Sontag usually being cited as central to this view of postmodernism as aligned with the political revolts of the 1960s. Such critics tend to see postmodernism as an irreverent, rule-breaking, populist challenge to the received conventions of the Western aesthetic tradition, somewhat along the lines of the oppositional political movements of the 1960s. Linda Hutcheon, one of the most effective apologists for postmodernist fiction, implicitly takes this tack when she argues that such fiction is centrally informed by a subversive challenge to authority, and especially to authoritative, official narratives of history. Thus, for Hutcheon, the paradigmatic form of postmodernist narrative is what she calls "historiographic metafiction," which reflexively calls attention to its own construction, but also, at the same time, calls attention to the assumptions upon which official accounts of history have been constructed by those in authority. Hutcheon argues, in fact, that postmodernism is subversive *by definition*. However, she finds little subversive potential in commercial television, which she sees as "pure commodified complicity, without the critique needed to define the postmodern paradox" (*Politics* 10). Television does not match her vision of postmodernism and therefore, according to her, is not postmodern—a conclusion that seriously calls into question her whole vision of postmodernism.

Arguing that "critique" is "crucial to the definition of the postmodern," Hutcheon acknowledges that this political element of postmodernism can be seen as part of "the unfinished project of the 1960s, for, at the very least, those years left in their wake a specific and historically determined distrust of ideologies of power and a more general suspicion of the power of ideology" (*Politics* 10). Of course, by the time of the 1960s, when such visions of postmodernism as somehow anti-ideological began to arise, more than a decade of incessant Cold War propaganda had made "ideology" almost synonymous with "communism." It is perhaps not surprising, then, that what coherence Eagleton does find in postmodernity has to do with a widespread suspicion toward the traditional ideas of the Left and with a sense that the rise of postmodernism has a great deal to do with the perception (accurate or not) of a historical experience of defeat of the Left in the West in the decades following World War II.

Anderson, in his investigation of the historical roots of the idea of postmodernism, finds a fundamental antisocialism at the base of most postmodernist thought. Discussing the well known suggestion by Jean-

François Lyotard that postmodernism is informed by a basic "incredulity toward metanarratives,"[6] Anderson offers a convincing argument that by "metanarratives" Lyotard really means only one metanarrative, that of classical Marxism. Further, Anderson argues that Lyotard's rejection of Marxism is part of a thoroughgoing rejection of all utopian alternatives to the existing capitalist order. Indeed, Anderson concludes that the various versions of postmodernism, as they developed in the work of thinkers otherwise as various as Lyotard, Ihab Hassan, Charles Jencks, and Jürgen Habermas, were united by a consistent antipathy toward the traditional utopian values of socialism and the Left: "Common to all was a subscription to the principles of what Lyotard — once the most radical — called liberal democracy, as the unsurpassable horizon of the time. There could be nothing but capitalism. The postmodern was a sentence on alternative illusions." (46)

Anderson's suggestion that postmodernism is rooted in pessimism and resignation contrasts dramatically with the vision of postmodernism as subversive that informs the work of critics such as Hassan and Hutcheon. Indeed, as a whole, the rich body of Marxist commentary on postmodernism tends to see the rise of postmodernist culture as aligned with (rather than opposed to) the expansion and transformation of capitalism after World War II. For example, David Harvey associates the rise of postmodernism with a fundamental transformation of capitalism into a post-Fordist mode of production after World War II. For Harvey, this new, more subtle and flexible form of capitalism extends the control of the economic system into areas (including culture) that had previously been relatively autonomous. Postmodernism, then, "signals nothing more than a logical extension of the power of the market over the whole range of cultural production" (62).

For Jameson, meanwhile, transformations in the capitalist economic system after World War II led to fundamental changes in individual subjective experience, accompanied by fundamental changes in the forms and themes of culture. Other Marxist critics have, however, warned against exaggerating the extent to which capitalism has changed in the postwar years, fearing that an emphasis on such changes might obscure fundamental continuities in the basic form of capitalist production. Even Harvey, for example, reminds us that, whatever changes capitalism has undergone in the postwar era, "we still live, in the West, in a society where production for profit remains the basic organizing principle of economic life" (121). Consequently, Harvey also concludes that, while postmodernist art may be a distinct phenomenon, "there is much more continuity than difference between the broad history of modernism and the movement called postmodernism" (116). Alex Callinicos is even more insistent on this continuity, doubting that postmodernism exists at all, except in the minds of certain theorists — largely because he doubts the reality of postmodernity as a genuinely new historical stage.[7] For

Callinicos, meanwhile, postmodernism is again antisocialist, and the invention of postmodernity is intimately linked to a "rejection of socialist revolution as either feasible or desirable" (9). That is, he sees the idea of the postmodern as the invention of theorists who would seek to argue that history has entered a radical new stage, in which the long tradition of Marxist critique, rooted as it is in the prior, modern stage, has been rendered ineffectual, if not entirely irrelevant.

Julian Stallabrass is even more unconvinced of the usefulness of most postmodern theory, which he feels obscures the real conditions of economic exploitation through an emphasis on textual phenomena that have little to do with reality. Stallabrass, in fact, concludes that postmodern theory "produces an inverse image of what is taking place in the real world, and while reality flaunts the most blatant counter-examples in its face, it nonchalantly continues on its way as though this blindness was a matter of principle" (10). In particular, Stallabrass, like Eagleton, is skeptical of postmodern celebrations of plurality and diversity, which may be good in theory but which do not, for Stallabrass, have much to do with the reality of material life in the contemporary world. He concludes that "there is much to be said for the postmodern utopia of diversity, but unfortunately its existence is not one of them" (10).

Teresa Ebert also worries that postmodern theory obscures the economic realities of the contemporary world. She grants that capitalism has undergone changes since World War II but insists that "the most important point to be made about the shifting patterns of production and employment is that they are still grounded on the basic structural relations of capitalism — *the expropriation and exploitation of living labor (surplus labor) for profit*" (112, Ebert's emphasis). In light of this basic continuity, Ebert suggests that there are two separate strains in postmodernist thought, which she labels "ludic" postmodernism and "resistance" postmodernism. The ludic strain, for Ebert, is complicit with capitalism, while the resistance strain retains the ability effectively to critique capitalism. In addition, Ebert argues that the two strains can be distinguished by their different views of the recent history of capitalism. Ludic postmodernism, she argues, envisions postmodernism as the product of a break in the evolution of capitalism so radical that all previous history (including the history of Marxist critique) is rendered irrelevant. Consequently, ludic postmodernism "articulates the emergence of what it considers to be entirely new social configurations: New Times, postindustrial society, consumer society, post-Fordism, all of which are seen as postproduction, postclass, postgender, and, frequently, posthistory" (132–33). Resistance postmodernism, with which Ebert aligns her own work, emphasizes the historical continuity in the development of capitalism, seeing the postmodern era not as the product of a radical break in history but of the historical evolution of capitalism, which constantly finds "new articulations of the relations of production. The extraordinary superstructural changes that we mark as postmodernism are simply new mediations of the fundamental social contradictions resulting from the division and exploitation of labor" (133).

French poststructuralists (such as Lyotard and Baudrillard) and "post-Marxists" (such as Ernesto Laclau and Chantal Mouffe) are the crucial figures in the ludic postmodernism outlined by Ebert. However, Ebert is also highly critical of the work of Jameson, which she feels is based on a monolithic version of postmodernism that leaves essentially no room for effective critique of or resistence to the dominance of global capitalism. Moreover, she feels that Jameson's association of postmodernism with a new phase in the history of capitalism tends, in the mode of ludic postmodernism, to emphasize historical discontinuities. However, Jameson's (and Mandel's) elaboration of the notion of late capitalism (very much in the Marxist tradition of Lenin's vision of imperialism as a new stage in the history of capitalism) in no way suggests a fundamental discontinuity in the basic facts of capitalist production of profit through exploitation of surplus labor. Indeed, one of Jameson's central criticisms of postmodernism is its emphasis on discontinuity and its consequent inability to think in terms of coherent, continuous historical narratives of the kind that underlie his own thought. Moreover, Ebert's critique of Jameson ignores his own dogged insistence on the necessity for seeking utopian alternatives to the existing order and his consequent rejection of the "total systems" visions of postmodern theorists such as Michel Foucault precisely because they lack any viable utopian dimension.

Still, it is clear that Ebert's elaboration of two opposed strains in postmodernist thought very helpfully illuminates certain aspects of postmodernism that Jameson's more totalizing view does not—just as Jameson's more focused view makes coherent certain aspects of postmodernism that Ebert's work does not. Indeed, many analysts of postmodernism have detected competing tendencies of the kind Ebert indicates. Ebert herself draws directly upon a similar distinction between ludic and resistance postmodernism made earlier by Mas'ud Zavarzadeh and Donald Morton.[8] The notion of these two opposed modes of postmodernism also closely resembles the oppositions outlined by Hal Foster, who suggests that postmodernism involves competing impulses of progressive resistance to and reactionary celebration of the capitalist status quo (xi–xii), and Gerald Graff, who outlines "the two postmodernism," one a celebratory strain and the other a more anxious, critical strain (55–59).

Perhaps the most sophisticated discussion of competing impulses within postmodernism remains that by Andreas Huyssen, who reviews the earlier visions of critics such as Foster and Graff, but provides a more thorough (and more historical) description of the complex sources of different postmodernist impulses. In so doing, Huyssen also produces his own account of a contrast between a purely affirmative postmodernism and a postmodernism that maintains an effective critical dimension. Huyssen's best known and most widely cited argument is that postmodernism is informed by a democratic challenge to received notions of a "great divide" between High and Low Culture, notions that for Huyssen most modernist artists not only accepted but sought to maintain. Further, Huyssen sees modernism as centrally informed by an attempt to "ward off" the threat posed to "genuine" art by mass culture, which he also sees as symbolically associated (for the modernists) with the threat of the feminine.

However, Huyssen's analysis is anything but a simple celebration of the liberating democratic impulses of postmodernism. On the one hand, Huyssen locates the rise of postmodernist art amid the pop art movement of the 1960s, concluding that "from the beginning ... the most significant trends within postmodernism have challenged modernism's relentless hostility to mass culture" (188). At the same time, this alignment of postmodernism with pop always threatens to reduce postmodernist art to the status of mere commodity, especially in the United States, where the cultural rebellion entailed in the experimental art of the 1960s, while reacting against the gray conformity of the 1950s, was not accompanied by any coherent program of radical social and political transformation (169). Indeed, Huyssen notes the rapidity with which the Western culture industry began to exploit new marketing opportunities produced by the pop art explosion of the 1960s (141–42).

Nevertheless, Huyssen believes, pace Jameson, that "the wholesale writing off of postmodernism as a symptom of capitalist culture in decline is reductive, unhistorical and all too reminiscent of Lukács' attacks on modernism in the 1930s" (199). One of Huyssen's central ideas is that the direct predecessor to postmodernism in Western cultural history is not modernism, but the avant garde.[9] As such, postmodernism inherits many of the critical and oppositional energies of the avant garde. In the 1960s, in particular, these energies were aimed at the entrenched visions of modernism (such as in the American New Criticism) that had been institutionalized in the 1950s. However, complicating the picture still further, Huyssen is careful to distinguish between modernism itself (as it was practiced and experienced by the modernists of the early twentieth century) and these institutionalized visions of modernism from the 1950s, which, for Huyssen, are profoundly reactionary, based on a cultural elitism that reinforces inequalities on the basis of class, race, and gender that have long informed the capitalist culture of the West. In addition, Huyssen argues that this conservative, institutionalized version of modernism cannot be separated from the climate of the Cold War, in which modernism became enshrined as the official example of the superiority of Western High Culture to both Western mass culture and Soviet socialist realism (which was itself always intended as mass culture, not High Art). For Huyssen, the "revolt of the 1960s was never a rejection of modernism per se, but rather a revolt against that version of modernism which had been domesticated in the 1950s, become part of the liberal-conservative consensus of the times, and which had even been turned into a propaganda weapon in the cultural-political arsenal of Cold War anticommunism" (190).

Huyssen argues that the inherited avant-garde tendencies of post-modernism challenged hegemonic visions of modernism from the 1950s, but they did so from the weakened position of an avant garde that had already largely lost its battle against the institutionalization and com-modification of art. Following the important analysis of Peter Bürger, Huyssen notes that, by the time of the rise of postmodernism, the politi-cal energies of the avant garde had largely been spent because the once-shocking techniques of avant-garde art had already been absorbed and appropriated by advertising and other forms of commodified culture. For Huyssen, then, the postmodernist culture of 1960s had in turn ex-hausted much of its critical energies by the 1970s, leading to the rise of a "largely affirmative postmodernism which had abandoned any claim to critique, transgression or negation" (189). At the same time, Huyssen also argues that a new, potentially critical form of postmodernism also arose in the 1970s, differing substantially from the avant garde and basing its oppositional strategies on a "new creative relationship between high art and certain forms of mass culture" (194). Thus, while Huyssen does not entirely dismiss the notion that postmodernism might develop in genu-inely oppositional ways in the future, he characterizes the explosion of postmodernist art in the 1960s as "the closing chapter in the tradition of avantgardism," as "the endgame of the avantgarde and not as the radical breakthrough it often claimed to be" (164, 168).

Huyssen's recognition of the two-sided nature of so many aspects of postmodernism represents an attempt at a genuine dialectical analysis of the phenomenon. Indeed, he specifically places his work in the Marxist dialectical tradition: "Just as Marx analyzed the culture of modernity dia-lectically as bringing both progress and destruction, the culture of post-modernity, too, must be grasped in its gains as well as in its losses, in its promises as well as in its depravations" (200). Meanwhile, for Huyssen, the need for a dialectical approach to postmodernism indicates that Jameson's vision of postmodernism as directly aligned with late capital-ism, "overstates the case" (235 n.4). However, Huyssen himself probably overstates the case for anticapitalist tendencies in postmodernism that derive from the avant-garde tradition and that are closely associated with the youth and pop art movements of the 1960s. For example, Matei Calinescu is much more skeptical than Huyssen about the subversive power of avant-garde art, even at its height; and he is far more negative than Huyssen himself about the remaining political threat posed by the avant garde by the 1960s. In particular, he argues that, by the 1960s,

avant-garde art had been thoroughly appropriated as popular entertainment with no critical power:

The avant-garde, whose limited popularity has long rested exclusively on scan-
dal, all of a sudden became one of the major cultural myths of the 1960s. Its of-
fensive, insulting rhetoric came to be regarded as merely amusing, and its apocalyptic outcries were changed into comfortable and innocuous clichés. Ironically,
the avant-garde found itself failing through a stupendous, involuntary success.
(120–21)

Calinescu's skepticism toward the avant garde is matched by Huyssen's own warnings about the commodification of pop art and Thomas
Frank's doubts about the 1960s counterculture in general. For Frank, in
fact, the complicity between 1960s consumer capitalism and the counterculture goes far beyond the mere appropriation of the latter by the former. Instead, he argues that the counterculture of the 1960s was largely
produced by capitalism, creating new products and new marketing opportunities more than genuinely new social and political ideas.

Frank demonstrates that American capitalism, largely through images
disseminated in television (and other) advertising, helped to create the
widely accepted notions that the 1960s were a time of liberation from the
conformist routinization of the 1950s and that the presumably hip 1960s
counterculture was a "life-affirming opponent of mass society" (14).
Given that some critics (Hassan, Hutcheon, to an extent Huyssen) seem
virtually to equate the subversive impulses of postmodernism with 1960s
counterculture, Frank's equation between this counterculture and consumer capitalism calls these impulses into question and supports
Jameson's vision of postmodernism as the cultural logic of late capitalism.

In addition, if neither the avant garde nor the counterculture of the
1960s is necessarily anticapitalist, it is also the case that capitalism itself
contains extremely complex and contradictory impulses. Indeed, one of
Marx's central arguments was that capitalism was powerful enough as a
historical force to overwhelm every competing system with which it
came into contact, but that capitalism contained the seeds of its own destruction and would ultimately produce its own downfall. In short,
Jameson's totalizing vision of postmodernism as the cultural logic of late
capitalism is not necessarily simplistic, defeatist, or nondialectical. Instead, this vision still allows for a variety of competing impulses (including anticapitalist ones) within postmodernism, because capitalism itself
contains such impulses.

What might seem potentially simplistic about Jameson's model is his
insistence on the hegemony of postmodernism in contemporary Western
(and even, to an extent, global) culture. It is surely the case that vestigial
energies from previous cultural forms, such as realism and modernism,

still exert a considerable influence, even at the beginning of the twenty-first century, after decades of presumed postmodernist hegemony. However, whether this obvious fact really contradicts Jameson's model may be largely a question of terminology. After all, Jameson himself has discussed the ongoing availability of cultural alternatives, especially in the Third World and among marginal groups in the West. Hegemony, in fact, never implies total and absolute power, but merely more power than the competition. And this is especially the case in the realm of the aesthetic.

As Eagleton repeatedly reminds us in his historical survey of philosophies of the aesthetic, the whole notion of the aesthetic as we know it is a thoroughly bourgeois idea that arose in conjunction with the rise to power of the bourgeoisie as the ruling class in modern Europe. Yet Eagleton also suggests that there is something inherently problematic, unruly, and uncontrollable in the aesthetic that nevertheless gives it considerable subversive potential: "The aesthetic as custom, sentiment, spontaneous impulse may consort well enough with political domination; but these phenomena border embarrassingly on passion, imagination, sensuality, which are not always so easily incorporable" (*Ideology* 28). Eagleton here may underestimate the ability of capitalism to incorporate rowdy impulses, as Frank's discussion of the close complicity between consumer capitalism and these, drugs, and rock 'n' roll counterculture of the 1960s indicates. Still, his remarks do support the notion that this complicity does not mean that there was absolutely *no* oppositional power in the counterculture — or in a postmodernism that might be thoroughly aligned with the logic of late capitalism.

Just as postmodernity may simply be the latest stage of modernity, it may well be that postmodernism is best understood not as an entirely separate cultural phenomenon, but as a sort of historical amalgamation that includes the accumulated cultural phenomena that came before it. Thus, from one point of view, Best and Kellner are probably correct in insisting that modern/modernist ideas remain dominant at the end of the twentieth century, when postmodernism is still emergent. However, if one views postmodernity as the latest stage of modernity and postmodernism as an accumulation that *includes* modern ideas, then this broader form of postmodernism is indeed dominant. Here, of course, I draw upon Williams's well-known formulation of the notion of residual, dominant, and emergent historical forces (*Marxism* 121–27). According to this model, any particular period of history may be dominated by specific tendencies and phenomena, but the effect of residual forces from previous eras can still be felt. Moreover, the effect of newly emergent forces, not yet fully formed, will at any time be felt as well. In the realm of culture, this model applies particularly well in the years following World War II, when modernism, through its institutionalization in the Western academy, came into focus as the dominant aesthetic, at least in certain academic circles, while a residual realism remained powerful, and indeed was dominant in other, broader circles. Postmodernism, meanwhile, was beginning to emerge, but was not yet fully developed or understood as a new cultural phenomenon. By the end of the 1960s, however, one could argue that postmodernism, by absorbing, extending, and transforming the earlier realist and modernist modes, had become a new form of dominant within which modernism and realism were both residual (and new emergent forces were presumably present, though not yet recognizable). However, this new postmodernism was a particularly weak dominant, a sort of coalition government of culture, in which modernist and realist impulses remained extremely strong.

Of course, my vision of postmodernism as a historical accumulation of competing cultural impulses may simply be another way of looking at the plurality and multiplicity that have informed so many characterizations of the postmodern, though it does add an important historical dimension to postmodernist plurality. Indeed, in considering the sources of this plurality, we need to consider the simple fact that the first half of the twentieth century probably produced as many texts in as wide as variety as all of previous history. As a result, the artists and writers of the second half of the twentieth century inherited at least twice as much cultural capital as their modernist predecessors, who, in turn, inherited far more cultural capital than any of *their* predecessors. And this situation grows only more dramatic with the explosion in cultural production of the second half of the twentieth century, an explosion in which the new phenomenon of television plays a very central role. Thus, one important source of postmodernist plurality is the sheer volume of cultural production in the postmodern era, combined with the availability of far more inherited cultural resources than had been available in any previous era.

To view postmodernism as a product of historical accumulation suggests the possibility that one might view the competing impulses within new cultural impulses that arose after World War II and the residual impulses of earlier eras. In particular, I would like to argue that the "resistance" postmodernism of Zavarzadeh, Morton, and Ebert is best thought of as primarily a residual pre–World War II modern impulse, while their "ludic" postmodernism might be better described as postmodernism "proper," that is, as the new aspect of modern Western culture that first appears in the period after World War II, during the era of the emergence of late capitalism.

In pursuing this historicist vision of postmodernism—and by reading television in the context of the movement of modernity into a new "postmodern" stage—I will, of course, be employing a totalizing metanarrative of cultural history of the kind that has often been seen as anathema to the postmodern worldview. I do so knowingly and with conviction. After all, such metanarratives are not necessarily invalid simply because much postmodern thought rejects them. Indeed, following

Anderson's conclusion that postmodernist hostility to metanarratives is often little more than a thinly disguised hostility to socialism, I will want to argue that the recent rejection of these metanarratives is largely a consequence of the anticommunist hysteria of the Cold War years and that, with the Cold War ostensibly over, we probably want to interrogate its premises rather than merely continue to accept them.

Having said that, it is still the case that my own Marxist methodology essentially places my position in the pre–World War II era of "classical" modernity. Again, however, I would argue that this positioning is a virtue, not a weakness, in that it gives me a stable ground upon which to view the transition from classical modernity to postmodern modernity marked by the rise of American television as the most powerful cultural force on our planet. Moreover, the effectiveness of Marxist approaches to postmodernism has been well established. Much of the best and most illuminating theorization of postmodernism has been done by Marxist critics such as Jameson, Eagleton, Harvey, Callinicos, and Anderson, whose firmly modern positioning gives them the critical distance necessary to see postmodernism in ways that theorists firmly situated within the phenomenon (such as Hassan, Lyotard, and Jacques Deleuze) have been unable to do.

However, while situating my work in the tradition of Marxist metanarratives, I will modify the usual metanarrative of Western cultural history to bring the importance of television more clearly into focus. It is, by now, fairly conventional to see Western literary history of the past two centuries as proceeding through three basic phases or periods, in which the modes of realism, modernism, and postmodernism serve as the respective cultural paradigms. There are, of course, fundamental problems with this model, not the least of which is that these three modes are not really comparable in terms of the influence they exerted during their "dominant" periods. Realism, rising to power with the European bourgeoisie whose worldview it so well expressed, became a genuine dominant, especially in England, by the end of the eighteenth century and remained so through the next century, despite a short-lived challenge by Romanticism (which was itself thoroughly bourgeois, and thus not nearly as radical as its practitioners sometimes liked to think) in the first half of the nineteenth century. Realism also survived the first stirrings of modernism in the second half of the nineteenth century. Indeed, despite these stirrings, and despite the explosion of modernist artistic production in the first three decades of the twentieth century, modernism never became a genuine dominant. The central figures of the British novel in the first decades of the twentieth century were not James Joyce and Virginia Woolf and Joseph Conrad, but H. G. Wells and Arnold Bennett and John Galsworthy.

In fact, modernism remained a marginal movement through its most productive years, though it did achieve a belated centrality of sorts due to its canonization in the 1950s, after most of the major modernists had either died or ceased to produce important modernist work. Postmodernism, meanwhile, emerged just as modernism was being canonized, quickly superseding its predecessor in overall cultural power, while still not achieving the kind of dominance that realism had achieved in the nineteenth century. Realism, in fact, remained the baseline of all Western artistic production through the twentieth century. Modernism thus achieved its most striking effects through a contrast to realism (and, indeed, often seemed simply to be seeking a higher form of realism), while postmodernism gained power through its difference from both realism and modernism.

Of the three modes of realism, modernism, and postmodernism, only the first was literally dominant as a mode of cultural production during the periods with which it is normally associated. It would be much more accurate to say that each of these modes was the dominant mode of cultural *innovation* during its period, each mode providing, in its respective period, the most exciting and influential energies for *change* in cultural production, without completely supplanting the underlying realist matrix. Of course, given the emphasis on innovation and change in capitalism, it is easy to see why these modes of artistic production would come to be regarded as the main elements in Western cultural history. On the other hand, this distinction between dominant modes of production and dominant modes of innovation helps to explain the impressive achievements and far-reaching influence of the English realist novel of the eighteenth century and the French realist novel of the nineteenth century, when each, respectively, became for a brief time the dominant mode of both aesthetic production and aesthetic innovation.

In short, basic Western assumptions about culture and aesthetics have changed far less in the past two hundred years than the realism-modernism-postmodernism model of cultural history would seem to imply, just as television is not nearly so radically different from the novel as has been widely supposed. The movement from realism to modernism to postmodernism was not a procession of radically different and discontinuous phases (in the mode of the *epistemés* of Foucault), but as a much more continuous process of layering, in which realism remained an underlying dominant, while realism and postmodernism were added as progressive complications. And it does not require an appeal to vulgar economism to see that this cultural continuity is closely related to the fact that capitalism itself has remained the single most important factor in determining the texture of life in Western society during the modern period, even though capitalism itself has passed through distinct phases. Thus, without implying historical discontinuities, one can relate the realist heyday of the nineteenth century to the classical industrial phase, modernism to the imperialist phase, and postmodernism to the "late" or global consumerist phase of capitalism, as long as one recognizes that these phases are essentially second-order effects that leave intact certain basic assumptions and structures of the capitalist system, just as the rise of modernism left intact many of the basic assumptions of realism.

The realism-modernism-postmodernism model is extremely useful as a heuristic device for organizing the vast data of cultural history, especially if viewed as a process of historical accumulation rather than a sequence of difference stages. Even then, however, the model should not be taken too literally, especially as the entire story could be constructed in an entirely different manner. For example, the period of the rise and dominance of realism as a cultural mode might alternatively be described as the period of the rise and dominance of the novel as a literary form. Among other things, this focus reminds us, as Ian Watt already did in his seminal study of the rise of the novel over forty years ago, that the intertwined rise of realism and the novel was related both to the rise of the bourgeoisie as the new ruling class in Europe and to a number of technological and economic factors. The novel, after all, could not have become the dominant genre of Western literature without dramatic advances in print technology and without the growth of a sophisticated capitalist system for production, marketing, and distribution of the products of this new technology. And realism, most likely, could not have become dominant without the novel.

Moreover, if the rise of realism closely corresponds to the rise of the printed novel, then it is also the case that the modernist period is closely synchronous with the appearance of the new medium of film, which was also made possible by new technological advances and new systems for the delivery of that technology to the public. Indeed, many observers at the time clearly regarded film as the quintessential modernist form, an attitude that can be detected, for example, in Walter Benjamin's classic essay, "The Work of Art in the Age of Mechanical Reproduction." In any case, film supplanted the novel as a dominant form, especially in the United States, in ways that modernism never supplanted realism. Thus, by the beginnings of the golden age of Hollywood in the 1930s, vastly more people viewed a successful film than had ever read the notoriously successful novels of Walter Scott or Charles Dickens.

Of course, the cultural power of Hollywood was established largely within a basic realist matrix, with Hollywood directors developing an invisible editing style that furthered an illusion of reality and departed radically from the modernist cinema of Eisenstein or the German expressionists. Even so, the golden age of Hollywood film was short lived. By the end of the 1950s, television had supplanted film as the most powerful cultural medium in America, corresponding very closely to the rise of postmodernism as a new cultural mode. One might, then, replace (or at least supplement) the realism-modernism-postmodernism model of cultural history with a media-based novel-film-television model, a move that results in far more than a change of terminology. The realism-

modernism-postmodernism model is based essentially on printed literature and thus does not well account for the impact of the new technologies of film and television. As a result, considering these technologies
brings entirely new phenomena into focus. For example, if film reached
larger audiences and thus had a cultural power that the novel never had,
television very quickly went far beyond film, both in the number of
viewers and in the amount of time individual viewers were exposed to
the medium.

The novel-film-television version of modern cultural history fits in
well with the notion of historical accumulation, as each new form appropriated its predecessors, building a larger and larger repertoire. Film, for
example, drew on the novel as a principal source of raw narrative material, while incorporating realism as a basic aesthetic within which it explored new (and largely modernist) modes of representation that were
appropriate to the new medium and the system of production and distribution that promoted it. Television, in desperate need of "content" for its
rapid expansion, devoured everything in its path, including both the
novel and film, both realism and modernism, adding new elements from
popular culture as well.

Thus, television again converges with postmodernism, both being the
result of historical accumulation and both drawing upon the cultural
heritage of the past, though it is also the case that both tend to do so in an
ahistorical way, treating the past as a sort of museum—or perhaps department store is more apt—of images to be rummaged through and
used at will. Thus, the two historical models I have elaborated converge
as well, making television a conglomeration of images and styles taken
from literature and film, but also a conglomeration of images and techniques taken from realism, modernism, and postmodernism. I argue in
the following chapters, however, that television programming did tend,
on the whole, to become more and more purely postmodernist over the
course of the second half of the twentieth century. Alternatively, using
the terminology of Ebert, Zavarzadeh, and Morton, postmodernist television tends more and more toward the ludic pole as time goes by.

My interest, in the following chapters, is in programs that still show
tendencies I regard as modern, or that Ebert, et al., might regard as examples of resistance postmodernism. I should add, however, that I do
not necessarily find much in the way of genuine resistance, in the political sense, in the programming I discuss, or in commercial television programming as a whole. However, I do believe that signs of an ongoing
modernist strain, with a potential for utopian critique of the status quo,
can be detected here and there in a certain anxiety that worries about the
current condition of things, even if it does not really suggest systemic alternatives.

In order to trace some of the historical developments in American
television programming in the second half of the twentieth century, I be-

gin my discussions in the following chapters through an exploration of
The Twilight Zone (which began airing in the 1950s) and end with a discussion of *The X-Files* (which was still on the air at century's end). In particular, *The Twilight Zone*, which aired in 138 half-hour episodes from
1959 to 1964 (plus 18 full-hour episodes in the fourth season), was situated at the very end of the long 1950s and represents the culmination of a
number of trends that were important during that period. As I will argue
in Chapter 2, *The Twilight Zone* often aspired to the condition of serious
art, reflecting a strong modernist influence. In addition, the program
strained against the routinization and alienation that were such crucial
phenomena in American culture in the long 1950s, showing at least the
rudiments of a critique of the negative consequences of American corporate culture. If *The Twilight Zone* was often anxious about the directions
in which American capitalist society was moving, it also reflected many
of the typical Cold War-related anxieties of the long 1950s. However,
perhaps because the anxieties of the period were all too immediate and
real, *The Twilight Zone* tended to mute its anxious modernism (or resistance postmodernism) with a strong note of irony that tended toward the
ludic. Indeed, many episodes of *The Twilight Zone* were overtly comic
and playful, though such episodes were almost invariably among the
weakest.

Vague gestures toward critique notwithstanding, the ideology of *The
Twilight Zone* was quite consistent with that of the 1950s liberal consensus. It was thus not until the advent of *The Prisoner* (first broadcast in
Britain in the fall of 1967 and in America in the summer of 1968) that a
genuinely strange (in my sense) television series would be aired. In fact,
The Prisoner (recalling Samuel Johnson's concerns about the oddness of
Tristram Shandy) was so strange that it could not survive for long on
commercial television. As I discuss in Chapter 3, *The Prisoner* was very
much a work of the 1960s, reflecting many of the concerns of the period.
Moreover, it addressed those concerns in an entirely serious (and anxious) manner, reflecting its fundamentally modernist matrix. In particular, *The Prisoner* addressed many of the same concerns as the French
poststructuralism that was emerging at much the same time, though
much French poststructuralism reflected a more ludic brand of postmodern thought than did the series.

The Prisoner was accompanied by an array of other Cold War-related
dramas, the most successful of which, including *The Avengers* (another
British import that began airing in Britain in 1961, but did not appear in
the United States until a run from 1966 to 1969) and *The Man from
U.N.C.L.E.* (1964 to 1968), tended much more toward the ludic, display-
ing a superficial (or even campy) interest in style that marked them as far
more distinctively postmodern than was *The Prisoner*. In the meantime, a
full-blown strain of ludic postmodernism had emerged on American
television with the appearance of *The Flintstones* on ABC in the fall of

1960. The first prime-time animated series, *The Flintstones* clearly built upon the success of the Disney animated classics of the 1950s. However, *The Flintstones* was essentially an animated sitcom, and much of its humor was clearly aimed at adult audiences. It was, as McNeil notes "little more than an animated version of *The Honeymooners*," the now-legendary Jackie Gleason sitcom-within-a-variety show that ran, in different incarnations, from 1952 to 1970 (290).

The Flintstones was quintessential ludic postmodernism. It was, in a sense, a one-joke show, virtually all of the humor (or at least all of the strangeness) deriving from the incongruous projection of twentieth-century characters and situations into the show's prehistoric context. This radical postmodern collapse of historical distinctions clearly produced a certain defamiliarization that potentially helped audiences to see contemporary phenomena in a new light. However, the comic tone of the show ensured that this defamiliarization would be simply amusing, rather than troubling. There was very little in the way of anxiety in *The Flintstones*, which might account for the fact that it remained a prominent part of American popular culture throughout the remainder of the twentieth century (including the release of a feature-length film version, with live actors, in 1994), despite the fact that the initial series was cancelled in 1966.

The high camp of the *Batman* series (1968–1970) ended the 1960s proper on a thoroughly ludic note. Meanwhile, *The Flintstones* paved the way for later animated series such as *The Simpsons*, which has run on the Fox Network from 1990 into the next century. *The Simpsons*, like *The Flintstones*, was an animated sitcom, but one with a much sharper satirical edge that poked fun at various aspects of American life, while simultaneously having a great deal of fun with the sitcom form itself. Indeed, if *The Flintstones* was an animated version of *The Honeymooners*, then *The Simpsons* was, to an extent, an animated version of Fox's *Married ...with Children*, which went on the air in 1987 and lasted more than a decade. Both series self-consciously lampooned the usual conventions of the sitcom form, twisting those conventions in ways that potentially produced a certain cognitive estrangement, but again doing so in a way that was almost entirely ludic. However, in the reverse of what one might expect, the animated *Simpsons* series contains potentially subversive social commentary (including extensive commentary on animation and on television) that goes well beyond that of *Married ... with Children*.

The ludic strain is also dominant in the notorious *Beavis and Butt-head*, which began in 1993 and soon gained a large youth following because of its seemingly transgressive irreverence toward conventionally acceptable social behavior — and the conventions of broadcast television. Along with its successor, *South Park* (which began airing on Comedy Central in 1997), *Beavis and Butt-head* owed much of its success to its violation of the expectations of animated programming, expectations that had largely been established in Disney features from *Snow White* (1937) to *Aladdin* (1992). There is, of course, nothing truly subversive about either *Beavis and Butt-head* or *South Park*, both of which portray transgressive behavior as immature, if not downright stupid. Both series are clearly postmodern, in the ludic sense, and both revel in television intertextuality. Indeed, the highly allusive *South Park* irreverently drew on all sorts of cultural resources, including *Beavis and Butt-head*, which was clearly one of the inspirations for the *Terence and Philip* series that the *South Park* characters watch so faithfully, mesmerized by the constant flatulence of the title characters. Meanwhile, *South Park* did the crude animation of *Beavis and Butt-head* one better, stretching it to a minimalist extreme that, among other things, mocked the elaborate animation of the Disney features.

By the 1990s, in fact, the ludic strain of postmodern television had become almost entirely dominant, so that even the strangest of strange TV came to be dominated by this strain—which is another way of saying that the transition from a classical modern to a postmodern sensibility had been greatly advanced. In Chapter 4, I discuss *Twin Peaks*, perhaps the strangest (at least in the usual sense of the word) program ever to appear on American commercial television. However, I argue in this chapter that *Twin Peaks*, despite its seemingly dark subject matter, was mostly ludic. Its strangeness was designed more to titillate and delight audiences than to trouble them or to make them view the world in new and different ways.

Finally, in Chapter 5, I discuss *The X-Files*, which I see as a sort of sequel to *Twin Peaks*, but one which learned important lessons from its predecessor to achieve much greater (and more prolonged) commercial success. In particular, *The X-Files* produces its postmodern effects within a fundamentally realist matrix and thus avoids estranging audiences who still regard realism as "normal." In moving from *The Twilight Zone* and *The Prisoner* to *Twin Peaks* and *The X-Files*, I thus trace the growing importance of the postmodern paradigm within modernity, while arguing that the increasing dominance of the postmodern paradigm can be seen in the increasing prominence of the ludic strain within postmodernism. At the same time, phenomenon such as the persistence of realism in *The X-Files* indicate important underlying continuities in American culture, as the modern worldview of both realism and modernism proper remains powerful.

2

The Twilight Zone and American Society in the Long 1950s: Between the Modern and the Postmodern

The 1950s, as a decade, have come to be the focus of a number of nostalgic longings, generally based on the notion that it was a simple and peaceful time when traditional values prevailed and the world still made sense. This nostalgia itself, as Jameson has noted, is a postmodern phenomena: it ignores much of the historical reality of the 1950s, instead picking and choosing images that produce the desired memory of a better day. The later representation of the 1950s on television has, of course, greatly contributed to this phenomenon. For one thing, as David Halberstam notes, the fifties nostalgia craze of later decades was inspired less by the reality of the 1950s than by the idyllic visions promulgated in the decade's television programming, especially in idealized family sitcoms, such as *Leave It to Beaver* and *The Adventures of Ozzie and Harriet* (514). For another, nostalgia for the 1950s was greatly promoted by later series, such as the long-running *Happy Days* (1974–84), whose very title indicates its nostalgic reformulation of the 1950s (though the series is actually set in the early 1960s).

Indeed, the 1950s have also come to be regarded as the "golden age" of television itself, a phenomenon that Frank Sturcken places primarily in the live programming of the period 1946–1958. But much of the recorded programming of the 1950s is fondly remembered as well, with programs such as *I Love Lucy* (first broadcast in the 1951–52 season) establishing formats and conventions that would last for decades. *I Love Lucy* became the model for the TV sitcom for years to come, though the genre already had a long history on radio. It was also of crucial importance to the direction of the television industry: in an era dominated by live programming, it was the first successful network series to be entirely filmed (in a fringe Hollywood studio), thus paving the way for such developments as reruns and syndication.

Thus, while *I Love Lucy* was a formulaic sitcom, it was an innovative series that helped to establish the formulas to which it adhered. It was, in fact, already postmodern. For example, like all programs broadcast on commercial television, *I Love Lucy* was continually interrupted by commercials (in this case, largely commercials for cigarette manufacturer Philip Morris). But the series was also plural and formally fragmented in ways that went beyond commercial intrusions. As I have noted, the nature of the television medium makes the boundaries of individual texts permeable in ways that books, contained in single bound volumes, or films, shown in an enclosed theater or distributed on self-contained videocassettes or DVDs, are not. Thus, viewers who tuned their newfangled TV sets to CBS on Monday nights in the 1952–53 season were likely to experience the program not in isolation, but as part of a stream of programming in which *Lucy* was preceded by *Talent Scouts* and followed by *It's News to Me*. Similarly, in its own 9–9:30 pm Eastern time slot, *Lucy* was part of a television environment that included the simultaneous broadcast of a film on ABC and the suspense-thriller anthology *Lights Out* on NBC[1]. Thus, even in an era before remote controls and proliferating cable channels would lead to a radical increase in the fragmentation of the experience of television viewing, audiences had an opportunity to make choices among programs in ways that are unique to television, or at least to television and radio.

As a whole, then, early network television, despite the relative simplicity of most individual programs and the relatively small array of choices offered to viewers, already reflected (and probably contributed to) the growing complexity and fragmentation of American society in the long 1950s. Indeed, television programming in the 1950s was, in many ways, especially fragmented given the prominence of anthology series such as *Playhouse 90, Kraft Television Theater* and, eventually, *The Twilight Zone* that were broadcast on a regular schedule but that featured new and different casts and scenarios in each episode. Many of these anthologies, as their titles indicate, were modeled on live theater and thus had strong roots in the modern era. Indeed, in a gesture toward modernist cultural elitism, they were generally envisioned as "prestige" or "quality" entertainment, designed to bring the cultural experience of the live stage to a national audience, many of the members of which had little or no opportunity to see live theater, especially with the kinds of elite professional casts that were featured on these shows. On the other hand, some anthology series of the 1950s, most notably *Alfred Hitchcock Presents* (1955–66 in various incarnations) and *The Twilight Zone*, were distinctively new forms of entertainment, even though they included elements derived from theater, film, radio, print, and television predecessors. Indeed, one of the most striking (and postmodern) aspects of such series was their sheer plurality, as they drew on multigeneric and multimedia forms to present audiences with something not quite like anything they had seen before.

The intertextual (and multimedia) character of *Alfred Hitchcock Presents* was especially obvious, given the clear attempt to link the series to Hitchcock's growing reputation as a film director. After all, during the run of the series, Hitchcock would produce such film classics as *The Wrong Man* (1956), *Vertigo* (1958), *North by Northwest* (1959), *Psycho* (1960), and *The Birds* (1963). I have argued, in *The Post-Utopian Imagination*, that such films contain numerous elements of an emerging post-modernism, and I think the same can be said for the series. For example, Hitchcock himself (though he directed only twenty of the hundreds of episodes of the series) appeared onscreen at the beginning and end of each episode, in a motif clearly reminiscent of Hitchcock's famous cameos in his own films. The series, like the films, thus included an inherent (postmodern) confusion of ontological levels, mixing the "real" Hitchcock with fictional stories and characters. However, the continuing presence of Hitchcock provided a unifying center that provided at least a partial stay against the confusion of the series's emergent postmodern fragmentation.

This fragmentation also involved a mixture of modes: the dark tales of violence and crime tended to have an ironic or even comic twist, and Hitchcock's own highly ironic commentaries added an additional comic element. Such mixtures of modes and genres were again a clear sign of incipient (ludic) postmodernism, even if they were also a sign that television censors (and sponsors) during the period looked askance on anything unremittingly dark or pessimistic. Of course, in Hitchcock's case, the sponsors themselves were often the butt of the humor. He tended to end his introductory remarks with a side thrust at the sponsors, which, at the time, surely reminded audiences of the tendency of Hollywood, in films such as *Will Success Spoil Rock Hunter?* (1957) to dismiss television as aesthetically inferior because of its commercial interruptions — as if the American film industry had not been driven by commercial considerations from the very beginning.

Hitchcock's barbs at his own sponsors contained a clearly postmodern element of ironic self-consciousness, even though they were hardly subversive and certainly presented no threat to the structure of commercial television, or of late capitalism itself. Indeed, the series was ultimately quite conservative and adhered to the standards of the time quite firmly, as when Hitchcock tended, at the end of each episode, to assure audiences that the criminals portrayed in the preceding episode had been apprehended and punished for their crimes. Again, however, there was a certain tongue-in-cheek quality to these reminders, making clear that these gestures toward conventional morality were just that — gestures, and highly ironic ones at that.

Such self-conscious irony is the sign of a mature (and secure) medium and reflects the speed at which television programming (and television audiences) matured in the 1950s. Still, for all of its innovation and complexity, *Alfred Hitchcock Presents* showed television audiences a world with which they were already familiar. If the focus on crime stories reflected a desire for danger and adventure in the highly routinized environment of 1950s and early-1960s America, it also addressed the anxieties of an increasingly affluent audience that criminals and other undesirables might threaten their newfound wealth and financial security. Meanwhile, there was little that was really innovative about the look of the series, despite the participation of the *auteur* Hitchcock, who tellingly employed the crew from the television series to film *Psycho* precisely because he did not want that film to look artistic.

The Twilight Zone, which consciously strove for a literary texture, was a different matter. This literariness can be seen, among other things, in the distinctive stamp that principal writer and executive producer Rod Serling put on the show, a stamp that helped to place the series firmly in the flow of 1950s culture. Serling had already established his ability to strike veins in the American consciousness with now legendary teleplays such as "Patterns" (broadcast live on *Kraft Television Theater* on January 12, 1955, then again on February 9 of the same year) and "Requiem for a Heavyweight" (broadcast live on *Playhouse 90* on October 11, 1956).[2] The latter, the second episode ever of *Playhouse 90*, swept the year's major Emmy Awards and helped to establish the critical reputation of that series, even though the first episode had been something of a flop. Incidentally, that first episode, "Forbidden Area," was also written by Serling (based on the novel by Pat Frank); though unsuccessful, it was also extremely topical, dealing with Cold War paranoia by focusing on the sabotage of American nuclear bombers during the Cold War.

Serling would try the Cold War thriller again (and more successfully) with his screenplay for *Seven Days in May* (1964). But it was *The Twilight Zone* that established his reputation once and for all. Indeed, *The Twilight Zone* is probably more closely associated with Serling than any other show in television history was associated with any writer, partly because he had already established a lofty reputation before the show began, partly because he was the show's executive producer, and mostly because of his memorable on-screen narrations at the beginning and end of each episode. As a result, these narrations, like those of Hitchcock in *Alfred Hitchcock Presents*, provided a strong sense of continuity to the episodic series. In fact, Serling provided an even stronger stabilizing center because of his perceived status as the "author" of the series. Of course, Serling did not write every episode. For example, Charles Beaumont and Richard Matheson, for example, wrote more than three dozen episodes between them. Both of these writers scripted episodes that are among the series' best, but this fact did little to diminish the popular view of Serling as the creative force behind the series.

This sense of *The Twilight Zone* as emanating from the pen of a brilliant author probably did a great deal to enhance its reputation as being more literary and artistic than typical television fare. In some ways, the series was rather formulaic: each episode begins by setting up an extraordinary situation, usually involving science-fiction or supernatural motifs; the middle part of each episode dramatizes and elaborates on this situation; each episode then ends with a surprising (and, presumably, thought-provoking) twist that makes the situation even more interesting than it had originally appeared to be. Indeed, the situations and ideas explored in the series were interesting enough that the formulaic structure did very little to diminish the popular (and critical) perception of the show's creativity and brilliance, especially because the unusual, fantastic, and far-fetched scenarios put forth in the various episodes always retained a clear sense of relevance to contemporary reality, their strangeness merely serving as a defamiliarizing device that helped to provide insights into and perspectives on a number of the concerns of the late 1950s and early 1960s.

Indeed, *The Twilight Zone* is primarily a work of satire, and one that is quite often reminiscent of Bakhtin's various discussions of the important genre of Menippean satire (or the "menippea"), which he regards as a crucial generic forerunner of the modern novel. In *Problems of Dostoevsky's Poetics*, Bakhtin emphasizes that "the use of the fantastic in Menippean satire is internally motivated by the urge to create extraordinary situations for the testing of philosophical ideas" (114). Further, he notes that these ideas are not necessarily mere abstractions, because "the menippea is generally concerned with current and topical issues" (118). At the same time, these issues are defamiliarized through the use of "a special kind of experimental fantasticality: ... observation from some unusual point of view, from on high, for example, which results in a radical change in the scale of observed phenomena of life" (116). And this defamiliarization is enhanced by the inclusion of playfully "abrupt transitions and shifts" (118). Finally, for Bakhtin, Menippean satire is an especially carnivalesque genre and thus includes all of the characteristics that he typically associates with the carnival, including a fundamental ambivalence, an irreverent attitude of rule-breaking and boundary-crossing, and a tendency to reverse or ignore typically observed hierarchies.

Though sometimes in a muted way, *The Twilight Zone* contains all of these elements. Obviously concerned with the fantastic and with creating unusual perspectives, it often engages current and topical issues from the long 1950s, including the nuclear arms race. It also follows the social criticism of the decade in calling attention to the dehumanizing consequences of the rapid capitalist expansion that went on during the decade. These consequences, as I have outlined in *Monsters, Mushroom Clouds, and the Cold War*, crucially include alienation (in the classic Marxist sense) and routinization (in the sense also referred to by Max Weber as rationalization), or the sense that every aspect of life, even the most "private," is being increasingly regimented to meet the gray-flanneled needs of capitalist economic expansion.

Many episodes of *The Twilight Zone*, especially those written by Serling, addressed the theme of routinization, as had "Patterns," in which a ruthless company head drives his more humanistic vice president to his death, thus producing a sharp critique of the corporate ethic of the 1950s, a sort of harder-edged *Man in the Gray Flannel Suit*. *The Twilight Zone* often similarly treated corporate culture as soul-destroying. Thus, two of the best known episodes of the series, "Walking Distance" (first aired on October 30, 1959)[3] and "A Stop at Willoughby" (May 6, 1960) both involve protagonists who attempt to escape from the grinding, cutthroat routine of their work as advertising executives by escaping into fantasy visions of a slower-paced, small-town pastoral past. Workplace routine is also at the heart of the difficulties suffered by the protagonists of such episodes as "Mr. Bevis" (June 3, 1960) and "The Mind and the Matter" (May 12, 1961). Finally, one of the very last episodes, "The Brain Center at Whipple's" (May 15, 1964), served as a summary of numerous workplace concerns. In the episode, Whipple, a heartless company head, replaces all of his employees with machines in order to increase profits. Then, in a final plot twist of the kind that occurs in nearly all episodes of *The Twilight Zone*, Whipple discovers that he himself has been replaced by a robot, played by Robby of *Forbidden Planet* fame.

"Requiem for a Heavyweight," with its story of a broken-down prizefighter who is treated merely as a financial asset, explored similar themes; it also anticipated the central role played by boxing in *The Twilight Zone* episodes such as "The Big Tall Wish" (April 8, 1960) and "Steel" (October 4, 1963, written by Matheson). These boxing stories recalled such film noir classics as *Body and Soul* (1947), *Champion* (1949), and *The Set Up* (1949) in their suggestive treatment of the dog-eat-dog world of boxing as a metaphor for the competitive ethic of capitalism. Thus, when ex-boxer Steel Kelly (Lee Marvin) stands in for his broken-down robot in a bout against another robot fighter, he does it purely for the money. He then gets beaten to a pulp in a reminder of how hard it is for people to compete with machines in the technological society of modern capitalist America. "The Big Tall Wish," meanwhile, comments on the phenomenon of routinization when a young boy (Steven Perry) with seemingly magical powers to make his wishes come true is unable to wish a battered prizefighter (Ivan Dixon) to victory in a key match because the boxer simply cannot believe in the magic of such wishes. Afterward, the boy decides to give up wishing altogether, because "there ain't no such thing as magic" in the routinized world of modern America.

Meanwhile, the noirish aspects of these boxing episodes provide a reminder that, if *The Twilight Zone* serves as a sort of capstone for the famed science-fiction films of the 1950s, it is also often reminiscent of film noir, itself at least partly a reaction against capitalist routinization. Meanwhile, as if to finish off its sweep of 1950s film genres, many episodes of *The Twilight Zone* are either Westerns or war stories. One of the most postmodern aspects of the show, in fact, is its strongly multigeneric nature, a characteristic that Bakhtin also consistently associates with Menippean satire and other "carnivalized" genres, including the novel. For Bakhin, genres are not mere formal structures, but carriers of specific ideologies. Indeed, for him, much of the dialogic power of the novel derives from dialogic confrontations among the different worldviews that meet within the multigeneric texture of the novel.

Of course, film noir, with its characteristic ambivalence in the face of extreme situations, is already itself a carnivalized genre. It was also an especially important predecessor to *The Twilight Zone*. Numerous episodes had a distinctive film noir look, perhaps partly (as with the films themselves) for budgetary reasons, but no doubt largely because the hundreds of films noirs made during the 1940s and 1950s had already demonstrated that dim lighting and exaggerated shadow effects could produce precisely the air of mystery and foreboding that *The Twilight Zone* was trying for. Many episodes of *The Twilight Zone* were thematically reminiscent of film noir as well, often focusing on petty criminals, struggling boxers, and various other losers and little guys of the kind who appeared so regularly in film noir. "The Four of Us Are Dying" (January 1, 1960) is paradigmatic of these episodes. It features Arch Hammer (Harry Townes), a small time chiseler who has only one thing going for him: the ability to change his appearance to resemble anyone he chooses. In the episode, set in a nightmarish noir landscape reminiscent of the dystopian Pottersville of *It's a Wonderful Life*, Hammer assumes a series of identities (a trumpet player, a gangster, a boxer) that reads like a roll call of typical film noir characters. He then meets his doom, shot down in the street—in a case of mistaken identity.

If "The Four of Us Are Dying" recalls a number of standard noir motifs (as well as a typical 1950s anxiety over the stability of personal identity), some *Twilight Zone* episodes even seemed to recall specific films noirs. For example, "The Hitch-Hiker" (January 22, 1960) was based on a radio play that had originally been broadcast on *The Mercury Theatre on the Air*, with Orson Welles (later to play such an important role in the evolution of film noir) in the lead role. But the *Twilight Zone* episode is also reminiscent of film noir classics such as Edgar G. Ulmer's notorious *Detour* (1945). Serling, in his closing voiceover, even describes the episode as a "detour though the Twilight Zone." Meanwhile, the episode also recalls the 1953 film of the same title, the only 1950s film noir to have been directed by a woman, Ida Lupino. And Lupino herself starred in the

Twilight Zone episode, "The Sixteen-Millimeter Shrine" (October 23, 1959), which, with its theme of a has-been movie star living in the past, could not help recalling *Sunset Boulevard* in its depiction of the inability of ex-movie queen Barbara Jean Trenton (Lupino) to find a place for herself in the contemporary world.

"The Sixteen-Millimeter Shrine," with its out-of-place protagonist, also addressed the theme of alienation. Indeed, *The Twilight Zone* addressed the twin themes of alienation and routinization perhaps more vividly than any other science-fiction artifact of the long 1950s. Marc Scott Zicree, introducing his *Twilight Zone Companion*, argues that the popularity of the show was due to its unique focus on the theme of alienation, which he describes as "the great dilemma of our age" (n.p.). But the show also focused to an equal extent on the theme of routinization, and its appeal surely derived in large measure from its ability to suggest that the universe still contained a great deal that was strange and mysterious, despite the routinized nature of American life in the 1950s. In the process, *The Twilight Zone* allowed Serling, after years of battling censors over his controversial, socially conscious scripts for shows such as *Playhouse 90*, to treat topics that he would never have been allowed to treat on television in a more realistic context.[4] Indeed, the series as a whole nicely illustrates the way in which politically engaged writers in the 1950s were forced to use techniques of indirection, making their comments through genres, such as science fiction and crime fiction, that were typically regarded as unserious, and thus unthreatening.

In its treatment of such issues, *The Twilight Zone* displayed a strain of modernist social consciousness, clearly believing that it could make a difference. The focus on alienation, described by Jameson as quintessential modernist concept and experience, also indicated a modernist inclination at the heart of the show (*Postmodernism* 90). From its initial pilot episode, ("Where is Everybody?" airing October 2, 1959), which used the loneliness of solo space flight as a allegory of the dangers of alienation, to the very last episode ("The Bewitchin' Pool," June 19, 1964, written by Earl Hamner, Jr.), in which two children dream of escaping into a pastoral fantasy world to get away from the routine of their affluent parents' bourgeois bickering, the series consistently focused on alienation, along with routinization, as crucial themes that concerned American culture in the long 1950s.

One of the *Twilight Zone* episodes that best encapsulates the twin themes of alienation and routinization is "The Lonely" (November 13, 1959). As the episode begins, James A. Corry (Jack Warden) has been convicted of murder (though he swears it was self-defense) and sentenced to serve fifty years of imprisonment on a barren asteroid. He is dying of loneliness, Serling's opening voiceover tells us, while Corry himself, as the episode begins, complains of the mind-numbing routine of the place, where "all the days and the months and the years are the same." The unfortunate Corry is, for a time, relieved of both his loneliness and his boredom when a compassionate spaceship captain drops off a female robot (named Alicia), which looks entirely human. In fact, the directions that come with Alicia suggestively tell us, "to all intent and purpose this creature *is* a woman. Physiologically and psychologically, she is a human being." Alice thus challenges the boundary between human and machine, a motif that would later be central to cyberpunk science fiction, cited by numerous critics (including Jameson) as a quintessential postmodernist cultural phenomenon.

Initially appalled by the robot, Corry slowly warms to Alicia and falls deeply in love with her, especially since she so directly reflects his own interests and strikes him as an extension of himself. In other words, he is so alienated that he cannot relate to anyone who is a legitimately separate subject, but can relate to a robot, which is merely an object. Later, Corry is pardoned and the spaceship returns to take him back to earth. Unfortunately. he can only take fifteen pounds of luggage, so he is told that Alicia must be left behind. When he protests that Alicia is not luggage, but a woman, the captain provides a shocking reminder of her Otherness by pulling out his gun and shooting the robot in the face, destroying it and revealing a mass of circuits and wiring. They won't be leaving behind a woman, the captain tells Corry, just his loneliness.

Airing the very next week after "The Lonely" was another classic, "Time Enough at Last" (November 20, 1959). In this episode, one of several to deal with the prospects of nuclear holocaust, mild-mannered, myopic bank teller Henry Bemis (Burgess Meredith) is the ultimate alienated individual, understood by no one, and tormented by both his domineering boss and his hectoring wife. In particular, neither the boss nor the wife can understand Bemis's love of reading, which clearly serves for him as an avenue of escape for routinization, but which serves for them as something that marks Bemis as abnormal. As Serling's opening voice-over puts it, Bemis's passion for the printed page is constantly being thwarted by "a bank president and a wife and a world full of tongue-cluckers and the unrelenting hands of the clock."

The Twilight Zone, however, supported such passions, and a love of books and literature is central to several episodes of the series. Bemis is thus presented sympathetically throughout the episode, despite the fact that his devotion to books has radically increased his alienation from the world around him. Desperate for a chance to get a little reading done, Bemis symbolically locks himself away from the world in the bank vault so he can read without interruption during his lunch breaks. One day, while he is in the vault, a nuclear attack destroys the entire city, and perhaps all of human civilization. But Bemis emerges unscathed, saved by the thick metal walls of the vault. At first, even though he is able to find plenty of food and other necessities, he feels despair at being the last man on earth, reminding us of the protagonist of "Where Is Everybody?" He even considers suicide. Then, however, he discovers that most of the books in the public library have survived. He suddenly realizes that the nuclear attack was a godsend: now he can have all these books to himself, with all the time in the world to read them and no one to interfere or complain. He joyously begins to arrange the books in stacks, planning out his reading for years to come.

At this point comes the episode's famous, heart-rending conclusion: Bemis drops and shatters his thick glasses, without which he is blind. Now, with no one to help him, with no ophthalmologists or optometrists or opticians left alive to provide him with a new pair of glasses, Bemis is helpless and all those books are worthless. It's not so easy to live without other people after all, an alienation-related theme that resounds through many episodes of the series. For example, a similar theme informs the less successful episode, "The Mind and the Matter" (May 12, 1961), in which the bitterly alienated protagonist gains the power to make everyone else on earth disappear, then relents and brings them back when he discovers life alone is even worse.

At the same time, the typical *Twilight Zone* protagonist is very much alone in the face of the strange circumstances that confront him or her. And these protagonists are typically treated sympathetically, in keeping with the individualist ideology that permeates the series—and American television programming as a whole. One of the best illustrations of this motif is "The Obsolete Man" (June 2, 1961), a companion episode to "Time Enough at Last." In "The Obsolete Man," the protagonist's love of books again places him in opposition to the official values of his society. Here, a lone librarian, Romney Wordsworth (again played by Meredith, providing an intertextual link that emphasizes the parallel between Wordsworth and Bemis), confronts a totalitarian dystopia that declares both the librarian and the books he so loves obsolete and useless. Thus, books again are glorified, and the episode, in High Enlightenment fashion, holds up printed culture as a bastion of individual liberty and natural enemy of totalitarianism.

"The Obsolete Man" is one of *The Twilight Zone*'s most interesting looking episodes, employing exaggerated expressionistic sets to enhance the dystopian atmosphere of the episode, in which the State exerts total control over the minds of its citizens, having banned all books, all religion, and all independent thought. The episode begins as Wordsworth is pronounced "obsolete" by a chancellor of the State (played by Fritz Weaver), a judgment that carries with it a penalty of death. In this thoroughly commodified and routinized society, nothing that does not have immediate instrumental value can be tolerated. Serling's opening monologue, meanwhile, emphasizes the symbolic nature of this State, declaring that it "has patterned itself after every dictator who has ever planted the ripping imprint of a boot on the pages of history since the beginning of time." This boot image probably derives most directly from Orwell's

Nineteen Eighty-four, but it also reaches back to Jack London's *The Iron Heel* (1907), placing the episode in a long dystopian tradition. There are historical references as well, as when the chancellor (employing a confused equation between fascism and communism that was a central motif in American Cold War propaganda) later identifies both Hitler and Stalin as his predecessors, though declaring that neither went far enough in eliminating undesirables.

Though it is not entirely obvious in the actual episode, director Elliot Silverstein has stated that the texture of the hearing in which Wordsworth is declared obsolete was partly inspired by the infamous Army-McCarthy hearings, a fact that suggests that this dystopian State, while overtly linked with Nazi Germany and the Stalinist Soviet Union, may also have a great deal in common with the United States. Indeed, if the lonely Wordsworth is a paradigm of alienation, this society is the ultimate in routinization, a fact that Wordsworth well recognizes, complaining to the chancellor that "your State has everything categorized, indexed, tagged." However, other than such vague hints at criticism of American society in the 1950s, "The Obsolete Man" is pure orthodox Americanism. It presents Wordsworth (not surprisingly, given his surname) as a paragon of Romantic individualism, upholding the values of religion, traditional culture, and human rights in the face of a dystopian regime so extreme that few viewers would be likely to relate it to their own United States. Indeed, the political commentary of *The Twilight Zone* is quite consistently attenuated by the series's ultimate orthodoxy, something that might also be said for the cultural criticism of the long 1950s. At the same time, the orthodoxy of *The Twilight Zone* is consistently destabilized by unstated hints that all is not well with the American way of life, leading David Cochran to declare that the series "destabilized, deconstructed, and subverted the certainties and eternal verities of the dominant Cold War worldview" (198).

The post-holocaust theme of "Time Enough at Last" and the dystopian theme of "The Obsolete Man" illustrate the way in which numerous *Twilight Zone* episodes paralleled the science-fiction films of the 1950s. For example, numerous episodes of the series dealt with invasions from outer space or with voyages to outer space, frequently making use of leftover props from films such as *Forbidden Planet*. One of the most interesting of these, "The Monsters Are Due on Maple Street" (which originally aired March 4, 1960), shows the mob mentality of small-town America when faced with the possibility of invasion from outer space (or Russia, or the Third World), much like the film *It Came from Outer Space* (1953). On the other hand, *The Twilight Zone* often treated the motif of alien invasion parodically, suggesting the way in which the series was moving toward a postmodern skepticism concerning the paranoia of the previous decade. Thus, both Martian and Venusian invaders comically play with the vanities of the lowly Mr. Dingle in "Mr. Dingle the Strong"

(March 3, 1961), while Martian and Venusian invaders compete with one another in "Will the Real Martian Please Stand Up" (May 16, 1961), as the humans in the episode bicker among themselves, each suspecting the others of actually being aliens.

Quite a few episodes of *The Twilight Zone* recalled films such as *The Incredible Shrinking Man* (1957), *The Amazing Colossal Man* (1957), and *Attack of the 50 Foot Woman* (1958) by dealing with an opposition between the tiny and the huge, or even with individuals who suddenly shrank or grew. But such episodes were also reminiscent of the Menippean giants of satirists such as Rabelais and Swift. In "The Last Night of a Jockey" (October 25, 1963), Mickey Rooney plays a diminutive jockey who wishes to be big, then gets more than he bargained for by becoming a ten-foot giant, thus ruining his career. In the ironic alien-invasion episode "The Fear" (May 29, 1964), two earthlings in a remote locale are apparently menaced by gigantic aliens. It turns out, however, that the aliens are really tiny and were only attempting to appear to be huge as a way of defending themselves from the much larger earthlings. Thus, in a typical *Twilight Zone* plot twist, it is revealed at the end that it is actually the earthlings who are the terrifying giants: we have met the Other and he is us.

A somewhat similar Menippean fascination with extremes in size (along with carnivalesque reversals of those extremes) went into the making of "The Little People" (March 30, 1962), in which an earth astronaut tyrannizes a planet populated by tiny people the size of ants, only to be replaced as the planet's ruler when a spaceship bearing giants the size of mountains lands there. Another episode along the same lines was "The Invaders"(January 27, 1960, written by Matheson), in which we see a lone woman in a remote farmhouse as she is menaced by tiny invaders from outer space. In the end, she manages to crush the invaders through the sheer force of her superior size and strength, and we are naturally relieved that this human has triumphed over the alien menace. Then, however, we learn that invaders are actually astronauts from earth who have landed on this planet of terrifying giants.

Such reversals, suggesting the relativism of all perspectives, provide key instances of the way in which *The Twilight Zone* serves as an important marker of the postmodern turn taken by American culture, and particularly American science fiction, in the long 1950s. In fact, *The Twilight Zone*, despite its lingering love of the Western literary tradition and its modernist aspiration to the condition of High Art, contains some of the clearest signs of the beginnings of postmodernism in the long 1950s, especially in its persistent self-conscious irony and in its incessant interrogation of conventional boundaries, such as those between Self and Other and between Reality and Fiction.

Sudden reversals in perspective, reminiscent of Bakhtin's descriptions of carnivalesque inversions, were a favorite motif of *The Twilight Zone*, including a number of episodes in which astronauts fly off to a seemingly distant planet—which turns out to be earth.[5] Other role-reversal episodes included "A Quality of Mercy" (December 29, 1961), in which a Japanese-hating American lieutenant suddenly finds that he has switched identities with his Japanese counterpart, and "The Eye of the Beholder" (November 11, 1960), a classic episode that employs a particular *Twilight Zone* favorite, a reversal of the normal and the abnormal. Given the 1950s obsession with normality, it is not surprising that this episode also focuses on the terrors of enforced conformity for individuals who can't conform even if they try. In the episode, a horribly disfigured woman has undergone plastic surgery and waits to have the bandages removed from her face, hoping that her appearance has been restored to normal. Throughout the episode, careful lighting and camera effects prevent us from seeing the faces of the doctors and nurses who attend her until the very end, when they remove the bandages and discover to their horror that she remains as disfigured as ever. Then we finally see her face, the face of a perfectly normal, even beautiful (by our standards) young woman.[6] In this world, however, that appearance is horrifying—in contrast to the "normal," which is now revealed in the distorted pig-like visages of the doctors and nurses.

"The Eye of the Beholder," as the title indicates, thus reminds us of the relativity, not only of beauty, but of normality, and of the distinction between Us and Them. At the same time, it provides a commentary on the 1950s demand for conformity. This dystopian society insists that everyone fit in, so, due to this failure to correct her different appearance, the woman is to be exiled to a land of misfits. She rushes screaming from the operating room and runs down a hallway dominated by a giant video screen on which a pig-faced dictator, recalling both Orwell's Big Brother and the One State of Zamyatin's *We*, extols the virtues of a "glorious conformity," including "a single law, a single approach, a single entity of people, a single virtue, a single morality."[7]

A particularly effective interrogation of the line between normality and abnormality occurs in the famous episode "Nightmare at 20,000 Feet" (November 11, 1963, written by Matheson). Here, the normality vs. abnormality opposition is couched specifically within the framework of the central 1950s concern over the difference between the sane vs. the insane. In this episode, airline passenger Bob Wilson (a pre-Kirk William Shatner) is flying home after spending six months in a sanitarium recovering from a nervous breakdown that occurred on a similar airline flight. In the course of the flight, Wilson spots a monster out on the wing, attempting to sabotage the engines. Wilson's efforts to alert the crew and the other passengers, including his own wife, of the danger go to no avail, especially as the monster manages to fly off out of sight whenever anyone other than Wilson looks out on the wing. Eventually, a desperate Wilson swipes a pistol from a sleeping policeman who happens to be on board the plane, then opens the emergency exit (which is conveniently beside his seat) and shoots and kills the monster, saving all on board the plane. In the process, Wilson is nearly sucked out of the plane by the release of pressure, and he ends the episode being taken off to a hospital on the assumption that he has suffered another breakdown.

Luckily, evidence of the monster's sabotage is left on the wing of the plane, and there are hints at the end of the episode that this evidence will eventually prove Wilson's sanity. However, what makes this episode truly special is the way in which Wilson must prove his sanity not to others, but to himself. In a role perfectly suited to Shatner's signature manic acting style, Wilson is clearly concerned through most of the episode that he might really be hallucinating. Thus, unlike Miles Bennell and John Putnam, normal Joes who simply can't get anyone to listen in alien-invasion films such as *It Came from Outer Space* and *Invasion of the Body Snatchers* (1956), Wilson's primary battle is an internal one. And his final victory consists, not in proving his sanity to others, but in proving it to himself. The episode thus nicely dramatizes the way in which the 1950s emphasis on normality, beyond turning neighbor against neighbor, turned individuals against themselves, forcing them to feel all the more alienated through internal mistrust of their own orthodoxy.

The Twilight Zone's interrogation of the boundary between normal and abnormal is part of a larger project of deconstruction of conventional polar oppositions, the very name of the series indicating a realm in which the normal distinction between opposites, such as darkness and light, has been blurred, recalling a similar blurring in the Bakhtinian carnival. It is in this consistent program of deconstruction that the series is at its most postmodern. This interrogation took a number of forms, perhaps the most typical (and most postmodern) of which involved the deconstruction of boundaries between different levels of reality. Particularly relevant to an understanding of this motif is Brian McHale's distinction between the epistemological concerns of modernism and the ontological concerns of postmodernism. McHale argues that modernism is fundamentally based on an epistemological quest for a truth that is felt to exist, no matter how hard it might be to find. Postmodernism, on the other hand, is informed by a much more radical doubt about the very existence of truth. The shift, McHale concludes, involves a "shift of dominant from problems of *knowing* to problems of *modes of being*" (*Postmodernist Fiction* 10, McHale's emphasis). In particular, postmodernism, for McHale, is informed by a sense that reality itself is an artificial human construct, not a preexisting objective target for epistemological inquiry. He thus cites the work of sociologists, such as Peter Berger and Thomas Luckmann, who "regard reality as a kind of collective fiction, constructed and sustained by the processes of socialization, institutionalization, and everyday social interaction, especially through the medium of language (*Postmodernist Fiction* 37).

For McHale, such insights contribute to the tendency of postmodernist fiction to depict shifts from one ontological level to another, as when authors appear as characters in their own fictions or when fictional characters supposedly enter the real worlds of their authors. A quintessential example of a text built around this kind of boundary crossing occurs as early as 1939, in Flann O'Brien's *At Swim-Two-Birds*, and such crossings would become quite common in postmodernist fiction by the 1960s. McHale does not mention *The Twilight Zone* in either of his books on postmodernism, but that series often depicted such ontological leaps, which are a particularly good way to produce just the sort of ironic twist for which *The Twilight Zone* was famous, a lesson that later generations of postmodernist writers seem to have learned well.

Any number of episodes of *The Twilight Zone* involve shifts between ontological levels that are normally considered to be strictly separate. One subset of this phenomenon—and a favorite motif in the series—involves confusion between the animate and the inanimate. One particularly common science-fiction version of this confusion occurs in a number of episodes in which robots are indistinguishable from humans (or vice versa), including "The Lonely," "Steel," "The Mighty Casey" (June 17, 1960), "The Lateness of the Hour" (December 2, 1960), "I Sing the Body Electric" (May 18, 1962, written by Ray Bradbury), "In His Image" (January 3, 1963, written by Beaumont), and "Uncle Simon" (November 15, 1963). Even more central to *The Twilight Zone*, however, were episodes in which the blurred line between animate and inanimate was the one between life and death, much in the mode described by Bakhtin when he notes that "carnivalized" genres tend to focus on "a naked posing of ultimate questions on life and death" (*Problems* 134). To some extent, such confusion is the typical stuff of ghost stories and shows the way in which *The Twilight Zone* often drew upon the horror and fantasy genres in addition to science fiction. Indeed, several episodes are relatively conventional ghost stories, including "The Grave" (October 27, 1961), in which a slain gunslinger may (or may not) get revenge from beyond the grave, "Death's Head Revisited" (November 10, 1961), one of several *The Twilight Zone* episodes dealing with Nazism, and "The Changing of the Guard" (June 1, 1962), in which the ghosts of several former students of a distraught teacher convince him that his life has not been spent in vain.

But even the ghost-story motif has its connections to science fiction. As McHale points out, a serious interrogation of the realm of death is one of most striking concerns of postmodernist fiction (*Constructing* 267). Many episodes of *The Twilight Zone* that deal with death and the afterlife do indeed have a postmodernist quality. But their blurring of fundamental boundaries is also reminiscent of Bakhtin's discussion of the carnivalesque and of Menippean satire, which he notes often takes place in the "nether world" and involves "dialogues at the threshold separating different planes of existence" (*Problems* 116).

In *The Twilight Zone*, even seemingly straightforward ghost stories, such as "The Passersby" (October 6, 1961), were based primarily on the difficulty of making an unequivocal distinction between the living and the dead. In this episode, one of several dealing with the American Civil War, survivors trudging down a road eventually realize that they are actually among the dead, concluding with the appearance of Abraham Lincoln, the war's last casualty. In a somewhat similar fashion, Nan Adams (Inger Stevens), the protagonist of "The Hitch-Hiker," finds out only after a week of encounters with a mysterious, supernatural hitchhiker, that she has been killed in an auto accident. Meanwhile, in "A Nice Place to Visit" (April 15, 1060, written by Beaumont), one of the series's numerous be-careful-what-you-wish-for episodes, different levels of death (i.e., heaven and hell) become confused. Here, small-time hood Rocky Valentine (Larry Blyden) is gunned down by police, only to awake in a seeming paradise, where his every wish comes instantly true. Eventually, Valentine concludes that he is in heaven, only to realize that there is nothing more boring and oppressive than having all his desires routinely and automatically met. In a motif that can be taken as a clear commentary on the downside of American prosperity in the 1950s, he finds that routinization makes life even in heaven almost unbearable. Of course, it turns out in the end that Rocky is actually in hell, not heaven, but that only makes the potential critique of American society all the stronger. Nevertheless, the episode ultimately endorses the central (anti-utopian) ingredient of the consumerist mentality that was still gaining momentum at the end of the long 1950s: satisfaction is death; always want more.

In other episodes, it turns out to be possible (in various ways) to cross the boundary between life and death. For example, in "A Passage for Trumpet" (May 20, 1960), Joey Crown (Jack Klugman) visits the land of death, learns some valuable lessons (especially from the angel Gabriel), then opts to return to life. In "The Last Rites of Jeff Myrtlebank" (February 23, 1960, written by Montgomery Pittman), the title character (James Best) returns from the dead, coming back to life in the midst of his own funeral, leading to a not surprising consternation among his small-town neighbors. In "A Game of Pool (November 13, 1961, written by George Clayton Johnson), legendary pool player Fats Brown (Jonathan Winters) returns from the dead for a match with challenger Jesse Cardiff (Jack Klugman). Cardiff wins, gaining claim to Brown's title as the world's greatest pool player. Too late, he realizes that he must also die, taking Brown's place in similar challenge matches in the future. In "One for the Angels" (October 9, 1959), salesman Lew Bookman (Ed Wynn) manages to wow death itself with his sales pitch, convincing a personified Mr. Death (Murray Hamilton) to take him instead of a little girl from the neighborhood.

"Little Girl Lost" (March 16, 1962, written by Matheson) is a pure science fiction take on the notion of different levels of reality. In this episode, a little girl accidentally falls through a portal into another dimension, forcing her parents (with the convenient help of a neighborhood physicist) to scramble to bring her back to this world. More postmodern were the various episodes of *The Twilight Zone* that involved shifts between fiction and reality, as in "The Sixteen-Millimeter Shrine." For example, episodes such as "Perchance to Dream" (November 27, 1959, written by Beaumont) and "Twenty-Two" (February 10, 1961) involve spillovers from the world of dream (especially nightmares) into the world of supposed reality, recalling Bakhtin's suggestion of the importance of dreams, daydreams, and other unusual psychic states in the Menippean satire (*Problems* 116). "Shadow Play" (May 5, 1961, written by Beaumont) takes this motif to its ultimate, suggesting that what we know as reality is in fact merely the dream of one Adam Grant (Dennis Weaver). In this episode, Grant has been found guilty of murder and condemned to death, but he is convinced that it is all just his recurring nightmare. District Attorney Henry Ritchie (Harry Townes) rejects this claim as nonsense, but newspaper reporter Paul Carson (Wright King) begins nervously to wonder if Grant might be right—and if his execution will mean the end of them all, as they are all merely characters in the dream. Finally, Carson convinces Ritchie to stop the execution on the grounds that Grant is insane, but it is too late: the switch is pulled, not only electrocuting Grant, but leading to the disappearance of Ritchie, Carson, and everything else, leaving only a blank screen. Never fear, however. The nightmare is a recurring one, so, seconds later, it begins all over again, with Grant back in the courtroom being sentenced to death.

In "The After Hours" (June 10, 1960), the ontological confusion occurs between humans and department-store mannequins. Indeed, the central figure, Marsha White (Anne Francis), is a mannequin who discovers only late in the episode that she is not human. This play on the sometimes disturbing resemblance between humans and mannequins is also central to "The Dummy" (May 4, 1962), in which a ventriloquist's dummy takes charge of the act and changes places with the ventriloquist (played by Cliff Robertson). This episode also played on the widespread sense among Americans in the 1950s of being helplessly in the control of larger forces, much like a puppet or ventriloquist's dummy. The creepiness of humanoid commodities is also central to "Living Doll" (November 1, 1963, written by Jerry Sohl, though credited to Beaumont), in which a child's talking doll turns out to be not only animate, but murderous. "Five Characters in Search of an Exit" (December 22, 1961) also builds on the doll motif. Combining its titular allusion to Pirandello (and perhaps Sartre) with a minimalist set that might have come from Beckett, the episode features five characters who find themselves trapped inside an essentially featureless cylinder. In the end, they discover that the cylinder is a barrel in which donated toys are being collected for Christmas — and that they themselves are dolls who have been donated.

This episode clearly reflects anxieties about personal identity in the long 1950s. One of the episodes that reflects this anxiety best is "In His Image" (January 3, 1963, written by Beaumont), which explores this theme through a confusion between humans and robots. In this episode, protagonist Alan Talbot (George Grizzard) begins to hear odd electronic sounds in his head, then goes berserk and throws an old woman in the path of a New York subway train, killing her. Later, with no memory of this event, he takes his new fiancée, Jessica (Gail Kobe), for a tour of his hometown, only to discover that the town does not match his memories of it. They return to New York, where Talbot again hears the electronic noises, barely escapes attacking Jessica, then is hit by a car, opening a large gash in his arm. Talbot looks at the gash, but sees no blood; instead, he sees wires, lights, and transistors. Talbot, it turns out, is a robot. Eventually, he learns that he has been created (only eight days earlier) by Walter Ryder, Jr., for whom he is an exact physical double. Unfortunately, there is a flaw in Talbot's design that causes him to undergo periodic attacks of homicidal madness. Stunned, Talbot asks Ryder the classic question, "Who am I?" "You're nobody," Ryder replies. "Nobody at all." After some additional suspense and confusion, we finally learn that Ryder has managed to deactivate Talbot, whom he now replaces in the relationship with Jessica.

Talbot's shock at discovering that he has no authentic identity directly anticipates the dissolution of identity that Jameson and other observers have seen as a crucial characteristic of postmodernism. This motif is also central to the episode "Person or Persons Unknown" (March 23, 1962, written by Beaumont), which again involves an ontological confusion between dreams and reality. Here, protagonist David Gurney (Richard Long) awakes to find that no one knows him and that all evidence of his previous existence seems to have disappeared. Insisting on his apparently nonexistent identity, he is committed to an asylum, where he has other unsettling experiences, only to awake again and realize he has been dreaming this troubling loss of his identity. His wife now recognizes him as well, confirming that he is who he thinks himself to be. The problem is, he doesn't recognize her — she looks nothing like the woman he remembers as his wife.

Such suggestions of the instability of personal identity anticipate the similar instability that is central to postmodern conceptions of subjectivity, while at the same time reflecting the particular sense of individuals in the long 1950s that they were somehow living inauthentic lives. An early example of episodes treating this motif was "The Four of Us Are Dying," in which Arch Hammer's shape-shifting ability destabilizes his identity. Able to become anyone at all, he is essentially no one. An even more unsettling disturbance of identity occurs in "Mirror Image" (February 26,

1960), in which Millicent Barnes (Vera Miles) spots an exact duplicate of herself waiting in the same bus station. Amid vague suggestions that the double may have somehow spilled over from an alternative reality into this one, Barnes is eventually taken away by police, assumed to be insane. But then Paul Grinstead (Martin Milner), a man who had attempted to help her, spots a duplicate of himself as well and thus realizes that there is more going on here than hallucinations on the part of Barnes.

Some of the most effective crossings of ontological barriers in *The Twilight Zone* involved a postmodern perception of the growing penetration of American society by the media. One of the most typical examples of this motif is "The Sixteen-Millimeter Shrine," which not only looked back on *Sunset Boulevard*, but also anticipated Woody Allen's *Purple Rose of Cairo* (1984) in that Barbara Jean Trenton literally ends the episode by escaping the routine of her "real" life and entering the world of one of her films. In a somewhat similar mode, "Showdown with Rance McGrew" (February 2, 1962) turns from film to television, allowing Serling to satirize the medium in which he had such success, but with which he enjoyed such an uneasy relationship. This episode combines mixtures of ontological levels with time travel, another favorite *The Twilight Zone* motif. Here, TV Western star Rance McGrew (Larry Blyden) suddenly finds himself in the real Wild West, where the real Jesse James (Arch Johnson) complains about McGrew's misrepresentation of the West in his work. In the end, James returns with McGrew to the present, now assuming the role of McGrew's agent so that he can make sure that, in the future, McGrew takes only roles that show the West as it really was.

One of the more effective of these ontological-shift episodes is "A World of Difference" (March 11, 1960, written by Matheson), which also intermixes the supposedly fictional world of film with the supposedly real world of everyday life. In this episode, businessman Arthur Curtis (Howard Duff) is going about his normal workday routine when someone yells, "Cut!" and Curtis suddenly realizes that his office is actually a movie set. The people around him appear to be members of the film crew, and, despite his protestations to the contrary, they insist that "Curtis" is merely a character in the film, being played by declining film star Jerry Raigan. Curtis rushes about, frantically attempting to substantiate his identity but is unable to locate his wife or anyone else who can verify that he is in fact a real person and not merely a fictional character. Finally, Curtis/Raigan's aberrant behavior causes the studio to cancel the production. He rushes back to the set, which is now being dismantled, thus removing the last link to the life he remembers. Then Curtis/Raigan pleads for help from some unspecified force, leading to the sudden restoration of his reality: he is back in his office, which now really *is* his office. Meanwhile, Raigan's agent arrives on the set, only to find that Raigan has disappeared. Thus, the restoration of Curtis's identity on one ontological level apparently leads to the loss of Raigan's on another.

"A World of Difference" (July 1, 1960, written by Matheson) is one of the most clearly postmodernist episodes of the entire series. This episode again turns on a confusion of the ontological difference between "reality" and the world of theater (and television), while again suggesting the instability of individual identity. This episode involves the most common type of postmodernist ontological confusion, a blurring of the ontological boundary between an author and his characters. In this episode, playwright Gregory West (Keenan Wynn) is able to bring his characters to life simply by recording their descriptions on tape. Tired of his domineering wife, Victoria (Phyllis Kirk), he seeks refuge by conjuring up the warm, affectionate Mary (Mary La Roche), a beautiful blonde, who provides him with calming companionship whenever Victoria isn't around. When the wife catches them in the act, West attempts to explain that Mary is merely a fictional character, an explanation that leads Victoria to conclude that he is insane, even when he appears to demonstrate his ability. When she declares her intention to have him committed, he turns the tables by revealing that Victoria, too, is a fictional character, showing her the tape on which her description is recorded. The incredulous Victoria seizes the tape and tosses it in the fireplace, destroying the tape and thus causing herself to cease to exist. A frantic West rushes to his dictating machine to recreate Victoria, but, after thinking for a moment, decides to bring Mary back as his wife, instead. There is an obvious potential for readings of this episode as misogynistic, but it ends on a charming note, with one last amusing ontological crossover. Serling appears in West's study to deliver his ending narration, which annoys West, who then burns Serling's tape, causing him to disappear, thus bringing the episode to an ironic, reality-blurring close as Matheson's character West turns out to be the creator of Serling, the creator of the series for which Matheson created West.

This final touch of ontological confusion also ended the first season of *The Twilight Zone*—and in an entirely appropriate manner, calling attention to the postmodernist (and carnivalesque) blurring of the distinction between reality and fiction that would come to be such a hallmark of the series. Indeed, this phenomenon entered the national consciousness and the national language of America. Decades later, Americans who found themselves in situations that seemed too bizarre to be real would still be saying that they felt as if they were in the Twilight Zone, perhaps at the same time intoning the distinctive "da-da-da-da" of the show's well-known theme music. Of course, the postmodern age of late capitalism being what it is, this feeling would come to be less an extreme circumstance and more the ordinary condition of everyday life. *The Twilight Zone*, then, can be taken, not only as summary of the concerns of the long 1950s, but as a remarkably prescient foreshadowing of things to come.

If the boundary crossings of *The Twilight Zone* recall the seemingly extreme transgressions of the Bakhtinian carnival, the ultimate ideological orthodoxy of the series, with its celebration of liberalism, calls attention to the fact that the carnivalesque, in the age of late consumer capitalism, has become not a temporary escape from everyday routine but the very texture of that routine. It is not for nothing that Twitchell refers to contemporary culture as "carnival culture" or that Stallabrass employs an allusion to Rabelais as the title of his book on contemporary mass culture. Of course, once carnival itself is routinized, it is difficult to see how carnivalesque images can serve any longer as an escape from routine, or as subversive in general. Here, then, Bakhtin's discussions of carnival would appear to cease to be relevant to contemporary postmodern culture. However, Gary Saul Morson and Caryl Emerson have argued (convincingly, I think) that Bakhtin's utopian vision of carnivalesque emancipation in the Rabelais book seems to have been an aberration in his own thought, which typically emphasizes, in a rather antiutopian mode, that social change is a long and tedious historical process. In fact, they conclude that the utopianism of *Rabelais and His World* is so odd (relative both to Bakhtin's overall work and the utopian tradition in general) that it might, in fact, be a disguised form of anti-utopianism. Thus, for Morson and Emerson, this utopianism "appears to designate something close to its opposite: an idealization of unremitting skepticism and unending change without a goal" (94).

Seen in this way, the Bakhtinian carnival would appear to be an image of capitalism itself, which would make it an ideal metaphor for a postmodernism that is the cultural logic of late capitalism. In short, the presentation of seemingly transgressive images on commercial television (MTV may be the paradigm here) is not necessarily transgressive at all but merely reinforces the individualist consumerism of the prevailing culture, much in the way that Thomas Frank has demonstrated a close complicity between the 1960s counterculture and the images that were being purveyed in American advertising in the 1960s. Thus, it may not be surprising that one of the strangest programs of the 1960s, *The Prisoner*, in many ways seems out of step with (and highly critical of) the counterculture of the time. Much of this criticism emanates from lingering modernist impulses within *The Prisoner*, impulses that also often make the program seem skeptical of the contemporary French poststructuralism with which it otherwise had so much in common. I discuss this phenomenon in the next chapter.

3

The Prisoner: The Modern, the Postmodern, and French Poststructuralism in the 1960s

After the demise of *The Twilight Zone* in 1964, a number of other series vied to continue its legacy on American television. One of the more successful of these was *The Outer Limits*, which actually appeared in 1963, while *The Twilight Zone* was still on the air, then lasted until 1965. *The Outer Limits* sometimes created genuine terror and suspense. However, it lacked both the variety and the thoughtfulness of *The Twilight Zone*. It was essentially an alien invasion show, with aliens who were generally evil, terrifying, and unequivocally Other. As such, the series was more in the spirit of the alien invasion films of the 1950s than of *The Twilight Zone*. It responded to a number of Cold War anxieties, but in a way that did relatively little to create the kind of cognitive estrangement that might encourage audiences to look on the Cold War in new and different ways.

The science fiction series of the 1960s was *Star Trek*, which ran for only three seasons (from 1966 to 1969), but which would become an indelible part of American popular culture for the remainder of the twentieth century, spawning an entire industry of merchandising, sequels, and spinoffs. *Star Trek* was notable for its relatively upbeat tone and for its suggestions that advances in science and technology really might eventually lead to better lives for human beings. *Star Trek* also stood out for its liberal politics and espousal of international and interracial cooperation. For example, Spock, the human-Vulcan hybrid, became the most beloved figure on the series, radically undermining the human-alien dichotomy of *The Outer Limits* and other conventionally paranoid Cold War alien encounter stories. However, for all that, *Star Trek* was not really strange TV, in the sense that it did very little to produce the kind of troubling defamiliarization that might genuinely lead to the reconsideration of received ideas. Neither was it, in itself, markedly postmodern: not only did the series project genuine historical change in coming centuries, but each episode was driven by a relatively coherent narrative in which definable problems were susceptible to clear solutions.

The first series after *The Twilight Zone* to achieve genuine cognitive estrangement was probably *The Prisoner*, the late-1960s British television series that was eventually to become a cult favorite of both American and British viewers. The tone of the series, a postmodern generic hybrid of science fiction and spy drama, is set in the first episode, when the nameless protagonist (played by Patrick McGoohan) finds himself suddenly transported to a strange, surreal village, where he is trapped in the grip of powerful forces he can neither understand nor overcome. In fact, once an insider in the power elite, he how finds himself in much the same predicament as most of the rest of the population of the capitalist West. On the one hand, the huge, mysterious forces at work in the global Cold War seemed beyond the understanding or control of mere individuals. On the other hand, the inexorable growth of Western capitalist economist in the two decades since World War II had led to an unprecedented penetration of every aspect of life by capitalist organization, leading to a mind-numbing regimentation and Weberian routinization of both physical and psychic experience. The Prisoner, however, defies the forces that hold him in their grip, declaring that he "will not be pushed, filed, stamped, indexed, briefed, debriefed, or numbered." He thus becomes a champion of individualism in an era when individualism was widely celebrated, but in which these celebrations clearly responded to an anxiety that true individuals were a thing of the past.

This potential contradiction is built into the series, in which the defiant refusal of the Prisoner to submit and conform can be taken either as heroic and inspirational or pointless and foolish, depending on one's point of view. This undecidability was a key element of the program, leading Buxton to declare it "undoubtedly the most enigmatic series of all time" (93). In this and other ways, the series resonated with the contradictory concerns of its time. In this chapter, I want in particular to explore the numerous concerns that the series shared with contemporary debates in French intellectual circles, which were at the time in the midst of the turn from structuralism to poststructuralism, a turn that itself can be taken as a marker of the ongoing historical transition to the postmodern era of modernity.

It is no accident that *The Prisoner* was roughly contemporaneous with the arrival of Continental "theory," especially of a French structuralist and poststructuralist variety, in the Anglophone West. After all, French theory is informed by a posthumanist, postindividualist sense that the stable, autonomous subject of bourgeois ideology is a myth and that individual subjects are not just controlled, but actually constructed by impersonal forces larger than themselves (such as "language"), forces that the subject can thus subsequently never entirely escape or resist. In America, the arrival of French theory can be located in October, 1966, when a symposium entitled "The Languages of Criticism and the Sciences of Man" was held at Johns Hopkins University — one month after the premiere of *Star Trek* on American television. The structuralist invasion that began with this conference came just as the French themselves were beginning to shift into a more poststructuralist phase, and French thinkers such as Jacques Derrida and Michel Foucault subsequently became major influences on American intellectual life primarily as poststructuralists. American literary criticism took on an especially strong Derridean accent in the 1970s as American academic critics turned to deconstruction in search of theoretically sophisticated alternatives to a New Criticism the woeful limitations of which were becoming all too clear. Foucault's more socially engaged version of poststructuralism would ultimately overtake Derrida in importance in America, while French thinkers such as Jean-François Lyotard, Guy Debord, Jean Baudrillard, Gilles Deleuze, and Félix Guattari would make central contributions to the theorization of postmodernism itself.

Debord and Baudrillard would make particularly strong contributions to the evolution of Jameson's thoughts on postmodernism, but almost all of these thinkers share with Jameson a certain sense that some great, global historical process (i.e., the Enlightenment) was, by the end of the 1960s, nearing completion. If, for Jameson, postmodernism occurs when capitalist modernization has completed its drive toward global hegemony, then for Debord the "society of the spectacle" is the culmination of the historical capitalist drive toward commodification of everything. "The spectacle," writes Debord, "is the moment when the commodity has attained the *total occupation*" of social life" (#42).[1] Baudrillard would then extend Debord's notion of the spectacle to envision a hyperreal world so thoroughly saturated with simulations that the idea of a basic reality behind those simulations has lost all meaning.

For Baudrillard, in fact, the society of the simulacrum represents such a new and powerful turn in human history that conventional resistance to official power becomes pointless. However, Debord (at least until late in his life, in the 1990s) remained rooted in a Marxist tradition in which humans are envisioned as making their own history. One could, then, view the competing interpretations of the Prisoner's individualist rebellion as an opposition between Debord (for whom such a rebellion would have a point) and Baudrillard (for whom such a rebellion could represent nothing but still another simulacrum). According to Best and Kellner, the difference between Debord and Baudrillard can also usefully be viewed as "a confrontation between modern and postmodern theories. At stake is nothing less than the possibility of interpreting and changing reality" (*Postmodern Turn* 104).[2]

This opposition can also be described as a confrontation between the long Marxist tradition of activism and an emerging postmodernist tendency toward quietist despair — or quietist celebration.[3] Here, one might recall Jameson's attempts to distinguish his own totalizing view of post-modernism from the "paranoiacritical" vision of Baudrillard and the "to-tal systems" approach of Foucault, for whom resistance to the carceral power that informs modern capitalist society tends merely to feed that power and to become "an integral and functional part of the system's own internal strategies" (Jameson, *Postmodernism* 203). Indeed, there are many ways in which postmodern theory can be seen as the antithesis of Marxism, though we should be careful in this case to distinguish be-tween postmodernity as a historical event and postmodernist theoriza-tions of that event.

Such theorizations, however radical they sometimes seem to want to be, quite often involve a basic anti-Marxist political resignation that places them quite thoroughly within the confines of Cold War discourse. Meanwhile, it is clear that both *The Prisoner* and the arrival of French the-ory in the American academy were part and parcel of that larger constel-lation of phenomena that we tend to describe as the "sixties," a period that actually extended, in the United States, roughly from 1964 to 1974, from the time the passing of the Civil Rights Act kicked the civil rights movement into high gear until the resignation of Richard Nixon in the wake of Watergate finally ended the anti–Vietnam War movement. If American critics of the 1960s were seeking alternatives to the New Criti-cism, it was partly because American college campuses in general were informed by an atmosphere of challenge to authority and a search for new solutions to old problems. A similar atmosphere prevailed through-out Western Europe and even extended to a Soviet bloc in which a new generation of youth seemed more drawn to blue jeans and rock and roll than to Marxism, Leninism, or any other established isms of authority.[4]

Given this widespread antiauthoritarian tone, it should probably come as no surprise that *The Prisoner*, potentially one of the most overtly antiauthoritarian programs ever to appear on commercial television, made its debut on ITV in September of 1967, approximately midway be-tween the landmark structuralism conference at Hopkins and the Prague, Paris, and Chicago upheavals in the spring and summer of 1968. In fact, the series premiered on American television precisely in the explosive summer of 1968—the first CBS broadcast occurring on June 1 of that year, three days before the shooting of Robert Kennedy in California. And its first run on French television ended in early May, one week be-fore the May 12 general strike that brought the demonstrations there to a near-revolutionary head.[5]

Granted, *The Prisoner* was dominated by the presence and vision of its star and executive producer, the suavely somber (though often bitterly sarcastic) McGoohan; as such, it had a very different feel than the carni-valesque "political theater" of the antiauthoritarian youth culture of the decade. Moreover, McGoohan's political vision was antiauthoritarian more in the right-wing, libertarian sense than in the vaguely (but only

vaguely) leftist sense of most of the leaders of the oppositional youth culture of the decade. In fact, *The Prisoner* went against the grain of the sixties in a number of ways, though it should also be said that going against
the grain was a quintessential strategy of the decade. For one thing, the
series opposed the trend, especially on American television, toward Cold
War spy dramas with an unproblematic anticommunist slant, which continued a long involvement of American television in Western Cold War
propaganda.[6] Thus, programs such as *The Man from U.N.C.L.E.* (1964–68),
I Spy (1965–68), and *Mission: Impossible* (1966–73) all depicted heroic
Western intelligence agents battling evil foes, usually from the Soviet
bloc. It should be noted, however, that the earlier British series *Danger
Man* (broadcast in the U.S. as *Secret Agent,* 1965–66) already showed a
tendency toward cynicism, depicting both sides in the Cold War (with
the exception of protagonist John Drake, played by McGoohan) as ruthless and corrupt, while at the same time inefficient and incompetent.[7]

All of these series owed a great deal to the immense popularity of the
James Bond films, which had begun with *Doctor No* in 1962 and which
were, by 1967, in their fifth installment (all starring Sean Connery as the
debonair Bond, aka Agent 007) with *You Only Live Twice.*[8] McGoohan's
portrayal of the rather suave Prisoner, in fact, recalls Connery's Bond in a
number of ways, including a vaguely Gaelicized British accent that
sounded similar to the Scottish Connery's, at least to American ears
(though McGoohan, oddly enough, had been born in Queens, New
York).[9]

But the Prisoner is no Bond. For one thing, he seems entirely celibate
and does not even appear to like women very much. For another, he is
constantly in the grip of forces more powerful than himself and generally
fails in his efforts to overcome his foes in the series. What's worse, he is
never able to determine just who his foes are, thus dismantling the simple good-guy-versus-bad-guy polarities of the Bond films. Though the
Prisoner is Bondishly dapper in some ways, he has no personal style, but
is generally forced to wear the slightly clownish uniform supplied to him
by his captors, emphasizing his lack of control over his own life. Indeed,
while one could see *The Prisoner* as conveying a strong individualist message, it certainly lacks the sense, in the Bond films and elsewhere in the
spy dramas of the 1960s, that all modern problems can easily be solved
by individual effort, as long as the individual involved is suitably heroic
and debonair. Instead, *The Prisoner* presents a world in which problems
are too complex even to be understood, much less solved, a notion that
probably resonated all too uncomfortably with the experience of many in
its viewing audience and surely contributed to the quick demise of the
series. As Wheeler Winston Dixon puts it, indicating the pessimism of the
series, but also making it sound very postmodern, the message of all seventeen episodes of *The Prisoner* can be summed up as "all is collapsed, all

is nothing, we live in the domain of the eye, and the always now. ...
Spectacle rules, character is non-existent" (C-9).

Still, *The Prisoner* is very much a series of the 1960s, though much
about the series has aged unusually well, just as French structuralist and
poststructuralist theory continue to resonate well beyond the initial de-
constructionist wave. Indeed, *The Prisoner* has many concerns in common
with French theory, even if it often seems to reach different conclusions
about those concerns than many French theorists. The pessimistic tone of
the series, however, resonates especially closely with much of the work
of Foucault, whose own gloomily eccentric political vision also often
seemed to tend toward the libertarian pole. But, if thinkers such as Foucault and a television series such as *The Prisoner* can be linked by their
simultaneous appearance in the 1960s, they can also be related as parallel
phenomena in the growth of postmodernism. In fact, most of the points
of contact between French theory and *The Prisoner* can probably best be
understood when viewed through the optic of postmodernism, a project
that might also help us better to understand postmodernism itself.

The first episode of *The Prisoner* (entitled "Arrival") begins as thunder
cracks and the protagonist speeds along a roadway in his small Lotus
sports car. He reaches London, drives into an underground parking ga-
rage, then walks up a long tunnel, eventually entering an office where he
has an angry (but inaudible) conversation with a bureaucratic-looking
man. We learn later that he is resigning from his job, apparently as some
sort of intelligence agent. Later, the protagonist goes back to his apartment, where he begins to pack his things. Suddenly, the room is flooded
with gas, and he loses consciousness, to awake in another apartment that
initially seems identical to the first. This one, however, is in a completely
unfamiliar setting, as he discovers when he looks out the window, ob-
serving an idyllic village, though one with a highly artificial look that
makes it seem oddly sinister.

The Prisoner awakes, in fact, in an elaborate prison, where he has
been taken because his former work has given him too much sensitive
information for him to be allowed to roam free after his resignation. Indeed, while the purpose of his imprisonment is never made entirely
clear, there are numerous suggestions that the village is being run by
British intelligence and that the Prisoner has been sent there on suspicion
that he may be preparing to defect to the Soviets, taking his knowledge
with him. However, the epistemological confusion of the series and the
paranoid climate of the Cold War are such that none of this is certain: at
times the Prisoner himself suspects that the village is being run by the
"other side" and that he has been taken there so that the Soviets can pick
his classified brain.

The Prisoner spends much of the rest of "Arrival" (and, for that matter, the rest of the series) trying to get his bearings and to determine
where he is so that he can get back to the "real" world. His inability to

determine his geographic position, represented most directly by the fact that none of the maps available in the village indicate the location of the village in relation to the rest of the world, can be taken as an extended allegory of the difficulty of cognitive mapping in the postmodern world. Indeed, the village carries no geographic or cultural markers that might indicate its location. Numerous motifs, in fact, act to reinforce the indeterminacy of this location throughout the series. In the "Free for All" episode, for example, the Prisoner is given an assistant who speaks a strange international language that seems to be cobbled together from various languages of the world, including a strong Russian influence. In that same episode, he is served a meal identified as "international" cuisine. "French?" he asks, always looking for clues to the nationality of his captors. "International," he is again told.

The exterior scenes in the village of *The Prisoner* were filmed on location at the Hotel Portmeirion on the coast of Cardigan Bay in North Wales. The Portmeirion is a sort of architectural museum, a portmanteau collection of buildings of different styles and from different periods, many of which preexisted in remote sites until they were torn down, shipped to Cardigan Bay, and reassembled on the hotel site. Though opened in the 1920s, the Portmeirion is thus in many ways an ideal postmodern setting, recalling Jameson's discussions of the fading of geographic distinctions between different locations in the postmodern world. "Place in the United States today," Jameson notes, "no longer exists, or, more precisely, it exists at a much feebler level" than in previous eras (*Postmodernism* 127).[10] The Portmeirion is also reminiscent of Jameson's discussion of the Westin Bonaventure Hotel in Los Angeles as a quintessential postmodern space. Jameson notes that the bewildering spatial layout of the hotel leads to a basic disorientation that, among other things, makes it extremely difficult to find one's way in or out. Then again, the overall conception of the Bonaventure tends to make entrance and egress irrelevant, as the hotel itself aspires to be "a complete world, a kind of miniature city" (*Postmodernism* 40). The Bonaventure thus becomes, for Jameson, a new sort of "postmodern hyperspace" that has "finally succeeded in transcending the capacities of the individual human body to locate itself, to organize its immediate surroundings perceptually, and cognitively to map its position in a mappable external world" (44).

All of these comments might apply quite directly to the village of *The Prisoner*, which is nothing if not disorienting and unlocatable, and which also aspires to the status of a self-contained miniature world, with its own stores, parks, restaurants, government buildings, telephone and power systems, and so on, but with no connection to the outside world. The village also echoes Jameson's close association between postmodernism and consumer society; it is a pleasant and beautiful prison, where all one's needs are met as long as one follows the rules, making it a microcosm of the world of consumer capitalism. As Christian Durante puts it, *The Prisoner* undermines the easy polarities of the Cold War by showing us that our "own supposedly liberal societies ... are gradually becoming treacherous, grey societies that will soon join the large battalions of totalitarian states" (20).

For Durante, the vision of *The Prisoner* lies "somewhere between Swift and Debord," and it is certainly the case that conditions in the village often recall Debord's vision of modern society as a "society of the spectacle" (22). It is perhaps not surprising that Debord's full elaboration of this concept was first published in 1967, the same year that *The Prisoner* first appeared on television. However, in many ways, especially for the Prisoner himself, conditions in the village resonates more with the work of Foucault than with that of any other French poststructuralist thinker — or with that of Marxist thinkers such as Jameson. This situation might not be surprising. Despite its complexities, *The Prisoner* is still very much rooted in the Cold War and still maintains a vaguely anticommunist stance, even if that stance resides more in a basic defense of individualism than a celebration of capitalism.

Viewed through Foucault's own bitter indictment of modern bourgeois society, *The Prisoner* may appear not only anticommunist, but anticapitalist as well; the village thus becomes an emblem of the carceral nature of the society produced by late capitalism, corresponding in almost every detail to the carceral society as described in the work of Foucault. For example, the protagonist, labeled "Number Six" by the powers that be in the village, is constantly under surveillance, and his occasional sense that he has the ability to escape the village is entirely illusory, suggesting the subtlety and invisibility of official power. However, as in the work of Foucault, any criticism of capitalism that might be found in *The Prisoner* comes without the added power of a utopian (especially socialist) alternative, thus seriously limiting its effectiveness as political critique.

Most of the inhabitants of the village, in fact, seem to think they are already in utopia. They certainly have no desire to escape. In fact, they live quite contentedly within the confines of the village, largely oblivious to the subtle system of controls that ensures their complete conformity with the desires of the official administration of this village. But, according to Foucault, the workings of systems of behavioral control in modern bourgeois societies are generally invisible, which is the secret to their immense efficiency. In *Discipline and Punish* (originally published in French in 1975), Foucault rewrites Marx's history of European society, maintaining the Marxist notion of stages of history, but replacing Marx's emphasis on economic systems, or modes of production, with an emphasis on "technologies of power," or the basic strategies through which power is exercised to ensure the obedience of the general population to the prevailing official ideology.

In particular, Foucault notes that the feudal aristocracy tended to exercise its power on the physical bodies of selected members of the citizenry, often in the form of spectacular displays that announced the ability of the aristocracy to dominate the bodies of its subjects, up to and including the taking of their lives. Foucault then traces the evolution of techniques of punishment into the modern bourgeois era, noting the decline in public tortures and executions but insisting that this decline was not simply a drive toward increased humanity and justice in the use of power. Instead, it was more a movement toward greater efficiency in the control of the populace through "disciplinary" techniques designed to obtain "voluntary" obedience through psychological manipulation based on effective use of extensive information about individual subjects. For Foucault, knowledge is, in a very literal sense, power, and his vision of the Catholic confession as the forerunner of the information gathering that informs modern carceral power is strongly reminiscent of the constant interrogations of Number Six in *The Prisoner*.

Held firmly in the grip of these subtle, but invisible, forces, most individuals have the illusion of freedom, while in fact they are acting within boundaries that are carefully established and maintained. In this sense, Foucault's description of this phenomenon accords closely with Althusser's Marxist notion of "interpellation" (or the "hailing of the subject"), and it may not be insignificant that Althusser was one of Foucault's teachers in college. For Althusser, individuals in bourgeois society are not merely controlled by the prevailing bourgeois ideology; they are literally created as subjects by the ideological forces that pervade the society around them and that are conveyed to the subject through a variety of institutions (collectively labeled by Althusser the "Ideological State Apparatus"), including the family, school, church, culture, and media.

Foucault's delineation of the carceral society corresponds quite closely to Althusser's notion of interpellation, even if Foucault works hard to avoid any semblance of Marxist vocabulary in his description. However, official power in Foucault's version seems even more mind-numbingly effective than in Althusser's, where a certain amount of subversion is nevertheless still possible. Of course, when that subversion occurs, official bourgeois society always has in hand a back-up strategy, through which institutions such as the police and the military (collectively labeled the "Repressive State Apparatus") can step in to employ physical violence to shore up the basic system of ideological control.

Here, Althusser's vision closely resembles that of the Italian Marxist Antonio Gramsci, who argues that the European bourgeoisie historically gained and have since maintained their power through a complex of political and cultural practices that convinced the more numerous "subaltern" classes willingly to accede to bourgeois authority as natural and proper. Thus, bourgeois hegemony resides principally in the ability of the bourgeoisie to obtain the "spontaneous" consent given by the great masses of the population to the general direction imposed on social life by the dominant fundamental group; this consent is "historically" caused by the prestige (and consequent confidence) which the dominant group enjoys because of its position and function in the world of production. (12)

If absolutely necessary, this consensual obedience can be supplemented by "the apparatus of state coercive power," that is, by institutions such as the police and the army, which use physical force to impose obedience "on those groups who do not 'consent' either actively or passively. This apparatus is, however, constituted for the whole of society in anticipation of moments of crisis of command and direction when spontaneous consent has failed" (12).

In many ways, this Gramscian-Althusserian model of a two-pronged bourgeois power works better than Foucault's vision of carceral power to describe the workings of power in the village of *The Prisoner*, where some resistance remains possible, despite the seemingly complete subservience of the general population. For example, in the first episode, Number Six looks on as a large, surreal, white balloon (identified in later episodes as "Rover") chases down and engulfs a man who appears to be some sort of subversive. Later, Number Six discovers that his own escape plans are continually foiled by Rover, which appears as necessary to exert physical force whenever psychological control fails. Rover, then, is the principal Repressive State Apparatus of the village, though there is also a collection of armed security guards who can be called upon as needed.

Ultimately, however, the psychological grip of official power in *The Prisoner* is so strong that such repressive tactics are seldom needed. In this sense, the situation there probably corresponds more to Foucault's vision of bourgeois society than to the visions of Althusser and Gramsci—which may be another way of saying that the series is informed by a postmodern mindset in which the ability to imagine utopian alternatives has been significantly curtailed. In any case, the close correspondence between the technologies of official power in the village and the workings of power in bourgeois society as described by theorists such as Gramsci, Althusser, and Foucault is highly important, because it suggests that conditions in the village are merely an extension of the conditions that prevail in the society at large. The series itself directly indicates this situation in a number of ways. For example, in his first interview with Number Two, his chief interrogator and a leading village administrator (the identity of Number One, the ultimate village authority, is a closely guarded secret), Number Six learns that he has been under surveillance his entire life, as Number Two shows him a number of photographs of various moments from his childhood onward, many of which he had thought to be entirely private.

This revelation indicates that the high-tech methods of surveillance being used in the village have in fact been used for decades in the world at large. Indeed, in the best tradition of the science fiction genre, futuristic technologies in *The Prisoner* are more important for what they tell us about the here and now than about far places and distant futures. Most of these technologies involve either surveillance or brainwashing, both of which had been growing concerns of the populations of the West during the Cold War years. Thus, much of the technology of *The Prisoner* echoes rumors of existing real-world capabilities, while also recalling earlier Cold War narratives such as John Frankenheimer's *The Manchurian Candidate* (1962), a classic paranoid tale of brainwashing.

On the other hand, the technologies envisioned in *The Prisoner* do sometimes look forward to later technological developments. In "A, B & C," for example, these technologies foreshadow the vision of William Gibson and other "cyberpunk" science-fiction writers of the 1980s and 1990s. Cyberpunk science fiction, frequently identified as a central postmodernist phenomenon, is centrally concerned with the development of computer simulations so effective that their "virtual reality" becomes virtually indistinguishable from actual reality.[11] In "A, B & C," the authorities of the village produce just such a virtual reality, employing a combination of film, drugs, and electronics to produce a series of simulations that place Number Six in situations in which they hope he will reveal what they want to know. Six, however, discovers and foils the plan, scoring one of his few victories and turning the simulated tables on his real captors by projecting a simulated reality in which it was Number Two himself who initially encouraged Number Six to resign.[12]

Virtual reality is even more central to the unique "Living in Harmony," an episode so strange and potentially troubling that CBS refused to broadcast it in the original run of the series on American television.[13] Viewers of this episode must have thought, initially, that they had tuned to the wrong channel, for it begins, not as the protagonist drives his custom Lotus toward London to resign his job as a secret agent, but as a man rides his horse through the American West, reaching a frontier town where he resigns his job as the local sheriff. The man, however, is McGoohan, starring as a nameless laconic Western stranger of the type Clint Eastwood had perfected a few years earlier in *A Fistful of Dollars* (1964). In a quintessential case of postmodern genre mixing, the episode proceeds, for more than forty-three minutes of its forty-nine minute running time, as a quite authentic Western (or at least as a postmodern pastiche of a Western), though the plot of the episode (in which the ex-sheriff finds himself trapped in a strange town, unable to leave) cleverly parallels the typical plots of all episodes of *The Prisoner*.

In the end, it turns out that the Western town and all of the events in it have been part of a virtual reality engineered by the village authorities, again using a combination of drugs and electronics. The virtual experience is designed, apparently, to put Number Six under so much stress (he is even "killed" in the end of the Western part of the episode) that he will finally crack. Again, however, Number Six turns the tables on his captors. He survives the episode with his psyche intact, though the two assistants working with Number Two to carry out the plan are both unhinged by their involvement in this all-too-convincing simulation and wind up dead.

If technology is used, in "A, B & C" and "Living in Harmony" to probe and manipulate the contents of Number Six's brain, a similar advanced technology is used in "The General" to place new contents in the brains of the entire village population, assuring their obedience to authority. In particular, the eponymous General, as Number Six discovers at the end of the episode, is a giant supercomputer that is the key to a new brain-washing technology.[14] This episode thus echoes the fears that some were already expressing about the potential use of computers as tools of an American national security apparatus that had, in the 1960s, turned its attention from the rooting out of Soviet agents to the surveillance and sabotage of antiwar and civil rights groups.

Perhaps even more importantly, the brainwashing that the General engineers involves the broadcast of special signals via the television screens that the inhabitants of the village spend so much of their time viewing. The episode thus anticipates similar motifs in later (highly postmodernist) works such as David Cronenberg's 1982 film, *Videodrome*, in which sinister behavior-modifying signals are broadcast via television. Number Six again spoils the plan and even destroys the General, but the implications of the episode are rather ominous, though also highly ironic, suggesting, via a television broadcast, the potential negative consequences of television viewing.

This motif, like so many others in *The Prisoner*, suggests that conditions in the village might not be much different from conditions in the world at large. Indeed, the true significance of the village throughout the series is its similarity to the world outside, even though Number Six doggedly persists in his attempts to return to that world. There is, however, a significant doubt in the series whether that return is even worthwhile. In "The Chimes of Big Ben," originally broadcast as the second episode in the series, Number Six apparently solves the puzzle of the village's geographic location when he learns that the village is in Lithuania. This finding also seems to answer the question of which side in the Cold War is running the village, suggesting that it is being run by the Soviets. He then ostensibly escapes to London, with the help of Nadia Rokowski (played by Nadia Gray), an Estonian woman who is also being held as a prisoner in the village. The entire escape turns out to be a ruse, however, and Nadia is working with high-ranking members of the British intelligence establishment in an effort to trick the Prisoner into revealing the real reasons behind his resignation. At the end, he remains in the village, thoroughly entrapped, though he foils the plan to learn his secrets, which, trusting no one, he refuses to reveal.

Such bogus escape attempts (which usually employ a woman assigned to win Number Six's confidence, then betray him) frequently occur in the series, beginning with "Arrival," in which a seemingly sympathetic woman offers Number Six an escape route, only to have that escape easily foiled by the village authorities, for whom she has been working all along. Such betrayals help to reinforce the paranoid, "trust no one" atmosphere of the series, though the central role played by women in such schemes also sometimes contributes to a misogynistic tone. Many of the women employed in this way are themselves victims, though that does not seem to be the case with Nadia, who may very well be a high-ranking Russian agent in addition to her work with British intelligence, suggesting that the village might even be a joint Soviet-British enterprise.

A central theme of "The Chimes of Big Ben" is the difficulty of distinguishing between Us and Them, even within the polarized climate of the Cold War. Moreover, the episode suggests a chilling reason for this difficulty: that there is very little (if any) real difference between the two sides. As Number Two tells the Prisoner early in the episode, "Both sides are becoming identical. A perfect blueprint for world order." This order, Number Two suggests, will be precisely that of the village, again making the village a microcosm of the larger world. Later, thinking he has returned to London with Nadia, the Prisoner himself questions whether there was any point to the return: "I risked my life and hers to come back here because I thought it was different. ... It is, isn't it? Isn't it different?"

I have argued elsewhere that much of the intensity of Cold War Us vs. Them thinking in the West grew out of a desire to be able to make and maintain clear polar distinctions amid the growing disorientation of a postmodern climate in which all such distinctions tended to collapse. Little wonder, then, that postmodern cultural products of the Cold War years often tended to challenge the simple dualities of Cold War logic.[15] Such distinctions certainly collapse in *The Prisoner*, where disorientation of all kinds is a central trope and where, among other things, Number Six consistently finds it difficult to distinguish between his captors and his fellow prisoners.

Even the central opposition of the series, that between the staunch individual, Number Six, and the repressive and impersonal authority of the village, sometimes threatens to collapse. Number Six seems to be presented in the series as an enlightened outsider who has escaped official indoctrination and is thus virtually the only one who can see the truth of the carceral conditions of the village. It is surely the case that viewers of *The Prisoner* are largely expected to identify with Number Six, but that the series has never attracted a truly large audience suggests that this identification (one of the central strategies through which television series garner viewers) has always been problematic. Part of this failure to attract a large audience might have to do with the unremitting pessimism of the series and the continual failure of Number Six's efforts to escape. And part of it might have to do with the fact that audiences, however much they sympathize with Six, are maneuvered into a position of sharing the desire of his captors to discover his secrets. After all, just why is he so important? Is there something we don't know?

The limited identification appeal of Number Six might also have something to do with the persona of the Prisoner. As played by McGoohan, Number Six is so single-minded in his devotion to escape that he has virtually no psychological depth. Moreover, his own behavior often seems as unrealistic and bizarre as the village around him. At times, he speaks in an emotionless robotic monotone. When he does express emotion, he tends to employ a mode of mocking sarcasm or to resort to theatrical (and obviously artificial) histrionics, with exaggerated rolling R's and stentorian proclamations that seem to belong more on the stage than in the real world, thus making Number Six a sort of postmodern simulation of a hero rather than a hero proper.

Then again, the emotional flatness and inauthenticity of Number Six are perfectly suited to the environment of the village. They are also typical of the characters of postmodernist culture, which tends to be informed, as Jameson notes, by a "waning of affect," or loss of emotion, which for Jameson is inseparable from large postmodernist phenomena such as the loss of historical sense and (even more fundamental), the dismantling of the stable individual subject (*Postmodernism* 10–16). In particular, for Jameson, individual emotional experiences such as anxiety and alienation were central to the phenomenon of modernism, but become largely irrelevant in a postmodern era where the "psychic fragmentation: of the subject produces an instability too radical to allow such emotional experiences to be maintained (90).

Elsewhere, Jameson employs Jacques Lacan's vision of schizophrenia as a metaphor for this postmodern experience of psychic fragmentation. The individual postmodern subject, according to Jameson, is too unstable to maintain a sense of continuous identity over time, thus becoming unable to link one moment to the next, much less to maintain a genuine sense of historical progression over long periods of time. Thus, the postmodern subject, like the Lacanian schizophrenic "does not have our experience of temporal continuity ... but is condemned to live a perpetual present with which the various moments of his or her past have little connection and for which there is no conceivable future on the horizon" ("Postmodernism and Consumer Society" 119).

Jameson's diagnosis here resembles that of numerous observers of postmodernism, though his negative vision of the fragmentation of the subject differs dramatically from that of French poststructuralist apologists for postmodern fragmentation such as Gilles Deleuze and Félix

Guattari (both notorious antagonists of Lacan, for whom clinical schizo-phrenia is an extremely painful and debilitating condition). In works such as *Anti-Oedipus: Capitalism and Schizophrenia* (originally published in French in 1972), Deleuze and Guattari see the schizophrenia of the post-modern subject as a potentially liberating experience that might lead to a positive redefinition of capitalist economies in libidinal, rather than ma-terialist, terms. In *The Political Unconscious* (1981), Jameson acknowledges that the project of Deleuze and Guattari has much in common with his own, but takes them to task for their glorification of fragmentation, which he associates with a politically debilitating postmodernist assault on totalizing modes of interpretation (21–23).

At least one episode of *The Prisoner*, "The Schizoid Man," explicitly thematizes the schizophrenic instability in individual identity associated by Jameson with the overall experience of postmodernism. In this epi-sode, the village authorities bring in an outside agent (Number Twelve) who looks exactly like Number Six and has been carefully trained to speak and act like him as well. Indeed, he is even more like Number Six than Number Six himself, who has meanwhile been conditioned to differ from his previous self in various ways. He is, for example, now left-handed, whereas before he had been right-handed. These changes have been made as part of an attempt by the authorities, led by Number Two, to try to convince Number Six that he is actually Number Twelve and that Number Twelve is the real Number Six.

Aided by Alison (Jane Merrow), another woman who has been enlisted to win the trust of Six, only to betray him, Number Two nearly succeeds in convincing Number Six that he is not who he thinks he is. We observe, through the course of the episode, the gradual fragmentation of Number Six's confidence in his own identity, a process the obvious terror of which hardly lends support to the Deleuze-Guattari vision of schizo-phrenia as liberating. Meanwhile, there is a special irony in the way the Prisoner begins to cling to the number 6 as a marker of his identity, even though he has staunchly refused, in previous episodes, to accept this numeric designation. Eventually, Six discovers the plot and turns the ta-bles on Number Twelve, who is subsequently killed by Rover in the con-fusion of identities. Number Six then impersonates Number Twelve and nearly succeeds in bluffing his way out of the village, but a telltale slip lands him right back where he started, as usual. Nevertheless, the overall thrust of the episode is to suggest that individual identity might not be as stable and unambiguously defined as we would like to think, while the ultimate circularity of the plot leaves Number Six again trapped in the perpetual present that is the temporal fabric of the village.

Individual identity is also destabilized in "Do Not Forsake Me, Oh My Darling," in which a brilliant scientist has invented a machine that allows the minds of two different people to be interchanged. However, the scientist, Dr. Seltzman (Hugo Schuster), has disappeared before revealing his process for reversing the exchange. Feeling that Number Six is the only man who can locate Seltzman, the authorities devise a plan to transfer Six's mind into the body of the "Colonel" (Nigel Stock), a loyal agent. They then release the new Number Six (in the Colonel's body) and allow him to return to his home in London, knowing (especially after a little well-placed conditioning) he will do anything to track down Seltzman in an effort to get his own body back, while they plan to follow Six to the scientist.

Ace agent that he is, Six succeeds, of course, and the authorities follow him to Seltzman, then bring them both back to the village. There, Number Six's mind is returned to his own body, but Seltzman manages to outwit the authorities, transferring his own mind into the body of the Colonel and then escaping, leaving the Colonel's mind in Seltzman's own dying body. Once again, then, Six escapes to the outer world only to find that he remains under strict surveillance and is hardly free. Meanwhile, the science-fiction motif of mind transfer resonates with the other high-tech methods of mind control and manipulation used by the village authorities at various points in the series. In *The Prisoner*, such amazing technologies have almost entirely negative implications, due to their sinister use by official power in both the village and the world at large, a use the continuity of which reinforces the notion that the village is not fundamentally different from the world around it and that Number Six's dogged efforts to escape are essentially pointless. Thus, in the episode "Many Happy Returns," he actually succeeds in escaping back to London, only to have the British authorities promptly return him to the village. There are, in fact, signs that the entire escape was engineered by his captors as a way of breaking his spirits by raising his hopes, only to dash them.

Such episodes again recall the work of Foucault, in which power functions as a total system, leaving essentially no effective path of escape or mode of resistance. Indeed, for Foucault, those who do not conform (to whom he refers collectively as "delinquents") actually do the work of official power by serving as counter-examples that help to reinforce the obedience of the bulk of the population. It is certainly the case, in *The Prisoner*, that Number Six is the most unhappy inhabitant of the village, so that his travails, far from igniting a general rebellion, might merely suggest to the other inhabitants that they are well served to remain docile and submissive.

From this point of view, it is clearly in the interest of the powers that be in the village to have delinquents such as Number Six in their midst, a fact that, according to Foucault, bourgeois society recognizes by instituting practices that are designed to ensure a continual supply of delinquents. It is in this sense that Foucault refers to the technologies of power in bourgeois society as "productive," rather than "repressive," and his various works trace a long history of the productive use of delinquency in modern society. In *Madness and Civilization* (first published in French in 1961), Foucault argues that, during the Enlightenment, discourses of madness sought not only to identify madness as a category of delinquency, but to produce a clearly labeled subpopulation of madmen against whom the rational norm could be identified. In *The History of Sexuality: An Introduction* (first published in French in 1976), Foucault describes the way in which the Victorians, far from seeking to stamp out perversion, produced an explosion of discourses on sexuality, one of the results of which was to produce and identify a subpopulation of "perverts" from whom those with "normal" sexuality could be differentiated.

Most relevant to *The Prisoner* is Foucault's description of the functioning of the modern prison in *Discipline and Punish*. For Foucault, the modern prison system is not designed to stamp out crime but merely to establish an efficient system for the identification and surveillance of a population of delinquents, whose crimes can thus be kept within the limits of acts that are "politically harmless and economically negligible" (278). Moreover, the periodic imprisonment of these delinquents places them in an overtly controlled environment in comparison to which the more subtle controls at work in the society at large seem benign. "Normal" subjects are specifically defined as those who are different from delinquents. The "normal" social order, then, seems by definition to function differently than the order within the prison, thus obscuring the basic similarity between the prison and the society at large, just as the overtly carceral nature of the village in *The Prisoner* disguises the fact that similar technologies of control are in effect in the larger world.

In this same vein, the Foucauldian prison is oddly similar to theme parks such as Disneyland and Disney World, the obvious fictionality of which are designed, at least according to cultural critics such as Baudrillard, to make the outside world appear solid and real, when it is, in fact, nothing but a collection of simulacra—simulations that do not duplicate anything in reality. In this sense, theme parks such as Disneyland retrospectively appear as the direct forerunners of the virtual realities of cyberspace. For Baudrillard, Disneyland functions to encourage the general population to accept the reality of a consumer capitalist social world that is, in fact, "hyperreal," saturated with images and simulations:

Disneyland is there to conceal the fact that it is the "real" country, all of "real" America, which *is* Disneyland (just as prisons are there to conceal the fact that it is the social in its entirety, in its banal omnipresence, which is carceral). Disneyland is presented as imaginary in order to make us all believe that the rest is real, when in fact all of Los Angeles and the America surrounding it are no longer real, but of the order of the hyperreal and of simulation. (172)

The village of *The Prisoner* looks precisely like a theme park, particularly in the absence of reliable historical markers through a collapse of periods that combines a variety of futuristic high-tech devices with the Portmeirion's collection of buildings from a variety of different eras, all located vaguely in the past. This collapse of periods is a quintessential postmodern gesture. Moreover, as I note in *The Dystopian Impulse in Modern Literature*, the theme park as discussed by Baudrillard represents a particular kind of contemporary dystopian space, in which a seemingly utopian appearance conceals the carcerality of a basically dystopian reality. *The Prisoner*, in fact, places itself quite explicitly in the tradition of dystopian fiction. For one thing, the basic defiant-individual-versus-repressive-authority structure of the series corresponds precisely to the central format of dystopian fiction. For another, the series often resonates with specific dystopian fictions. For example, the insistence on the village authorities to label each of the inhabitants with a number recalls the reduction of individuals to numbers in the One State of Zamyatin's *We* (1924). Similarly, the enclosed confines of the village create very much the same sense of claustrophobic containment that prevails in the walled dystopian city that is the One State, though the brightly pleasant material conditions in the village are more reminiscent of the bourgeois dystopia of Aldous Huxley's *Brave New World* (1932). Finally, the simultaneous video broadcasts and video surveillance with which the village is saturated recall the ever-present vid-screens of George Orwell's *Nineteen Eighty-four* (1949).

The dystopian character of *The Prisoner* takes on a special significance in the context of the appearance of the series in the late 1960s. Thus, the series appeared precisely after the extinction of utopian energies in the long 1950s was essentially complete but before most of the brief resurgence of utopian energies in American culture of the 1970s (as described by Jameson in *Postmodernism*) had begun. As I argue in *The Post-Utopian Imagination*, the postmodern collapse of utopian imagination that occurs in the long 1950s is closely connected to a loss of confidence in conventional narrative structures, a phenomenon that is also related to the collapse of historical vision that Jameson sees as a crucial postmodern characteristic. In *The Prisoner*, this loss of narrative sense is reflected in the almost total lack of narrative progression, both within individual episodes and from one episode to another. As Alain Carrazé and Hélène Oswald put it, all of the episodes "seem to take place in an eternal present and to tell an uncompromisingly cyclical story" (45). Thus, each episode ends with the same distinctive "logo" of prison bars closing on a full-screen closeup of the face of the Prisoner, signaling that Number Six is still thoroughly entrapped in the village, having achieved nothing. Most (but not all) subsequent episodes then begin exactly like their predecessors, with the same opening sequence as the first one, through the point at which the Prisoner awakes in the village. They then proceed through Number Six's initial interrogation by Number Two, an interrogation that always proceeds according to the same script (ending with

Number Six's famous declaration that he is a free man, not a number), even though most episodes feature a new Number Two, in a move that indicates both the postmodern instability of individual identity and the constant movement toward innovation and change (as long as the underlying class structure is maintained) that is central to capitalism.[16] The repetition of this initial interrogation indicates the cyclical and repetitive nature of life in the village. Due to this lack of narrative progression, fans of the series have long debated the proper order in which the episodes (which were not initially broadcast in the order in which they were filmed) should be viewed. But the controversy is clearly an empty one: except for the first and last episode, the order is essentially irrelevant, and that is precisely the point.

Again, however, the series implies that this lack of narrative progression is not confined to the village, which continually serves as a microcosm of the larger world. Many of the episodes of *The Prisoner* present defamiliarized versions of various practices and institutions of the modern world, serving thereby to satirize those institutions by revealing their true character, free of the ideological obfuscation with which they are usually disguised. One of the most telling and powerful of these episodes is "Free for All," in which Number Six is encouraged by the current Number Two to run against him in the upcoming "democratic" elections. Because Number Six represents a genuine alternative, Number Two argues, his participation is needed to prove that the elections really are democratic. Though suspicious, Number Six is tempted, and eventually agrees to run.

The election, of course, is a sham, though in ways that tend to make us wonder whether all of the electoral processes we traditionally value so highly in Western "democracies" might be similarly meaningless. The campaign itself consists of nothing but clichés, both in the speeches of the candidates and in the vulgar (and completely orchestrated) demonstrations of their supporters. There is, in fact, something vaguely American about the circus-like campaign, and one often has the feeling in watching *The Prisoner* that much of the satire of the series is aimed at American vulgarity and excess. Associated institutions, such as the local "free" press that covers the campaign, are lampooned as well. In one telling scene, a reporter interviews Number Six, but ignores the answers given to the questions, preferring to supply his own, which are nothing but a series of platitudes. Meanwhile, the burlesque democracy of the village extends beyond the elections to the actual institutions of government, as when, in one scene, Number Six visits the village Council, a ludicrous sham democratic assembly.

To make matters worse, the powers that be in the village carefully work to guarantee that Number Six will not, in fact, be able to achieve any genuine change through his electoral efforts. For one thing, he is brainwashed and/or drugged at several points in the episode, thus ensuring his basic cooperation with the rules of this absurd political game. For another, the whole election turns out to have been a cruel joke, apparently designed as part of the efforts of the village authorities to break Number Six's resistance to their incessant efforts to extract information from him. Number Six easily wins the election, as it turns out, but this means nothing. Number Six (now nominally the newly elected Number Two) and his seemingly dull-witted assistant, Number 58, celebrate the victory by cavorting weirdly about in the control chamber from which Number Two orchestrates the activities of the village. Suddenly, though, 58 is revealed as another treacherous female: she becomes serious and begins slapping Number Six, bringing him out of his drug-induced stupor. He is then savagely beaten by security guards, while Number 58 assumes her place as the real new Number Two.

"Free for All" creates a sort of cognitive estrangement that potentially asks us to look at the workings of conventional authority through a new, more skeptical lens. "Dance of the Dead" extends this relentless defamiliarization of democratic institutions to the judicial system, as Number Six is placed on trial, ostensibly for being found in possession of an unauthorized radio receiver, but also for his general opposition to authority in the village. In this particularly dark episode, the authorities have dropped almost all pretence to democracy. For example, the electoral ruse of "Free for All" seems to have been dropped. At one point in the episode, Number Six remarks to still another new Number Two (this one female, played by Mary Morris), that her administration seems very effective, though it has no opposition. "An irritation we've dispensed with," she replies. "Even its best friends agree democracy is remarkably inefficient."

This Number Two, as this exchange perhaps indicates, seems even more ruthless and sinister than usual, which may have something to do with her gender, women typically being Number Six's worst antagonists in the series. The episode also features a certain Number 240, a woman who is assigned as Number Six's official observer, thus becoming another in the series of women who seem to establish a personal connection to Number Six, only to turn out to be working for the village authorities. In this episode, even the female cat that befriends Number Six actually belongs to Number Two. Realizing this, Number Six bitterly declares, "Never trust a woman. Even the four-legged variety," thus making particularly overt the note of misogyny that otherwise runs through the series in more subtle ways.

If the village political system in "Dance of the Dead" no longer even pretends to be democratic, it is also the case here that the judicial system makes few gestures toward justice. The trial of Number Six is conducted within the surreal atmosphere of a costume ball that is part of the village's periodic carnival celebration. Indeed, the entire trial is surreal, recalling a number of twentieth-century literary precedents, including the trial of Kafka's Josef K. and the trial of Leopold Bloom in the "Circe" chapter of Joyce's *Ulysses*. In this case, Number Six is to be judged, not by a jury of his peers, but by a bizarre three-judge panel of local citizens dressed, respectively, as Napoleon, Caesar, and Queen Elizabeth I, all apparently intended as figures of totalitarian power. Informed that he is to be judged by this panel, Number Six remarks that the situation is reminiscent of the French Revolution, to which Number Two quips, "They got through the dead wood, didn't they?" Number Two herself (dressed as Peter Pan) then serves as Number Six's defense attorney, a situation perfectly in keeping with the surreal nature of the trial, which, in addition to the potential evocation of Kafka and Joyce, possibly echoes (given the program's Cold War context) the notorious Stalinist show trials of the 1930s. However, the specific allusions to the French Revolution suggest Western referents as well, and the collection of personages represented by the judges comprises a sort of allegorical history of official power in Western Europe.

There is something very confused about this allegory, in which the conflation of the Roman Empire, the early British Empire, and the postrevolutionary French Empire ignores, in typical postmodernist fashion, the very real distinctions between these three historical phenomena. Meanwhile, the inclusion of the French Revolution (often viewed as the most important single event in the historical growth of modern bourgeois democracies) in this list challenges the distinction between democracy and totalitarianism. Similarly, the inclusion of Elizabeth I implicates the "Golden Age" of Elizabethan England (and, by extension, modern England, which many see as having been born in the Elizabethan Renaissance) in the sinister political forces behind the village.

This collapse of all historical periods into simultaneity is very much in keeping with the carnival atmosphere, in which time seems suspended, while all sorts of traditional boundaries and distinctions are dissolved. This carnivalesque atmosphere again recalls the work of Bakhtin. However, even more than in *The Twilight Zone*, carnival in *The Prisoner* is not quite the emancipatory motif it has often been seen to be in the work of Bakhtin, especially in *Rabelais and His World*, where Bakhtin portrays the carnivalesque imagery in the work of the fifteenth-century French writer François Rabelais as an effective challenge to the humorless and monologic authority of the medieval Catholic church.[17]

Bakhtin would ultimately become more important in the West for his theories of the dialogic properties of all language and for his theoretical elaboration of the special nature of the novel as a genre, especially as expressed in the essays collected in English translation as *The Dialogic Imagination* (1981). Moreover, as Morson and Emerson rightly point out, there is good reason to be skeptical of the apparent utopianism of the Rabelais book. Nevertheless, it was Bakhtin's exploration of the transgressive energies of the medieval carnival in *Rabelais and His World* that made the most important initial impact on Anglo-American criticism. In their important study *The Politics and Poetics of Transgression*, Peter Stallybrass and Allon White acknowledge their debt to Bakhtin's theories of the carnivalesque, noting that Bakhtin has in fact been the major figure in a widespread fascination with the notion of carnival among Western critics in the latter decades of the twentieth century. Bakhtin's book on Rabelais, Stallybrass and White suggest, "catalysed the interest of Western scholars ... around the notion of carnival" (6). And little wonder, given the extent to which the exuberant, exorbitant, transgressive, emancipatory rhetoric and imagery that most critics have associated with Bakhtin's readings of Rabelais resonated with the atmosphere on Western college campuses in the late 1960s.

On the surface, Bakhtin's carnival is a time of festive and exuberant plurality when normal social boundaries collapse and groups from different social classes and backgrounds meet and mingle freely in a mood of celebration and irreverence that runs directly counter to the cold, sterile, and humorless world of official medieval Catholicism. The carnival is a time when normal rules and hierarchies are suspended, when boundaries are transgressed, and when the energies of life erupt without regard for conventional decorum. However, the carnival in "Dance of the Dead" is anything but an emancipatory celebration that mocks authority. It is, in fact, a thoroughly administered function of the village authorities, announced in the beginning by the town crier, who proclaims that the carnival has been "decreed" by official order. Then again, the medieval carnival cited by Bakhtin was officially sanctioned by the very Catholic church to which Bakhtin saw its energies as being opposed. Noting this fact, numerous critics have challenged Bakhtin's use of the carnival as an image of transgression and emancipation, as when Terry Eagleton reminds us that carnival "is a *licensed* affair in every sense, a permissible rupture of hegemony, a contained popular blow-off as disturbing and relatively ineffectual as a revolutionary work of art" (*Walter Benjamin* 148).

In addition, the carnival of "Dance of the Dead" takes a particularly dark turn when Six is condemned to death for his individualism, then pursued by an unruly mob of village inhabitants intent on tearing him limb from limb. However, as Michael André Bernstein has pointed out, the medieval carnival on which Bakhtin bases his (ostensibly) utopian vision contained a dark and violent side. These carnivals, Bernstein notes, often "ended in a violence that proved devastating both to the actual victims and to the community as a whole" (36). Further, Bernstein argues, a recognition of this abject violence, which often focused on the most marginal and least fortunate members of the local citizenry, makes it very difficult to see the extreme violence in the works of writers such as Rabelais as mere examples of comic excess.

In its portrayal of the carnival as a tool of official power, "Dance of the Dead" clearly resonates more with the critique by Bernstein than with the work of Bakhtin, at least if one reads the ostensible utopianism of *Rabelais and His World* as genuine. The episode, in fact, offers an extremely pessimistic suggestion that even the most seemingly transgressive practices are, by the late 1960s, already thoroughly in the grip of official power, a suggestion that resonates with Thomas Frank's conclusions concerning the close association between consumer capitalism and the 1960s counterculture. As such, the episode offers a rejoinder to the carnivalesque aspects of oppositional politics in the 1960s, particularly as evidenced in the playfulness of American subversives such as Abbie Hoffman. "Dance of the Dead" also challenges, in advance, the widespread appropriation, by American critics in the 1970s, of Bakhtin's notion of the carnival as a key image of transgression and subversion.

If "Dance of the Dead" seems especially pessimistic in its portrayal of the absolute power of the village authorities and dismissal of the subversive possibilities of the carnival, it is also the case that some of the most seemingly optimistic episodes in the series have ultimately dark implications, again suggesting Foucault's pessimistic attitude toward the possibility of subverting carceral power. In "A Change of Mind," Number Six is the target of a plan to render him docile by a combination of drugging him and making him think he has been lobotomized. In this episode, perhaps more than any other, the medical treatment of "abnormal" behavior is crucially important as a tool of official power, recalling Foucault's highly skeptical treatment of modern methods of treatment for mental illness in *Madness and Civilization*. But Six emerges triumphant, regaining his usual defiance. Moreover, at one point the target of an angry mob for his aberrant individualist tendencies (he is declared "Unmutual"), Six manages to turn the mob against Number Two. Nevertheless, the vision of the village populace as a dangerous mob bent on the destruction of anyone who differs from the norm is particularly frightening, as is the realization that Six could well have been lobotomized were he not considered so "valuable."

In "It's Your Funeral," Number Six ostensibly scores one of his greatest victories by foiling a plot to assassinate Number Two, a plot that is designed to provide a justification for the village authorities to wreak revenge on the population of the village. Here, for the first time, Six acts primarily for the good of his fellow villagers rather than for his own individual purposes. Moreover, there seems, in this episode, to be a functioning underground organization of "jammers," who resist the village authorities by constantly discussing imaginary subversive plots, knowing they will be overheard by the village authorities, who will be forced to expend resources investigating the fictional plots.

Unfortunately, the effectiveness of the jammers is highly limited, because the authorities have already identified them and come to understand their strategy. The jammers thus function like the authorized delinquents of Foucault's carceral society; in fact, they are often used by the authorities for their own purposes, as when one of them (a young woman, of course, but this time apparently without her knowledge) is employed in an attempt to manipulate Number Six. Meanwhile, Number Six's "victory" is of equivocal value: he may have saved the villagers from reprisals, but his efforts are now suddenly directed in the highly problematic direction of preventing, rather than fomenting, subversion, even if in this case the subversion is being engineered by Number Two's successor.

"Checkmate," which was originally broadcast as the next episode after "Dance of the Dead," has similarly problematic positive resonances. Here, the grip of official power in the village seems much less absolute than usual. Indeed, the Prisoner is even able to enlist a handful of supporters (all male, of course) in his attempts to subvert authority and escape from the village. Early in the episode, in a scene reminiscent of Lewis Carroll, Number Six observes a chess match that is being played using live people as chess pieces, making quite literal a major theme of the series: that individuals are pawns in the hands of official power. Later, discussing the match with one of the players, Number 58, Number Six realizes that the strict differentiation between black and white chess pieces might also apply to the village population as a whole. He thus adopts a rigorous Us vs. Them logic, concluding that the inhabitants of the village can be neatly separated into those who are guardians, working in support of official power, and those (including Number 58) who are prisoners like himself.

But, again, this polar opposition is difficult to maintain. The rebellion quickly collapses, partly because the co-conspirators recruited by Number Six conclude that he is actually one of the guardians and thus abandon him. In other episodes, the defeat of Number Six seems to suggest the ultimate impossibility of a single man overcoming the authority of an oppressive society. But this motif has a potentially positive, even leftist, political lesson, suggesting the importance of collective action given the political impotence of the lone individual. In "Checkmate," however, an organized rebellion of multiple individuals is similarly doomed. As Carrazé and Oswald put it, in this episode, the Prisoner's "ultimate defeat seems all the more fraught with political significance for his world, the Village chessboard, but also for ours. His failure—a symbolic one—is that of all bids for collective freedom" (128).

With the obvious end of the series in sight, the last two episodes of *The Prisoner* move toward a conclusion, the inconclusiveness of which can be taken as another marker of the program's postmodernist skepticism. In the sixteenth episode, "Once upon a Time," Leo McKern returns as Number Two, having earlier played the role in "The Chimes of Big Ben." This time, Number Two is grimly determined to solve the problem of Number Six once and for all, leading to a cataclysmic psychological struggle with Six, but ending in complete and total defeat for Number Two. The acting in these scenes is so intense that McKern reportedly nearly suffered a heart attack during the filming. But Six seemingly emerges completely triumphant. Not only is Two vanquished (and apparently killed), but, at the end of the episode, the "Supervisor" (who often works for the Number Twos) agrees to take Number Six to see the mysterious Number One at last.

The stage is thus set for a final episode, in which Number Six appears poised to solve many of the riddles of the village. However, the last episode, "Fall Out," infuriated many viewers by refusing to supply simple answers and unequivocal closure. Indeed, this stunning final episode completes the final deconstruction not only of the opposition between the village and the world at large, but between Number Six and his captors in the village. Bewildered audiences were left with no stable verities on which to depend, no solid interpretive ground on which to stand. They were also given nothing to nourish the individualist longings that had propelled them through their viewing of the earlier sixteen episodes, rooting for the virtuous, free-thinking Number Six.

The episode begins with some of the strangest and most surreal scenes in the entire series, including a trial sequence even more bizarre than the one in "Dance of the Dead." While other forms of subversion are denounced during this trial, Six's own ultimate defiance of authority is applauded as a sign that he is the only true individual among them. As a reward, he is free to go. But first he must learn the identity of Number One, who turns out, in a confusing sequence, apparently to be Number Six himself, or at least a dark aspect of Number Six, whose identity is thus fragmented in true postmodernist style. Then begins an apocalyptic sequence of violent revolution and total chaos , leading to the evacuation of the village to the strains of the Beatles' "All You Need is Love," a musical choice the Brechtian irony of which tends to dismiss the sentiment expressed in the song, as well as the entire panoply of 1960s attitudes that it expresses.

Number Six at last escapes (along with others, including McKern's Number Two, who has returned from the dead) and returns to London. The escape, however, is highly problematic. When Six reaches his home, we discover that the door swings open automatically in the same telltale fashion as the door to his home in the village, suggesting that little has really changed and that he is still in the grip of the diabolical forces of which he is himself a part. Six then hops in his Lotus and drives away — into the standard opening sequence of the series, which thus apparently completes the loop and (in a favorite gesture of postmodernist narrative) returns him back to the beginning of the entire series, presumably only to do it all over again. The notion of progressive narrative sequence is destroyed once and for all, as is the illusion that the world is really any different from the village or that Number Six is really independent of the forces that run the village and the world.

The final episode, then, tends to reinforce pessimistic interpretations of the series, leaning more toward the postmodern pole than the modern, Marxist one. In this sense, the series was probably in step with the times, even though many would locate the ultimate triumph of postmodernism as beginning after the collapse of the French rebellion of May 1968. However, a close look at *The Prisoner* — and even *The Twilight Zone* before it — shows that elements of postmodernism were already beginning to appear in Anglo-American television programs well before 1968. On the other hand, that *The Prisoner* clearly takes its engagement with issues such as routinization and surveillance so seriously suggests that it still contained a strong dose of modern thinking. As a result of this continuing modernist seriousness, *The Prisoner* might have been a bit too much in step with its times, addressing anxieties of the period all too directly and uncomfortably — which might account for the fact that the series has gained greater popularity as a cult favorite in later decades than it did during its initial run on broadcast television. Indeed, by the end of the 1980s, many of the concerns of modernism had been around long enough to become the objects of irony and self-parody, which made it possible to view *The Prisoner* as almost campy and certainly less troubling. Moreover, later postmodernist series, such as *Twin Peaks* and *The X-Files*, would contain decidedly campy elements from the beginning, suggesting that the growth of postmodernism that was beginning in the 1950s had, by the end of the 1980s, virtually completed its conquest of Western televisual culture.

4

Strange Reaganism: Ludic Postmodernism as Cold War Allegory in *Twin Peaks*

Douglas Kellner argues, in *Television and the Crisis of Democracy*, that American television was particularly interesting in the 1970s because an unprecedented variety of ideas and viewpoints began to appear in commercial programs, partly due to the impact of the political upheavals of the 1960s. To support this point, Kellner mentions the new "miniseries" format, which inherently allowed for greater variety, but he also mentions regular weekly programs such as *Saturday Night Live* (which first appeared in 1975), in which satirical comedy was often aimed at political targets. Kellner is particularly impressed by the numerous series produced by Norman Lear during the decade, of which the best known and most widely watched was *All in the Family*, which ran from 1971 to 1983 and ranked first in the Nielsen ratings for its first five seasons. *All in the Family* certainly dealt with the political issues of the 1960s and 1970s, though with a comic twist. But Kellner is particularly interested in Lear's short-lived syndicated soap opera spoof, *Mary Hartman, Mary Hartman* (1976–77), which, for Kellner, "used humor and self-reflective irony to suggest that something was profoundly wrong with patriarchy and consumer capitalism" (*Television* 58).

Mary Hartman did indeed have something to say about the world of consumer capitalism, though it tended to focus on one aspect of that world: television itself. For example, many of the travails of the title character (played by Louise Lasser) came about because of her bovarystic tendency to approach the world via expectations derived from television, and especially from television advertising. Ultimately, then, *Mary Hartman* may have been most important for the way in which it marked the growing self-referentiality of American television from the 1970s forward. Thus, Steven Connor notes "the intensifying absorption of TV in its own forms and history," which brings us to "a view of TV as consti-

tuting the postmodern psycho-cultural condition—a world of simulations detached from reference to the real, which circulate and exchange
in ceaseless, centreless flow" (191).[1] For example, *Mary Hartman's* 1977
spinoff, *Fernwood 2-Night*, was a spoof of television talk shows—and thus
the forerunner not only of HBO's talk-show parody/sitcom *The Larry
Sanders Show* (beginning in 1992), but also of the increasingly self-
conscious and self-parodic turn taken by "real" talk shows, such as those
hosted by David Letterman, not to mention *Howard Stern*, which brought
the antics of the nationally syndicated radio shock-jock to the E! network
in a classic case of postmodern media-crossing.

If talk shows were ideal for this kind of self-parodic postmodern excess, then soaps were even more so. *Mary Hartman* spawned one direct
sequel, *Forever Fernwood*, which was essentially a continuation of the
same show, but with a title change necessitated when Lasser left the
show, forcing the producers to jettison Mary Hartman as well, by having
her suffer a breakdown on a television talk show. *Mary Hartman* was also
quickly followed by the much more commercial *Soap* (1978–81), which,
because of its controversial subject matter, initially triggered widespread
protests from various religious and ethnic groups. But *Soap* lacked the
satirical punch of *Mary Hartman*, and the protests soon died down when
it became clear that the show was mostly a mild-mannered and good-
humored spoof of the convoluted plots of daytime soaps. In fact, *Soap*
was successful enough to contribute to the quick appearance of
"straight" nighttime soaps, such as the long-running and immensely influential *Dallas* (1978–91) and *Dynasty* (1981–89), both of which enjoyed
an international popularity that made a major contribution to the global
hegemony of American television.

This wave of nighttime soaps had pretty well run its course by the
beginning of the 1990s, but it was soon followed by David Lynch's *Twin
Peaks*, which combined a basic soap-opera stock with ingredients of crime
fiction, horror fiction, and science fiction to produce a complex soup of
popular genres, flavored with a generous dose of modernist sound and
camera techniques derived from art films. *Twin Peaks* is thus one of the
leading examples of the way in which television programs, like the novel
as described by Bakhtin, are able to incorporate elements of numerous
genres within a single work. However, *Twin Peaks* performed such combinations in unprecedented ways and with an unprecedented self-
consciousness. Commercial television audiences had never seen anything
quite like it. When the two-hour pilot of *Twin Peaks* aired (as an ABC
Sunday Night Movie), it was an immediate sensation, partly because of
the artsy aura brought to the show by Lynch, who conceived the series
with TV veteran Mark Frost and who directed and cowrote the pilot.
Thus, the cult status of earlier Lynch films, such as *Eraserhead* (1976) and
(especially) *Blue Velvet* (1986), seemed to carry over directly to *Twin
Peaks*.[2] However, the formal subversions of *Twin Peaks* were accompa-

nied by little in the way of subversive political statements; if anything, the weirdness of the series conveyed a nostalgic call for a return to the values of the idyllic past, when life wasn't so weird. This nostalgia, in particular, is directed at the Cold War, when it was possible to view the world in terms of simple Us vs. Them dichotomies that are no longer tenable in the confused and multiple postmodern world of the 1990s.

The basic premise of *Twin Peaks* seems fairly simple. As the series begins, FBI Special Agent Dale Cooper (Kyle MacLachlan, who had also starred in *Blue Velvet*) is sent to the town of Twin Peaks, Washington, to investigate the murder of local teen queen Laura Palmer (Sheryl Lee). As Cooper's unconventional investigation proceeds, we learn that Laura had not been living the idyllic life most in the community had imagined. The good-girl homecoming queen of Twin Peaks high school, she had been the daughter of a prominent local attorney, who provided her with a pleasant suburban home and other accoutrements of upper-middle-class affluence. Virtually a walking stereotype of the "popular" girl in high school, Laura had been the girlfriend of Bobby Briggs (Dana Ashbrook), the quarterback of the high school football team. However, she had also been secretly seeing the working-class James Hurley (James Marshall). She had been living a much more shocking secret life involving drugs and prostitution as well.

As the show proceeds, we also meet various other locals and learn a great deal about their extensive eccentricities. Finally, we learn that the town itself would be a virtual embodiment of 1950s-style small-town American values were it not for the fact that it is threatened by numerous evil forces (many of them supernatural) from both within and without. This information, meanwhile, is conveyed via a number of postmodern techniques, the most obvious of which is the show's radical mixing of genres and moods. For example, the mood of the series can change in a heartbeat. One scene might feature Cooper and local Sheriff Harry S. Truman (Michael Ontkean) trying to solve a gruesome and abject murder, the next might feature the comic antics of characters such as Deputy Andy Brennan (Harry Goaz) and Lucy Moran (Kimmy Robertson), whose very names evoked two of the greatest stars of the television sitcom, Andy Griffith and Lucille Ball. Truman, meanwhile, is one of the "straightest" and most "normal" characters in *Twin Peaks*, yet his intrusive naming contaminates even his relatively ordinary activities with a corrosive irony. The characters themselves are similarly impure, and not just because many of them tend to be morally depraved. They can also change their basic characteristics from one moment to the next, exhibiting surprising behavior that is completely inconsistent with their prior characterization, much in the mode of the schizophrenic characters discussed by Jameson as typical of postmodernism.

For example, Laura Palmer is not the only citizen of Twin Peaks to have a secret life. Bobby Briggs may be the high school quarterback, but he is also a drug dealer and a killer; he may be Laura's boyfriend, but he is also having an affair with Shelley Johnson, the wife of Leo Johnson (Eric Da Re), who turns out to be one of his key drug suppliers. James Hurley, meanwhile, is an outsider who looks something like a juvenile delinquent, but turns out to be a paragon of virtue, at least relative to almost everyone else in Twin Peaks. In the course of the series, various other characters behave in complex and contradictory ways as well, as when Audrey Horne (Sherilyn Fenn), in a kind of reversal of Laura's behavior, first appears as a sultry high school vixen and bad girl, only to turn out, by the end of the series, to be a virgin, a paragon of virtue, and, like her reformed father, an environmental activist. Characters can suddenly change age, as when thirty-five-year-old Nadine Hurley (Wendy Robie) becomes a teenager again—not to mention suddenly being blessed with comically superhuman strength. They can also change gender, as when David Duchovny makes a memorable (especially in retrospect, after his *X-Files* fame) appearance as cross-dressing DEA agent Denis(e) Bryson. The scheming Catherine Martell (Piper Laurie) goes one better, changing both race and gender by assuming the identity of Mr. Tojamura, a Japanese businessman. And, speaking of Asians, there is the completely unreadable Josie Packard (Joan Chen), who constantly flip-flops between positions of good and evil, innocence and depravity.

Most of the specific eccentricities in the behavior of individual characters can be attributed to psychological complexity or intentional stratagems. Indeed, the fragmented identities of certain characters are literally attributed to schizophrenia, as in the case of both Mike (aka The One-Armed Man, aka Phillip Gerard, played by Al Strobel) and Windom Earle (Kenneth Welsh). Meanwhile, the particularly unpredictable nature of Josie Packard is a classic Orientalist comment on the inscrutability of Asians. Still, the cumulative eccentricity of the citizenry of Twin Peaks seems to go well beyond any such psychological or racialist recuperation. Some of the specific turns taken by various characters are purely parodic (emphasizing the zaniness of soap-opera plots in general) or satirical. Thus, when both Ben Horne (Richard Beymer) and daughter Audrey (the latter perhaps more sincerely) devote themselves to environmental activism late in the series, the motif can be taken as a Reaganesque jab at environmentalism in general, with its negative short-term impact on the logging industry in northwestern towns such as Twin Peaks. The patent silliness of Audrey's final scene, in which she chains herself to a security door inside the Twin Peaks Savings and Loan as a public protest, makes this satirical point rather obvious.

But one can also see the inconsistencies in the behavior of various characters as indicative of a schizophrenic (in Jameson's sense) postmodern sense of the fragmented and provisional nature of individual identity. Thus, Lisa Saaf sees these inconsistencies as signs of a "decentered" subjectivity typical of postmodernism (Reeves et al. 184–85). Indeed, I would argue that these inconstencies are often postmodern even when they have specific, identified causes. However, the fragmented, postmodern identities of *Twin Peaks* work largely because they stand in sharp contrast to the stability and integrity of the conventional bourgeois subject. In other words, the postmodern impact of the series depends upon the ongoing power of modern assumptions about individual identity, as does the series's postmodern play with genre, narrative, and closure, allowing for dialogic interactions between the legacy of Enlightenment rationalism and postmodern skepticism toward that rationalism.

This skepticism consistently undermines the basic detective story plot of the series, as does the combination of the detective story plot with elements of so many other genres. Much of the published criticism on the show thus understandably focuses on its dialogue with various traditional genres. For example, Melynda Huskey relates *Twin Peaks*'s exposure of the "criminal undercurrents in family life" to the tradition of the mid-nineteenth century "sensation" novel, of which Wilkie Collins's *The Woman in White* (1861) was a crucial founding example (248). Michael Carroll notes the program's use of the mythic quest narrative, especially as it figured in the culture of the United States in the nineteenth century. And Lenora Ledwon notes the numerous points of contact between *Twin Peaks* and the gothic tradition, especially in the program's frequent depiction of doubles, though she also argues that "Television Gothic is a distinctly post-modern form" (260). To this list, one might also add pornography, which might also be cited as an important element in *Blue Velvet*. Not only are numerous motifs in *Twin Peaks* potentially pornographic, but many scenes (despite the reputation of the series for a lush look unusual for television) have the cheesy look of low-budget adult films.[3] Meanwhile, the pornographic magazine *Flesh World* (containing, among other things, photographs of Laura Palmer) figures prominently in several episodes.

Indeed, virtually every aspect of *Twin Peaks* can be found in various traditional Western genres dating back to the nineteenth century or even earlier. However, as Ledwon suggests, the characteristics of these genres tend to be transmuted by their presentation within the environment of broadcast television. Beyond this, what is different, and unprecedented, about the series is the fact that characteristics of so many different genres are combined and juxtaposed within the framework of a single cultural product. In a sense, *Twin Peaks* is the ultimate postmodern television artifact, combining in a single program the Bakhtinian dialogic plurality that critics such as Jim Collins have seen as the most postmodern characteristic of the television, with its simultaneous broadcast of various programs in various styles and genres. Thus, much of the content of the roundtable discussion of *Twin Peaks* and postmodernism that ends David Lavery's collection of scholarly essays on the program focuses on its use of elements from various genres, including the horror film, the TV commercial, the sitcom, film noir, and, of course, the detective genre and the soap opera. As the introduction to the discussion puts it, "No popular genre, no morsel of culture, whether high or low, was safe from *TP*'s haphazard hunger" (Reeves et al. 175). And, as Herb Eagle puts it in this discussion, the show was marked by "a kind of generic montage" that might be considered the "structural dominant of postmodern style" (Reeves et al. 183).

If the detective story provides the basic plot of *Twin Peaks*, the soap opera clearly provides the basic texture, a fact of which viewers were repeatedly reminded in the early episodes by the tendency of many characters to spend much of their time watching *Invitation to Love*, a fictional television soap opera embedded within the soap opera of *Twin Peaks*. Among other things, this motif is poised to suggest that the soap operaesque behavior of the local citizens is partly conditioned by their exposure to the media, though the motif is never really developed, and *Invitation to Love* disappears in the later episodes. In the meantime, the detective story was also foregrounded as a generic model for *Twin Peaks*, at least during the first seventeen episodes, which were given a sort of narrative coherence by the efforts of Agent Cooper to solve the abject murder of Laura Palmer. The series thus drew upon two important strains in postmodern television: the self-parodic soap opera (of which *Mary Hartman* was the paradigm), and the postmodern crime drama, which featured predecessors ranging from the early *Alfred Hitchcock Presents* to immediate forerunners such as *Moonlighting* (1985–89), with its campy and self-referential crime solving, to *Miami Vice* (1984–89), which featured a flashy, but superficial, style that has made it a favorite example of postmodern TV for numerous critics.

None of these programs was a pure example of any genre. *Mary Hartman* contained elements of the crime drama, and in fact began with a mass murder in the opening episode. *Miami Vice* was as much about pop style as crimefighting. And *Moonlighting* featured conventional television crimes (and a great deal of televised violence), but the focus was really on comedy, self-referentiality, and the sitcom/soap-opera sexual tension in the relationship between the main characters, Maddie Hayes (Cybill Shepherd) and David Addison (a then little-known Bruce Willis).

But none of these earlier examples are quite as generically mixed as *Twin Peaks*, which revels in its confusion of genres and proliferating simultaneous subplots, each of which might jump from one genre to the next at any moment. In the beginning (and through the first seventeen episodes), *Twin Peaks* is roughly held together by the investigation into the murder of Laura Palmer. However, even this central plot proceeds in a haphazard and sometimes bizarre fashion, partly due to the unorthodox methods employed by Cooper to solve the crime.

The offbeat treatment of the detective story motif in *Twin Peaks* is one of the features that most clearly marks the series as postmodernist. Numerous critics, in fact, have identified detective fiction as a crucial element of postmodernist culture. Collins, for example, sees detective fiction as a crucial postmodern genre, but argues (making a point that well describes *Twin Peaks*) that postmodernist texts are generally characterized by a multigeneric environment in which detective fiction is placed in dialogue with other (often very different) genres. Thus, for Collins, Jean-Jacques Beineix's *Diva* (1981) is an excellent example of postmodernist film partly because of the way in which it sets the assumptions of its basic detective story plot in opposition to the radically different assumptions of nineteenth-century opera, establishing a dialog between popular culture and "High Art" (61).

Michael Holquist argues that the detective story may be the structural model "par excellence" for postmodernist fiction, suggesting that "what the structural and philosophical presuppositions of myth and depth psychology were to Modernism ... the detective story is to Post-Modernism." For Holquist the appeal of the detective story is its reliance on reason, on "the magic of mind in a world that all too often seems impervious to reason" (143). But he suggests that the postmodernist treatment of the detective story model is highly ironic, undermining the neat solutions to epistemological problems typically offered by the detective story genre. Thus, "by exploiting the conventions of the detective story such men as Borges and Robbe-Grillet have fought against the Modernist attempt to fill the void of the world with rediscovered mythical symbols. Rather, they dramatize the void" (155).

Holquist's argument is obviously quite relevant to *Twin Peaks*, with its numerous symbols of a manufactured mythology and its suggestion of an evil void threatening the quiet town of Twin Peaks. And Holquist's differentiation between modernism and postmodernism on the basis of the use of myth versus the detective story is not unusual, resonating in particular with Huyssen's comments on the increased acceptance of popular culture in postmodernism relative to modernism. His polar opposition between myth and the detective story is somewhat problematic, however. For example, one of Holquist's own central examples of the postmodernist reinscription of the detective story is Robbe-Grillet's *The Erasers*, a text that certainly participates in the detective story tradition, but that does so by invoking the mythical Oedipus as its principal intertextual exemplar of the detective.

William Spanos agrees with Holquist that a subversive dialog with the epistemological closure usually associated with the detective story is a crucial element of postmodernist fiction. However, Spanos goes a step further by suggesting that the rationalist epistemology of the conventional detective story is representative of a modernist ideology that sees the world as "a comforting, even exciting and suspenseful well-made cosmic drama or novel—more particularly, a detective story" ("Detective" 150). But Spanos's suggestion of epistemological closure in the modernist text is also questionable. For example, modernist classics like Franz Kafka's *The Castle* can clearly be read as parodies of detective story plots in which no closure is achieved.

Modernist texts, in fact, are quite generally characterized by a lack of neat closure. However, the undecidability of the endings of postmodernist fictions tends to be of a different kind. Relevant here is Brian McHale's argument that modernism and postmodernism can be distinguished precisely by their different attitudes toward such epistemological issues. However, more to the point in the case of *Twin Peaks* is my own argument elsewhere that the radical undecidability of postmodernist detective fiction frequently derives from a combination of the detective story (which seeks traditional epistemological closure) and the "fantastic" (which inherently makes such closure impossible). Here, I draw upon Tzvetan Todorov's important characterization of the fantastic as a mode in which it is impossible to tell whether seemingly supernatural events are genuinely supernatural or merely "uncanny," i.e., containable by psychological or other natural explanations. In a reading of Mario Vargas Llosa's *Who Killed Palomino Molero?* I conclude that "both detective fiction and the fantastic depend upon the active contribution of readers to achieve their effects, and in this sense both genres are paradigmatic of the emphasis on reader involvement in postmodernist fiction in general" (Booker, *Vargas Llosa* 161).

The importance of reader (or viewer) involvement in creating meaning from *Twin Peaks* is obvious, leading María Carrión to conclude that "the central theme of *Twin Peaks* is whatever each one of the viewers wants to name it" (243). And Diane Stevenson has noted the clear relevance of Todorov's discussion of the fantastic to *Twin Peaks* (70–71). The use of the detective story motif in the series would seem to be crucial to its functioning as a postmodernist cultural artifact, making it important to examine that motif in detail. At times, Cooper displays impressive abilities as a conventional detective, leading Sheriff Truman to compare the FBI agent to Sherlock Holmes. In the pilot, Cooper, Truman, and others watch a video shot of Laura and best friend Donna Hayward (Lara Flynn Boyle) during a picnic shortly before Laura's death. Cooper is then the only one who notices the reflection of a motorcycle in Laura's eye, suggesting that local biker James Hurley had been along on the picnic. But Cooper is more Amazing Kreskin than Holmesian detective, using psychic powers more than ratiocination to process clues. He processes a great deal of conventional evidence, but none of this evidence really leads anywhere. In fact, it eventually leads to the mistaken arrest of the town's leading businessman, Ben Horne, for Laura's murder.

Cooper eventually solves the crime (sort of), but does so largely through a series of dreams, visions, and intuitions, many of which he himself attempts to trigger by spiritual techniques. Thus, if viewers had mistakenly thought they were watching a conventional detective fiction, they were unequivocally disabused of this notion by the third episode, in which Cooper processes a list of potential suspects using a technique supposedly derived from Tibetan mysticism, of which he has subconsciously gained knowledge, apparently through his dreams. In this scene, as the name of each suspect is read off, Cooper throws a rock at a glass bottle, then categorizes the suspects according to the results of the throw: a miss, a hit that does not break the bottle, a hit that breaks the bottle.[4]

Should it really be possible for anyone to fail to recognize this scene as a wacky postmodern farce (thus taking it seriously as a Tibetan information-processing technique), the scene undercuts itself in a number of ways. For one thing, Cooper carefully measures off his distance from the bottle at 60 feet, 6 inches, precisely the distance from the pitching rubber to home plate in baseball. The comic nature of the scene is then further established as Cooper (whose fondness for a good cup of Joe has already been made clear) receives a cup of coffee offered him by Lucy. He takes one quick sip, then frantically spits the (seemingly foul) coffee out onto the ground. "Damn good coffee!" he exclaims enthusiastically. "And hot!"[5] From here, Cooper launches into a ludicrous lecture on Tibetan history, while the sheriff, Lucy, Andy, and the Native American Deputy Hawk (Michael Horse) listen with rapt attention, sitting on a bench and leaning forward in choreographed unison as Cooper begins his discourse.[6]

Meanwhile, Cooper's arm is remarkably erratic; though he hits the bottle twice (breaking it once), he also at one point misses it by several feet, causing the rock to bounce off a tree and plunk Andy directly on the forehead, sending him staggering about in the finest slapstick tradition. Finally, the entire scene is undercut by the fact that Cooper has constructed his list of suspects on a false premise. Laura Palmer had written in her diary on the day of her death that she was "nervous about meeting J tonight." We will eventually learn that she meant James Hurley, who turns out to have been her secret boyfriend, but who had nothing to do with her death. Not knowing this, Cooper has constructed a list of possible suspects whose first or last names begin with J, feeling that J might be the killer. Included on the list is "Jack with One Eye," about whom he has received an anonymous tip. But Jack, Cooper learns during the scene, is a place, not a person, "One-Eyed Jack's" being a bordello just across the border in Canada that happens to be owned by Ben Horne, who also owns Horne's Department Store and the Great Northern Hotel. In any case, the rock-throwing session points to Leo Johnson, at whose name Cooper breaks the bottle. However, this information makes absolutely no contribution to the eventual solution of the murder, in which Leo was not directly involved, whatever his other shady activities.

It was, indeed, in this third episode (directed by Lynch and written by Lynch and Frost) that *Twin Peaks* took its first irreversible turn toward genuine weirdness. If the rock-throwing scene is actually a red herring that leads nowhere (a kind of fish, we learn in a later episode, that Cooper doesn't much care for), a more genuinely weird scene later in this same episode actually does lead to the identification of the killer. Here, Cooper experiences a dream in which he is addressed by Mike, who warns him of the existence of Bob (Frank Silva), a murderous supernatural entity of pure evil. Then Cooper, suddenly twenty-five years older, finds himself in a surrealistic room surrounded by red curtains (the Red Room). A dwarf (aka The Man from Another Place, played by Michael J. Anderson) enters the room, while Cooper realizes that Laura Palmer, still young and beautiful, is sitting in a chair across from him. Both the dwarf and Laura (or a Laura lookalike) speak to Cooper in cryptic fashion and in strangely distorted voices (luckily translated for viewers in subtitles). Eventually, the dwarf begins to dance weirdly to a strain of cool jazz music of the kind that forms much of the distinctive soundtrack of *Twin Peaks*. Then Laura walks over to Cooper, kisses him, and whispers the identity of her killer in his ear. Cooper then awakes (with his hair standing comically on end, perhaps suggesting a post-dream erection) and calls Sheriff Truman, asking him to meet him for breakfast, because "I know who killed Laura Palmer," though he refuses to identify the killer over the phone.

The episode ends there, with the kind of cliffhanger for which the series would eventually become notorious—as when the first season ends with Cooper lying on the floor of his hotel room, apparently bleeding to death from multiple gunshot wounds. If Truman had to wait for breakfast to learn the identity of the killer, viewers had to wait a full week—for what would turn out to be pure anticlimax. At breakfast, Cooper delays things still further by taking time to order a hearty meal of griddle cakes with maple syrup and a slice of ham, proclaiming proudly, in TV-commercial fashion, that "nothing beats the taste sensation when maple syrup collides with ham!" When Truman impatiently demands to know who killed Laura Palmer, Cooper announces that he has had a dream that he believes to be a code: "Break the code, solve the crime," he explains. Then, after a scientific explanation of the physiological source of dreams, Cooper describes his strange dream of the night before, up to the revelation of the identity of the killer. Unfortunately, though, he has now forgotten the identity of the killer. "Damn!" exclaims the disappointed Truman.

Viewers might have agreed with Truman, but then the desire of many viewers to learn the identity of the killer was surely driven by precisely the sort of Enlightenment demand for simple and unequivocal answers that *Twin Peaks* seemed designed to frustrate. Indeed, Cooper's offbeat methods of detection make a mockery of the scientific-rationalist techniques employed by more conventional detectives, especially given that his methods ultimately work. These more conventional techniques, meanwhile, are represented in the series in the work of Agent Albert

Rosenfeld (Miguel Ferrer), who serves as a sort of counterpoint to the intuitive and spiritual Cooper. Rosenfeld is all business and all science, employing brilliant deductive reasoning and the latest techniques of forensic pathology to process the various bits of evidence unearthed in the investigation. Rosenfeld is also acerbic and hostile, taking every opportunity to insult the local rubes and hayseeds with his big-city wit—as opposed to Cooper, who immediately falls in love with Twin Peaks and its citizens. Indeed, Rosenfeld can be interpreted, at least in his early appearances, as a sort of allegorical representative of a heartless, dehumanized modernity, now intruding rudely into the pastoral space of Twin Peaks.[7]

Indeed, the sometimes idyllic depiction of the medium-small town of Twin Peaks (near the Canadian border) in the series would seem to involve the kind of specific local color that would set it apart from Jameson's vision of the lack of distinctive localities in the postmodern world, when the homogenization of life under late capitalism effaces the former distinctive identities of different regions. After all, the very title of the series seems to call attention to the importance of the distinctive setting in the town of Twin Peaks. Indeed, the series is punctuated with numerous shots of the natural beauty that surrounds the area. The towering North Woods that surround the town seem both awesome and serene, while the Great Northern Hotel (in which virtually every interior surface is covered by wood paneling to emphasize the setting in timber country) sits at the top of a majestic waterfall (Washington State's Snoqualmie Falls) that is shown several times in virtually every episode. One of the central motifs that establishes the strangeness of the series is the fact that Cooper seems as interested in learning about the local flora and fauna as he is in solving the murder of Laura Palmer. Thus, he repeatedly interrupts his criminal investigation to ask questions about the local plant and animal life, sighing dreamily when, for instance, he is informed that the trees he so admires are Douglas firs.

Yet the waterfall also has a vaguely dangerous look, while we are repeatedly reminded that something evil lurks in the nearby woods, however beautiful they may be. The natural setting thus also makes an important atmospheric contribution to the program's air of strangeness and to its continual suggestion that the line between good and evil, between beauty and horror, is a fine one indeed—if there is a line at all. This continual deconstruction of traditional dichotomies is an important part of the postmodern texture of the show.

A closer look at the Twin Peaks setting, however, shows that there is really no there there. We see the interiors of a number of the homes of the important characters, and we see the exteriors and interiors of a number of public places as well, including the Great Northern Hotel, the sheriff's office, the high school, a bank, a hospital, the Packard Saw Mill, Horne's Department Store, Big Ed's Gas Farm, the Double R Diner, and the

Roadhouse. But we rarely see any exterior public spaces (and then usually obscured by night and shown in little detail), and we never really see the town itself. Twin Peaks has a traffic light, but it seems to have few roads and virtually no traffic. Though supposedly a town of more than 50,000 inhabitants (51,201, says the sign welcoming visitors to the town[8]), Twin Peaks seems to have no shopping mall, no grocery stores, and virtually no children below high school age. Horne's seems to be the only department store, the Great Northern the only hotel (though there is a cheap motel on the outskirts of town), Big Ed's the only gas station. Meanwhile, it is impossible, based on the series itself, to map the town or to determine the relative locations of the various settings featured in the series, though fans have tried mightily at times, and speculative maps have been developed, suggesting the ongoing desire of postmodern audiences to be able to get their bearings in a traditional fashion.[9]

The town of Twin Peaks has no actual identity at all; its local color exists all on the surface and for essentially allegorical reasons. Thus, the regionalism of *Twin Peaks* is actually what Jameson calls "neoregionalism," which he identifies as a "specifically postmodern form of reterritorialization." For Jameson, this new form of regionalism is in fact a "flight from the realities of late capitalism," a ruse that is designed to "reassure North Americans as to the persistence of a distinctive regional or urban social life," while simultaneously attempting to "certify the microscopic and inconsequential — or rather what the state and the dominant institutions pronounce to be trivial and insignificant — as the space of real life" (*Seeds* 148–49).

Jameson's comments here are extremely helpful in explaining the strong sense that I have, while watching the series, that its regionalism is somehow bogus. In fact, Twin Peaks is not so much a town as a simulation of a town, or perhaps a simulacrum, as the typical American small town that it supposedly simulates no longer exists by 1990. Then again, the show is not necessarily set in 1990. One by-product of the relative lack of any overall view of the town is that there are few markers that would place the program in any particular historical period. The availability of computers and other advanced electronic technologies identifies the setting as essentially contemporary with the broadcast, but the community of Twin Peaks itself has a timeless quality, very much along the lines of the town in Lynch's *Blue Velvet*, often cited as a key example of the ambiguous historical referentiality of postmodern film. Note, for example, Norman Denzin's discussion of the film's refusal to identify its historical setting, freely mixing images that appear to derive from different historical periods: "This is a film which evokes, mocks, yet lends quasi-reverence for the icons of the past, while it places them in the present" (469).

Blue Velvet includes a number of inconsistent historical markers, though its principal historical mix is between the mid-1980s, when the film was made, and the 1950s, in which many of the characters seem to reside and for which the film shows a certain nostalgia — along the lines of the nostalgia (especially for the 1950s) that Jameson has identified as a crucial characteristic of postmodernism.[10] *Twin Peaks* employs similar mixtures, as when James Hurley goes through the entire series as a leather-jacketed, motorcycling personification of teen angst — in imitation of James Dean. Jimmie Reeves thus notes that the series "ostensibly takes place in the present, but retains a real fifties feel" (Reeves et al. 176). One might also note here the 1950s-style garb worn by the waitresses in the Double R Diner. However, the local psychiatrist, Dr. Jacoby (Russ Tamblyn), goes about in 1960s-style hippie garb, while other characters wear a variety of uniforms, plaid shirts, and other attire that is difficult to link unequivocally to any particular time period.

Twin Peaks also gets extensive mileage out of a confrontation between its apparent 1990s setting and the sense that Twin Peaks could potentially be a traditional enclave protected from the vicissitudes of history, with values that have remained unchanged for decades. The murder of Laura Palmer shatters this small-town tranquility and wrenches Twin Peaks violently into the flow of history. On the other hand, there are numerous suggestions that the traditional values of the town were themselves bogus all along: almost every event in the series reminds us of the corruption, lust, and venality that lie just beneath the calm surface of this (and presumably any) small town. Even the opening title sequence, which mixes peaceful images from nature with industrial images from the saw mill (including smokestacks spewing pollution into the pure northwestern air) effects a similar confrontation between timelessness and modernity.

Life in Twin Peaks would be perfect were it not for the evil that threatens the town from both within and without, a situation that directly replicates the logic of the Cold War, in which American society would supposedly be ideal were it not for the evil Soviets who menaced the American way from abroad and the sinister communist agents who threatened America from within. Even Cooper is at one point accused, though by the villainous Jean Renault (Michael Parks), of representing an intrusion of outside evil. As Renault points out (in his hokey French Canadian accent), it was only upon the arrival of Cooper in the community that things really got ugly: "Quiet people lived a quiet life. ... Suddenly the simple dream become the nightmare. ... Maybe you brought the nightmare with you." Given Lynch's apparent desire to represent Twin Peaks as a vaguely utopian enclave, relatively free of the contamination of modernity, it comes as no surprise that the community tends to win out in its encounters with the outside world. Cooper falls in love with the community and even begins shopping around for real estate. Rosenfeld, meanwhile, gets his come-uppance when his insults and coldly rational approach to the investigation become too much for Truman, who punches him out, causing him to fall on top of Laura Palmer's corpse in a clearly suggestive position.

Rosenfeld, the consummate by-the-numbers bureaucrat, then doggedly pursues the filing of an official complaint against Truman for assaulting a federal agent, though Cooper refuses to support him in this effort. But, when Truman again threatens violence in a subsequent confrontation, Rosenfeld suddenly changes character and announces that he is a pacifistic follower of Gandhi and King and that he will continue turning the other cheek no matter how many times Truman assaults him. His abrasive manner, he explains, comes about because he is a "naysayer and hatchet man in the fight against violence. ... I reject absolutely revenge, aggression, and retaliation. The foundation of such a method is love. I love you Sheriff Truman."

"Albert's path is a strange and difficult one," Cooper explains to the stunned sheriff, and that's not the only thing in *Twin Peaks* that is strange and difficult. In the postmodern world of the series, individual identities have no real content, so that characters are not constrained to behave consistently. But there are suggestions that Rosenfeld has been specifically changed by his encounter with Twin Peaks. For example, the information uncovered in this investigation is strange enough that Rosenfeld eventually concludes that his scientific techniques will never solve this particular crime. He thus urges Cooper to go on with his "vision quest," because he is the "only one with the coordinates" to deal with the peculiar circumstances of this case.

These coordinates, among other things, include the fact that the normal Aristotelian logic of the detective story does not seem to apply here, where the collapse of conventional either-or oppositions defeats any possibility of epistemological closure. This deconstruction of polar oppositions reaches its climax at the end of the last episode, when the central opposition between Cooper, as a force for good, and Bob, as a force for evil, also collapses. In one of the series's most overt dramatizations of the schizophrenic nature of postmodern subjectivity, Cooper ventures into the Black Lodge in an attempt to rescue Annie Blackburne (Heather Graham), his super-pure ex-nun new girlfriend (and also the newly elected Miss Twin Peaks). While in the lodge, Cooper finds himself split into two different entities, presumably a "good" Cooper and a "bad" Cooper. He then returns to the "real" world of Twin Peaks, at first seemingly restored to his original virtuous self. Then, in the last scene of the series, he regains consciousness in his room in the Great Northern Hotel and immediately asks, "How's Annie?" Assured that she is fine, Cooper weirdly charges into the bathroom to brush his teeth, then inexplicably squeezes the entire tube of toothpaste into the sink, after which he stares into the mirror and suddenly smashes his head into it. We then see the distorted reflection, not of Cooper, but of Bob, in the shattered mirror. The series then comes to a close with Cooper, apparently now possessed by Bob, repeatedly muttering, "How's Annie?" in an evil and sinister voice.

This ending, among other things, recalls that of *Oedipus Rex*, in which the investigation of the detective, Oedipus, leads to the revelation that Oedipus himself is the culprit responsible for the plague that has befallen Thebes. It is also strikingly reminiscent of the conclusion of *The Prisoner*, in which Number Six and his nemesis, Number One, turn out to be one and the same. Moreover, as with *The Prisoner*, the last episode of *Twin Peaks* leaves numerous questions unanswered, in addition to the eventual resolution of the battle between Cooper and Bob. How *is* Annie, anyway? Is Ben Horne, who was apparently just accidentally killed by Donna's "father," Dr. Hayward (Warren Frost), really dead?[11] Will Leo Johnson escape from the spiders of Damocles position in which he has been left by Windom Earle? Were Andrew Packard (Dan O'Herlihy), Pete Martell (Jack Nance), and Ben's daughter, Audrey Horne, killed in the apocalyptic explosion that has just occurred in the Twin Peaks Savings and Loan? Will James Hurley, who has headed for Mexico to "find himself" (after a brief involvement in a hasty side-plot involving adultery and murder) ever return? Will he resume his relationship with Donna? Will Big Ed Hurley (Everett McGill) ever get together with his true love Norma Jennings (Peggy Lipton) now that Ed's wife, Nadine has apparently returned to what passes, in her case, for normal?

These and other questions would never be answered, not even in Lynch's much-anticipated subsequent feature film, *Twin Peaks: Fire Walk with Me* (1992), which turned out to be a prequel detailing the days leading up to the death of Laura Palmer, while saying nothing about what happened subsequent to the final episode of the television series. But, given the logic of *Twin Peaks*, were these questions to be answered, they would only lead to still other questions. Thus, once the murder of Laura Palmer was solved, *Twin Peaks* tends to fragment in all directions, with uncertainties proliferating wildly. The subplots multiply almost geometrically, while there is now no main plot to hold them all together. As a result, the show becomes more and more postmodern, more and more strange. It also becomes more and more fragmented and incomprehensible. As a result, once devoted audiences (at heart still longing for some realist morsels to hold on to) began to scatter like rats deserting a sinking ship. Indeed, the spectacular rise and equally spectacular fall of *Twin Peaks* as a television phenomenon is now virtually legendary.

Many of the plots in the later episodes are still primarily the stuff of soap opera, though often taken to an extreme even for that inherently exaggerated genre. Also in the later episodes, Air Force Major Garland Briggs (Don Davis), the father of Bobby Briggs, becomes a more important character, increasing the importance of the science fiction motif with which he is associated. Formerly involved in a top secret government program to monitor radio transmissions from deep space, Briggs now becomes entangled with the forces of evil that haunt the woods around Twin Peaks. In the tenth episode, these transmissions, which had previously been mere gibberish, suddenly began to contain messages referring to Agent Cooper and also the phrase "the owls are not what they seem," which Cooper had previously heard from the enigmatic giant in his visions. Indeed, these transmissions turn out to be coming not from outer space, but from the woods around Twin Peaks, emanating from either the Black or the White Lodge. Then, in episode twenty, Major Briggs is suddenly abducted, possibly by aliens but apparently by minions of the alternative dimension in which the lodges reside. Learning of Briggs's disappearance, his superior warns Cooper that the event concerns top-secret matters that could potentially "make the Cold War seem like a case of the sniffles."

This suggestion—which might be taken as another example of the nostalgia of *Twin Peaks* for the good old days of the Cold War (and the 1950s)—never really goes anywhere, despite its seemingly important implications. Indeed, many motifs of the series are never really developed, no doubt partly because of its early cancellation. Still, the numerous loose threads left hanging at the end of the final episode are very much in keeping with the overall refusal of the series to provide clear and unequivocal answers to the questions it poses. Indeed, the lack of closure of the series is a key ingredient of its dialogic novelness, in the Bakhtinian sense, Bakhtinian dialogue never coming to an end because "there is neither a first nor a last word and there are no limits to the dialogic context" (*Speech Genres* 170).

In terms of closure, the key event in *Twin Peaks* is the investigation into the murder of Laura Palmer, which reaches a successful conclusion in conventional terms, but which, at the same time, shows just how inadequate and misleading such conventional terms can be. From the beginning, the investigation into Laura's murder is beset by a superabundance of clues, many of them pointing in contradictory directions. In fact, by the time Cooper arrives in Twin Peaks, he already knows a great deal about the crime in advance, having investigated the similar murder of Teresa Banks (Pamela Gidley) in the "southwestern part of the state" a year earlier. This prior knowledge then helps Cooper to gather evidence, because he knows just where to look and what to look for. Both crimes, as we eventually learn in *Fire Walk with Me*, were indeed committed by the same killer. But the identification of this killer turns out to be more troubling and less satisfying than fans of traditional detective stories might have expected.

Indeed, there is much that is troubling about the investigation into Laura's murder, including the abject nature of the crime itself, which seems so shocking in this peaceful community. Also a bit shocking are the numerous intrusions of the supernatural into the daily life of the tranquil community of Twin Peaks, though, again, these intrusions can be read as allegory, though an allegory with multiple indications. The same might be said about almost every aspect of the show, which is consistently informed by a campy excess and in which many motifs are so ridiculous in themselves that one often feels that they must surely be standing in for something else. For one thing, the supernatural forces of the show are almost always evil and thus, within the Cold War logic for which the show yearns, can be read as stand-ins for communism. For another, the presence of supernatural in the series suggests the existence of forces beyond human understanding and thus indicates the way in which, especially after the breakdown of the clear oppositions of the Cold War, the world is becoming more and more complex and inexplicable.

The most distinctive explanation for aberrant behavior in *Twin Peaks* is possession by evil spirits, especially the ever-lurking Bob. But this attribution of otherwise inexplicable behavior to Bob's supernatural agency can be read in various ways. Psychoanalytically, Bob clearly stands in for the dark forces of the Freudian unconscious, which, presumably, often determine our behavior without our conscious knowledge or control. But Bob can also be taken as a sign of the postmodern sense that individual subjects find themselves in the grip of large impersonal forces that are far beyond their understanding or ability to resist.

The most important example of possession by Bob involves Leland Palmer (Ray Wise), the prominent Twin Peaks attorney who turns out to have raped and murdered his daughter Laura. In episode seventeen, Leland is unequivocally identified as the killer, presumably answering the question "Who killed Laura Palmer?" that had at one time become a central mantra of America popular culture. There are also strong hints (though the series is extremely coy about actually stating it) that Leland had been sexually abusing Laura for years. In *Fire Walk with Me*, for example, Laura states that Bob has been "visiting" her since she was twelve, and the film actually includes one scene of a rape in which the identity of the rapist flickers between Leland and Bob.

The series thus potentially reveals one of the dirty secrets of the American family that was so beloved of the Reagan-Bush administration. However, by attributing the child abuse to the supernatural intervention of Bob, *Twin Peaks* removes this issue from the realm of the sociological and places it in the realm of the metaphysical — or at least the ambiguous. Meanwhile, the implications of the Bob motif are so ambiguous that simply identifying Leland Palmer as the physical murderer really solves very little. Are we to believe that Leland was literally possessed by an evil spirit and therefore simply another victim, not morally responsible for his deeds? Or is Bob merely an allegory of the intrusion of dark, inexplicable forces, not just into Leland's unconscious mind but into the once safe and sensible community of Twin Peaks?

The town of Twin Peaks potentially represents a utopian echo, however embattled, of a world that still made sense and in which reliable cognitive mapping was still possible. However, the inability of Lynch and the other creative forces behind the show to keep a straight face while attempting to represent Twin Peaks as a sort of rural utopia is especially significant. On the one hand, it suggests the weakness of the utopian imagination in late capitalist America; on the other hand, it suggests the continuing desire to think utopia, even if the result of this thought is a mangled, compromised, and thoroughly bogus one. Here, the context of the series in the midst of the first Bush administration is probably important. The show's placement of utopia in a small town with traditional values is pure Reagan-Bush. The suggestion that this utopia is surrounded and threatened by an empire of evil has obvious Reaganite sources as well, suggesting a nostalgic last-ditch attempt to revive the seemingly clear dualities of the peak years of the Cold War, even as the Soviet Union and its socialist allies were collapsing like a house of cards.

But this very collapse was one of the major reasons why, by 1990, it was no longer possible to maintain this Cold War allegory without a liberal dose of ludic self-conscious irony. Meanwhile, any small-town utopianism that might be detected in the series is thoroughly nostalgic, pointing back toward an idealized (and distorted) vision of what was, rather than pointing forward toward what might be, as any genuinely useful utopian vision should do. As Jonathan Rosenbaum points out, the "social orientation" of both *Twin Peaks* and *Blue Velvet* "consists basically of an infatuation with 1950s small town America and its dirty little secrets, coupled with a view of women that essentially regards them as either madonnas or whores." Rosenbaum then goes on to argue that this Reaganite orientation is not only reactionary, but banal, undermining the notion of *Twin Peaks* as an artistic breakthrough for television:

It seems useful to point out that with a sheriff and a federal agent as its principal charismatic male buddies, a sentimentality about homecoming queens that borders on gush, a Reaganite preference for the wealthy over the poor (and for WASPs over everyone else), and a puritanical Peyton Place brand of sociology, *Twin Peaks* is ideologically no different from other prime time serials. (25)

Rosenbaum is, I think, basically correct here. However, where *Twin Peaks* differs from *Dallas* and *Dynasty* is in its radical inability to take its own nostalgic Reaganite politics seriously. Rather than present a Reaganite view of the world, *Twin Peaks* wishes it could present a Reaganite view of the world, but seems to know, deep down, that such a view is so untenable as to be ridiculous. This phenomenon is especially clear in the show's attempts to draw upon the legacy of the Cold War, while simultaneously undermining the kind of polar oppositions upon which the

Cold War paradigm was centrally based. Even dichotomies as presumably basic as good vs. evil are constantly collapsing in *Twin Peaks*, where it becomes increasingly difficult to distinguish the good guys from the bad guys. Thus, in the abstract, metaphysical realm of the Black and White Lodges, there are suggestions that the two lodges are mutually implicated (or maybe even one and the same) rather than diametrically opposed. Similarly, the palindromic name of "Bob," the show's central personification of evil, suggests that the opposite of Bob is still Bob, an interpretation that is reinforced in the tumultuous final episode when the Man from Another Place, whose role is to drop cryptic clues for Cooper's interpretation, suddenly exclaims, "Wow, Bob, wow," extending the palindrome in the midst of a scene in which we learn that this dwarf is indistinguishable from his physical opposite, the mysterious giant (Carel Struycken), who also periodically appears in Cooper's visions to provide riddling clues.[12]

This continual collapse of seemingly stable oppositions greatly complicates any attempt to interpret the significance of any given motif in *Twin Peaks*. For example, while both the family and the American small town might seem sinister in *Twin Peaks*, it is really the deviation of the family and the small town (due to the influence of evil outside forces) from the Reaganite ideal that is sinister. Indeed, while the show almost seems to revel in the collapse of simple oppositions, it is consistently underwritten by a dread of this collapse and by a nostalgic longing for the days when such oppositions could still stand.

One of these oppositions is class, always an awkward topic in America. As Scott Pollard notes, Lynch's view of the world seems firmly rooted in the American middle class, and "the stable and stabilizing center of Lynch's vision is the middle class' own idealized image of itself" (301). Thus, the evil in *Twin Peaks* emanates not from the middle class, but from outside threats to the middle class, which is upheld as a center of virtue. For Pollard, then, *Twin Peaks*, like *Blue Velvet* and *Wild at Heart* (1990), is "a narrative of redemption which is meant to save the American middle class" (301). In short, the utopian resonances of the community of Twin Peaks are contained within the middle class and the American Way, which, for Lynch, are far more the true loci of utopia than any particular community, rural or otherwise. The threats to the American Way, meanwhile, come from the have-nots who might, at any moment, begin to demand their slice of the pie.

Pollard grants that all commercial television is, to an extent, designed to uphold and promote middle-class values. He argues, however, that Lynch's vision is particularly potent because of his paranoid sense that "unknown universal powers are out to get the middle class" (303). Stevenson is more specific, noting that Bob, like Frank Booth (the principal locus of evil in *Blue Velvet*) is clearly presented as a member of the underclass. Thus, "as Lynch conceives of normality in terms of the middle class, so he tends to imagine the threat to that normality as coming from the lower class" (74). Stevenson is, I think, very much on target here, though Lynch does, in *Twin Peaks* at least, seem to want to universalize these powers by depicting them as supernatural forces. Still, I would again argue that supernatural entities such as Bob and the Black Lodge are relatively transparent Cold War allegories of the real-world forces that threaten American middle-class serenity, including not only communism as a system, but also (and, perhaps, even more so) the unwashed masses of working people (especially, by 1990, in the Third World) for which communism is itself a sort of emblem.

The vaunted "artistry" of *Twin Peaks* can similarly be read as a sort of belated, almost nostalgic, appeal to the simple, Manichean dichotomies of the Cold War, in which modernist subtlety and sophistication were consistently held up as signs of the intellectual and moral superiority of the West to a Soviet bloc that was mired in a supposedly primitive and ideologically narrow-minded socialist realism. Of course, the various artsy techniques employed in the series seemed striking not because they were unprecedented (in both art films and modernist literature), but because they were unusual on commercial television and because so many different techniques were combined in a single program. Meanwhile, this artistry is presumably a sign of the making hand of Lynch as the modernist *auteur* and might thus militate against any view of the program as thoroughly postmodernist.

It is certainly the case that *Twin Peaks* employs a number of techniques that are reminiscent of both art film and modernist literature. However, these techniques appear within a campy, kitschy matrix that makes it very difficult to take them seriously as art. Indeed, *Twin Peaks* clearly takes *itself* much less seriously than modernist authors such as Kafka, Joyce, and Brecht. It even takes itself far less seriously than do the films of Lynch, as can easily be seen by the fact that, in the feature film that succeeded the series, the comic and campy aspects of the television series (for me, at least, precisely the elements that made it entertaining) were removed almost entirely, making for a fairly grim and baleful effort, despite the fact that it maintained the dwarves and giants and other silliness. I would argue that it is this lack of self-seriousness, combined with the television format and the multiplicity of techniques, that helps to identify *Twin Peaks* as more postmodernist than modernist and as more ludic than anxious or critical.[13]

Many aspects of *Twin Peaks*, especially the dream sequences, clearly draw upon the techniques of surrealism, while also harking back to the expressionistic dream sequences of classic films noirs such as *Murder, My Sweet* (1944).[14] The classic case here is the construction of the Red Room and of the Black Lodge as a whole, but, even in the more "realistic" scenes, the show often features a surprising juxtaposition of seemingly incommensurate materials, very much along the lines of surrealist collage, though again this aspect of the series is reminiscent of Bakhtin's vision of the novel as a collection of diverse materials. Incongruous images thus often intrude into even seemingly mundane scenes, as when, in the pilot, Cooper and Truman go into the bank to inspect Laura Palmer's safety deposit box. There, they enter an ordinary conference room to find a large buck's head (it has recently fallen from the wall, where it was mounted) lying atop the conference table. But this effect is comic, rather than shocking, and by 1990 the surprising juxtapositions of images in *Twin Peaks* probably reminded most viewers far more of television commercials or music videos than of André Breton.

The absurd quality of so many scenes and images in *Twin Peaks* is often highly reminiscent of the work of Kafka, while the juxtapositions of diverse materials and images are also reminiscent of something like Joyce's *Ulysses*, which employs a complex multiplicity of genres and styles that anticipates *Twin Peaks*. Formally, the modernist writer *Twin Peaks* recalls most directly is probably Brecht. As with Joyce, Brecht often imports a variety of materials from a wide array of sources (including popular culture) in constructing his texts. But Brecht is most important as a predecessor to *Twin Peaks* in the way so many elements of the series involve Brechtian techniques of alienation that seem designed to force audiences to engage the show on an intellectual level rather than merely becoming emotionally immersed in it. The patent ridiculousness of many events and characters already produces such an alienation effect, though one of the most obvious Brechtian elements of *Twin Peaks* is the acting, which is often so intentionally weird as to prevent audiences from forgetting that they are watching actors acting rather than real people living out their lives. Crucial here is the wooden acting of Kyle MacLachlan (who would surely have to play the lead role were they ever to make a film of the life of Al Gore), which is perfect for the role of Cooper, making his actions seem all the more peculiar. Moreover, the casting of MacLachlan provided an important intertextual link to *Blue Velvet*, in which he also starred. Other actors deliver over-the-top performances so exaggerated as to make impossible any direct emotional identification with their characters. Richard Beymer, at least in many scenes, falls into this category, as do Jack Nance, Wendy Robie, and the comic duo of Harry Goaz and Kimmy Robertson.

Still, the most Brechtian element of *Twin Peaks* might be the music of Angelo Badalamenti (who also did the music for *Blue Velvet* and *Wild at Heart*), which is extremely effective, but which never quite fits the scenes it accompanies, creating a classic alienation effect, much in the way the music of Kurt Weill complemented Brecht plays such as *The Threepenny Opera*. For example, the mismatch between the cool jazz that makes up so much of the score and the banal soap opera scenes that make up much of the content does a great deal to create the delicious air of weirdness that the show's creators were obviously shooting for.[15] This effect is enhanced by a postmodern crossing of ontological barriers that often occurs in the music, which quite frequently seems to be coming from the background score, only to turn out to be part of the scene itself. Indeed, Kathryn Kalinak identifies such crossings of music from the nondiegetic to the diegetic level as a key ingredient of *Twin Peaks* (85). Crucial here are the performances of Julee Cruise (a frequent Lynch collaborator who performed a haunting rendition of "Mysteries of Love" for the *Blue Velvet* soundtrack), whose singing is here inserted at the diegetic level by having various characters attend her live performances at the Twin Peaks Road House.[16] Further, while she does not actually mention Brecht, the Brechtian resonances are clear in Kalinak's suggestion that the inappropriate music of *Twin Peaks* "consistently short circuits the flow of affect between the spectator and the screen by sending mixed messages." For Kalinak, the music thus "functions ironically or parodically ... to effect a kind of distantiation" (89).

Twin Peaks, however, lacks the commitment of the socialist Brecht, whose plays are overtly designed as a contribution to a revolutionary overthrow of the capitalist system. Relevant here is Dana Polan's convincing argument that the plays of Bertolt Brecht employ much the same aesthetic strategies as Daffy Duck cartoons but have a far different significance because of their overtly political content. Polan, in particular, concludes that contemporary postmodern culture has no trouble accommodating "formally subversive art," because "as long as such art does not connect its formal subversion to an analysis of social situations, it becomes little more than a further example of the disturbances we go through every day. And a work of art that defeats formal expectations does not lead to protest against a culture that itself deals continually in defeating expectations" (351).

Twin Peaks seems to go out of its way to avoid connecting its formal subversions to an analysis of social situations, opting for a strangeness-for-the-sake-of-strangeness strategy that might be the postmodern equivalent of the nineteenth-century art-for-art's-sake movement. For example, the extensive arrays of doughnuts laid out meticulously on the tables in Sheriff Truman's office might be taken as an attempt to confine a craving for sensual pleasure within a capitalist rage for order and regimentation. Yet the absurd, surreal quality of these arrays conflicts with this rage for order, suggesting a contradiction at the heart of capitalist logic. The superabundant doughnuts might also serve as a sort of consumerist fantasy that simultaneously threatens to undermine itself by demonstrating a sort of waning of affect at the level of taste, in which postmodern consumers of food products require more and more sugar, more and more spice, to be able to taste anything at all. Meanwhile, the sheer number of these doughnuts (though their number tends to decrease as the series proceeds) might potentially be taken as a comment on the excesses of American consumerism in general.

None of these potential subversive readings is very convincing, however, largely because the arrays of doughnuts are laid out like still-life set pieces and seem to have no real function other than visual decoration, except for their contribution to a stereotypical running gag about the fondness of law enforcement officers for doughnuts. Any critique in *Twin Peaks* of consumerism, or of capitalism in general, is decidedly weak. There are actual thematic engagements with capitalism, particularly in the early episodes, in which Ben Horne (in league with his attorney, Leland Palmer) plots to gain control of the Packard Saw Mill so that he can build a golf club and resort (the "Ghostwood" project) on the site. But this motif, especially in Horne's comic attempts to secure investments from Norwegians and Icelanders, is far too silly to be taken seriously. Moreover, any instances of unscrupulous capitalist practices in *Twin Peaks* are attributed either to individual corruption (capitalism isn't bad—Ben is just a bad capitalist) or to metaphysical evil. The capitalist system, with its Reaganite fantasy world of smoothly efficient unregulated free markets, remains unscathed.

Meanwhile, the very multiplicity of the styles and genres that most clearly identifies *Twin Peaks* as postmodern (and that some might see as subversive) also identifies it as structurally consistent with capitalism. For example, while pluralism and dialogism, in Joyce's case, may pose inherent challenges to the monologism of colonialism or (especially) the Catholic Church, they do not necessarily produce preferable alternatives. And they are almost entirely ineffective as fundamental critiques of capitalism, which takes its life's blood from multiplicity, as Eagleton reminds us (*Illusions* 133).

That Eagleton's characterization of the plurality of capitalism could apply equally well to *Twin Peaks* should call into question any view that the series is subversive simply because it is strange. Of course, Eagleton's point is that postmodernism in general is structurally consistent with capitalism and that postmodern plurality poses no fundamental threat to the capitalist order. As he puts it (mentioning Margaret Thatcher, the British Ronald Reagan), "many a business executive is in this sense a spontaneous postmodernist" (133). And, though Eagleton does not mention Jameson here, this point is very much in line with Jameson's view of postmodernism as the cultural logic of late capitalism. Meanwhile, one might make very much the same point about Bakhtin's vision of the inherent plurality of the novel as a mere restatement of the emphasis on multiplicity that lies at the heart of bourgeois ideology. Thus, as Franco Moretti points out, Bakhtin's vision of the dialogic multiplicity of the novel "reproposes in the domain of literary criticism some of the basic tenets of liberal-democratic thought" (151).

Within the terms of my own characterization of the intertwined evolution of postmodernism and television, the entirely innocuous "subversions" of *Twin Peaks* are thoroughly ludic—and thus thoroughly postmodern, pushing the lingering modern elements of the series into the background. While the series appropriates numerous modernist formal techniques and certainly contains a great deal of extremely dark material that might potentially trigger anxiety and discomfort in viewers, these formal experiments and dark images remain almost entirely self-referential and seem designed to produce thrills (as if viewers were getting away with something by being able to see such strange programming on commercial television) more than chills. However, *Twin Peaks* was something of an extreme case, its quick death suggesting that it might have been a bit ahead of its time and thus even more decadent than the capitalist society around it. Even in the 1990s, realism remained the basic premise of American cultural production, while modernism remained a strong aesthetic force. That this was true can be seen in the much greater commercial success of *Northern Exposure* (1990–95), a sort of kinder and gentler (and politically liberal) version of *Twin Peaks* that took its small-town utopianism much more seriously and that, despite numerous self-reflexive, postmodern elements, featured realistic (and loveable) characters that gave viewers a stable footing for identification with the series.

Northern Exposure was similar to *Twin Peaks* in a number of ways, the most obvious of which was its focus on a big-city outsider who comes to a small and remote (in this case, *really* small and remote) northwestern town. In many ways, however, the series that can be compared most fruitfully to *Twin Peaks* is *The X-Files*, which began broadcasting on the fledgling Fox network in the fall of 1993. From the beginning, *The X-Files* resembled *Twin Peaks* in numerous ways, but retained a much greater realism, especially in its characterization, allowing viewers actually to identify with its protagonists, Mulder and Scully. It also retained at least the rudiments of political critique in its vision of shady international conspiracies pulling the strings of global society. However, *The X-Files* still involved strong ludic elements, making it a crucial example of postmodernism in the sense of a historical accumulation of realist, modernist, and postmodernist elements.

5

It's the Libidinal Economy, Stupid: *The X-Files* and the Politics of Postmodern Desire

The X-Files was first broadcast on September 10, 1993, on the fledgling Fox network. The new show was clearly regarded as an experiment, part of the ongoing effort by Fox to find new wrinkles that might help it break the broadcasting hegemony of the big three networks. At that, the experiment did not seem all that promising, especially after the commercial failure of *Twin Peaks*, with which it had so much in common. The show's conception was highly unusual; its creator-producer, Chris Carter, was relatively inexperienced; one of its stars was completely unknown; and the other star was perhaps best known for his role as a transvestite in *Twin Peaks*. Even Fox executives seemed unenthusiastic about *The X-Files*, placing most of their hopes for the upcoming season on another new series, a Western entitled *The Adventures of Brisco County, Jr.*, starring Bruce Campbell, an actor who had gained cult status by starring in the *Evil Dead* cult horror movies. But Fox gave its other new show a chance, airing it in the hour immediately following *Brisco County*, in the hope that it could ride on the coattails of that more promising series. *Brisco County* soon bit the dust, but the seemingly less promising *X-Files* would emerge by the 1994 season as a full-blown hit, then last into the twenty-first century, becoming for many *the* signature American television series of the 1990s.

The X-Files resembles *Twin Peaks* in many ways, though the much greater commercial success of the former can be attributed to a number of significant differences between the two series. For example, *The X-Files* recalls *Twin Peaks* in that it is stylistically self-conscious, establishing a distinctive noir look and often pursuing unusual formal experiments. Thus, some episodes are shot in black and white, while one episode, "Triangle" (6x03; November 22, 1998),[1] is shot in both black and white and wide-screen letterbox format, while employing long continuous

takes in the mode of the Alfred Hitchcock film *Rope* (1948). But the experiments of *The X-Files* are far less radical than those of *Twin Peaks*;
viewers tuning into *The X-Files* are far less likely to be discomfited or dis-
oriented by the mismatch between the look of the series and the way
they expect television to appear. The same might be said for the content,
in that *The X-Files* is far less thoroughly ludic than *Twin Peaks*, employing
plots, characters, and settings that are likely to be registered as much
more serious and realistic than those in *Twin Peaks*.

The basic premise of *The X-Files* is fairly simple. FBI Special Agent
Fox Mulder (David Duchovny) has managed to get himself assigned to
investigate the "X-Files," a collection of unsolved cases involving para-
normal phenomena, especially UFO sightings and alien abductions.
Though Mulder is an Oxford-trained psychologist, his abiding interest in
such phenomena (which seems to have been triggered largely by childhood trauma caused by the disappearance of his sister, Samantha, perhaps by alien abduction) has earned him the nickname "Spooky."
Mulder's odd interests have also led the FBI to assign fledgling agent
Dana Scully (Gillian Anderson) to work with him and to keep an eye on
him. A trained medical doctor with a reputation for dispassionate scientific objectivity, Scully is seen as a counter to Mulder's potential for excess — but also as a way of keeping tabs on him to prevent him from
probing into areas that are better left alone. Indeed, one of the crucial
premises of the series is that many of the cases in the X-Files involve a
vast international conspiracy carried out by The Syndicate, a mysterious
group that includes the participation of officials highly placed in the
United States government. However, other mysterious figures in the
government sometimes lend aid and support to Mulder and Scully, further complicating the picture. As the series proceeds, Scully remains the
voice of conventional reason, but she also begins to grant that Mulder's
theories might have more validity than she first believed, while Mulder
himself experiences occasional bouts of skepticism. In the meantime,
Mulder and Scully become genuine friends as well as professional allies,
their bonding and mutual respect providing one of the key elements of
the series.

The basic *X-Files* premise lends considerable flexibility to the show.
For one thing, Mulder and Scully become engaged in the investigation of
a number of strange phenomena. In the so-called monster-of-the-week
episodes, the two agents battle against werewolves, vampires, mutants,
and other relatively traditional supernatural creatures. Sometimes these
creatures are not even truly supernatural, but are merely particularly bizarre criminals, especially serial killers, adding still more flexibility to the
series. Meanwhile, early on, the series also establishes an arc of sequen-
tially connected episodes involving the complex interrelationship between the alien-invasion and government-conspiracy motifs. These so-
called mythological arc (or "mytharc") episodes are themselves ex-

tremely flexible, and what happens in a given episode is only loosely bound by what has gone before. Thus, these episodes go through a number of twists and turns; for example, The Syndicate sometimes seems to work hand-in-hand with the alien invaders, but at other times seems to be working to attempt to thwart the invasion and intended colonization of earth by extraterrestrials. At still other times, there are hints that the aliens don't exist at all, but are merely being used as a cover-up for the sinister activities of the Syndicate or the U.S. government.[2]

The continuity of these mytharc episodes provides a convenient framework for the evolving relationship between Mulder and Scully. It also seems to have furthered the relationship between the series and its devoted fans, providing an element that had been largely missing in earlier episodic series and entirely missing in anthology series such as *The Twilight Zone* and *The Outer Limits*. However, the use of such ongoing plot arcs had become important to series television in the 1980s with the growth of such sequential series as *Cheers*, *Wiseguy*, and *Twin Peaks*.[3] These mytharc episodes (which, through the 2000–2001 season, comprised a total of 61 out of 182 episodes[4]) are, in fact, the heart of *The X-Files*, producing the bulk of its most provocative ideas and images. For one thing, the general epistemological uncertainty surrounding the investigation into the complexities of the alien invasion-government conspiracy relationship provides one of the most postmodern elements of the show. In addition, the tendency of the mytharc to veer off in unexpected new directions contributes greatly to the lack of closure for which the series is widely known, while the continual suggestion that sinister forces, virtually beyond human understanding, are at work in the world, contributes to a very postmodern sense of difficulty in cognitive mapping.

It was appropriate that *The X-Files* would last into the twenty-first century, because the program serves, in many ways, as a kind of summa of strange TV in the twentieth century. Its science fiction premise takes advantage of the inherent ability of that genre to produce cognitive estrangement, while building upon an established tradition of science fiction television that includes *The Twilight Zone* and *The Prisoner* as two of its crucial founding texts. Meanwhile, the FBI crime investigation motif of *The X-Files* places it in the tradition of postmodernist television that began with *Alfred Hitchcock Presents* and includes *Moonlighting* and *Miami Vice*. By combining the science fiction and crime elements with a strong dose of the supernatural, *The X-Files* also became a direct successor to *Twin Peaks*. And Carter has been particularly open about the way he was influenced, in his conception of *The X-Files*, by the campily strange television movie *The Night Stalker* (1972), along with its sequel, *The Night Strangler* (1973), and a subsequent short-lived series, *Kolchak: The Night Stalker* (20 color hour-long episodes in 1974–75).

In some cases, the relationship between predecessor programs and *The X-Files* is quite direct. For example, *The Night Strangler* features a villain who has developed an elixir that bestows immortality, the only problem being that the elixir must be renewed every twenty-one years and that one of its ingredients is fresh human blood, which must (for some unexplained reason) be extracted from murdered young women. Thus, protagonist Carl Kolchak (Darren McGavin), a newspaper reporter working in Seattle, discovers, while investigating a series of recent murders, that similar series of murders have occurred every twenty-one years, dating back to 1889. In this, *The Night Strangler* directly precedes the very first monster-of-the-week episode of *The X-Files* ("Squeeze," 1x02; September 24, 1993), in which the villain must return every thirty years to extract the livers of human victims for his own immortality. In other cases, the link between *The X-Files* and its predecessors is more general. For example, *The Night Stalker* TV films and series resemble *The X-Files* in the general way in which the protagonist must overcome the resistance of official authority in his attempts to investigate supernatural crimes, a basic similarity that *The X-Files* acknowledges by having McGavin guest star as retired FBI agent Arthur Dales (who had originally, in the 1950s, started the project that ultimately became the X-Files[5]) in such episodes as "Travelers" (5x15; March 29, 1998) and "Agua Mala" (6x14; February 21, 1999).[6] This sort of allusive casting was used to acknowledge another predecessor when Roy Thinnes, who had starred as David Vincent, the lone voice crying out against the alien intruders of *The Invaders* (43 color hour-long episodes in 1967–69), appeared in several episodes of *The X-Files* as the Christ-like good-guy alien, Jeremiah Smith.[7] Finally, numerous members of the cast of *Twin Peaks* (in addition to Duchovny) have appeared in episodes of *The X-Files*.

These nods to predecessors represent only one example of the allusiveness of *The X-Files*.[8] Indeed, one of the principal reasons academic critics have been attracted to the program is its allusiveness, so reminiscent of the classics of modernist literature. Laced with stylistic and thematic references to film, television, and other works of popular culture, the show asks to be seen as a sort of culmination of twentieth-century American popular culture. Meanwhile, *The X-Files* offers academic critics a number of opportunities to talk about it in the same way that they have become accustomed to talking about works of literary modernism and postmodernism. In addition, the show provides opportunities for critics to discuss cultural phenomena that go well beyond the show itself, overcoming the vague uneasiness on the part of many professional scholars that a "mere" television show is not important enough to warrant serious efforts at analysis and interpretation.

That the most important allusions in *The X-Files* tend to be to other television programs can be taken as a sign of the postmodern acceptance of popular culture lauded by critics such as Huyssen. Indeed, *The X-Files* is consistently self-conscious about its own status as a television program—and even about its placement on the Fox network. Mulder, for example, likes to make occasional references to *The Simpsons*, while, in "Nisei" (3x09; November 24, 1995), Mulder acquires a bootleg tape of an alien autopsy that Scully describes as "even hokier than the one they aired on the Fox network." Meanwhile, one entire episode of *The X-Files*—"X-Cops" (7x12; February 20, 2000)—is shot as if it is an episode of the Fox "reality" show, *Cops*. Such moves again identify the series as postmodern, though *The X-Files* also alludes to films and works of literature, again suggesting its role as a kind of cumulative summary of modern American culture. Indeed, the commercial success of *The X-Files*, which far exceeds that of any of its important predecessors, can be attributed, at least in part, to the way in which it combines various elements of its predecessors.

This and other elements of *The X-Files* appear to identify the series as a quintessential example of American postmodernism. Thus, numerous critics have commented on the postmodern nature of the show's paranoid tone, self-conscious intertextuality, unstable epistemology, mixture of genres, and periodic forays into self-parody. Douglas Kellner's "*The X-Files* and the Aesthetics and Politics of Postmodern Pop" is perhaps the most concentrated argument for the postmodernism of *The X-Files*, while many commentators merely take the postmodernism of the series for granted and proceed from there. However, it is also the case that other critics are not so sure. Thus, Jimmie L. Reeves, Mark C. Rodgers, and Michael Epstein note that *The X-Files* displays certain postmodern characteristics, but conclude that, especially in its sincere treatment of its protagonists' search for the truth, the show is ultimately "almost militantly anti-postmodern," making it perhaps "the first truly post-postmodern television show" (34–35). Meanwhile, comparing *The X-Files* with *Twin Peaks* and other "cult" series, Reeves et al. conclude that *The X-Files* "takes a step backward" in a more conventional attempt to attract wide audiences (24).

Such disagreements about the postmodernity of *The X-Files* probably arise more from disagreements about the nature of postmodernism than about the nature of *The X-Files*. However, it is also the case that the series does situate itself within postmodernism in a particularly complex way. Eileen Meehan, for example, argues that the series contains both modernist and postmodernist elements, and in fact gains its principal energies from a tension between the two (126). Indeed, *The X-Files* displays, at one time or another, virtually all of the formal and thematic characteristics of postmodernist television, yet it does retain an earnestness that one might associate more with modernism. However, it is also important to recognize that the series generally presents its material, however strange, within a basically realist matrix.

Such overt appeals to the prior modes of realism and modernism make the aesthetics of *The X-Files* almost nostalgic, though such nostalgic gestures can be taken as a commodification of the past that is itself postmodernist. In any case, such combinations of aesthetic modes help *The X-Files* to display a simultaneous ability to create a sense of cognitive estrangement and to comment critically on the difficulty of cognitive mapping in the postmodern world by showing a nostalgia for earlier times when such mapping was easier. The various conspiracies, unsolved mysteries, and unresolved plots that inform the series suggest a world far too complex for comprehension by individual subjects. At the same time, this complexity does not necessarily constitute a postmodern dismissal of the possibility of understanding the world. In the world of *The X-Files*, uncertainty and complexity generally arise not from the fundamental nature of reality but from the machinations of specific agents (whether they be alien invaders, freakish monsters, or sinister conspirators placed high in the U. S. government) even if the exact nature of these machinations is not always, or even usually, possible to determine.

This motif is part of a larger phenomenon in which *The X-Files* presents a postmodern view of the world while simultaneously straining against and protesting certain characteristics of the postmodern age. The great theme of the show, I think, is desire, and the real question explored by the series is not about alien invasions and human conspiracies, but about whether desire is fulfillable or whether utopia is thinkable in any meaningful way at this point in American history. The science fiction and supernatural aspects of the show clearly address a desire for adventure and romance in the thoroughly routinized environment of late capitalism, a phenomenon also marked by the absolute flood of science fiction and supernatural thrillers that appeared in American theaters in the 1990s. Meanwhile, much of the utopian desire in *The X-Files* can be taken as a specific attempt to overcome the consequences of capitalism in terms of classic Marxist mediatory codes such as commodification and alienation. Here, in particular, one can see the professional activities of Mulder and Scully as a quest for the satisfactions of nonalienated labor, while the obvious romantic tension between the two addresses conventional sexual desire, but in ways that present their relationship as a potential counter to alienation that also helps to anchor both of their identities within the fragmented confusions of the postmodern world. Finally, much of the desire that lies at the heart of *The X-Files* is purely epistemological, and the strenuous attempts of the protagonists to find the truth that may or may not be "out there" can be taken as a fairly direct allegorical equivalent of the striving of the postmodern subject to make sense of the almost hopeless complexities of the contemporary world.

Thomas Frank's argument about the close affinities between consumer capitalism and the counterculture of the 1960s is particularly helpful in situating *The X-Files* with regard to such issues because the political mindset of the series seems to be informed by a basic 1960s-style liberal-ism—as opposed to the Reaganism of *Twin Peaks*.[9] Indeed, much of the appeal of *The X-Files* can be attributed to the way it resonates with the values of its namesake, the so-called Generation X, essentially a Madison Avenue creation designed to link the youth of the 1990s to the youth of the 1960s for marketing purposes (Frank 233–34). *The X-Files*, meanwhile, not only roots its own ideology in the 1960s, but opposes the work of Mulder and Scully to evil forces that have their roots in the 1950s. The program thus directly enacts the rejection of the 1950s by the 1960s that Frank sees as crucial to the evolution of both consumer capitalism and the counterculture. In any case, Frank's suggestion that the 1960s actually extended the penetration of capitalism into every aspect of American life helps to indicate the way in which, from the 1950s to the end of the twen-tieth century, individual lives were controlled more and more firmly by capitalism, rather than the reverse.

In short, the routinization of daily life was, in many ways, even more thorough at the end of the century than it had been in the 1950s, even if it was painted in brighter, shinier, and more varied colors. Meanwhile, the waning of affect discussed by Jameson as a crucial element of the post-modern experience can be related to a commodification and routiniza-tion of desire itself; programs such as *The X-Files*, which seem intended to provoke fear and anxiety in their audiences, are thus attractive not only because they serve as a counter to the routinization of everyday experi-ence, but because they at least help viewers to feel *something*, however packaged and fleeting. One could also argue that the nominal end of the Cold War at the beginning of the 1990s added significantly to this phe-nomenon by removing the only seemingly substantial enemy of global capitalism and thus rendering moot the strong element of romance that had been built into the Cold War vision of heroic battle against an evil empire. Thus, by the 1990s, Americans remained vaguely anxious that sinister forces (generally located in the Third World) were still out there, threatening the comfort and affluence of the American way. Yet, in an-other sense, the real anxiety plaguing American society at the end of the twentieth century was that no such threats were really serious, that there were no more glorious victories to be achieved, no more frontiers to con-quer.

Relevant here is Jameson's argument that postmodernist culture, ex-emplified by cyberpunk science fiction, is informed by a dissolution of older oppositions such as those that allowed groups such as the working class to be firmly positioned as "Other" in the bourgeois imagination. Postmodern thought, however, is characterized by a "weakening if not outright disappearance of just this category of specieslike difference" that forces ever more exotic visions of Otherness, such as the alien or the cy-borg (*Seeds* 152). Bourgeois society, it seems, needs others against which to define itself, even as it finds those others threatening and even terrifying. All those monsters, aliens, and supercharged serial killers that lurk in the shadows of The X-Files address this complicated situation quite directly, and much of the doubleness of the series derives precisely from the doubleness of American desire for safety and comfort, on the one hand, and danger and adventure, on the other. The particular fascination of The X-Files with the motif of government conspiracy (largely derived from memories of Watergate) would seem, perhaps surprisingly, to identify the American government as one of these new exotic Others.[10]

That Mulder and Scully themselves work for the government merely demonstrates the instability of Us vs. Them categories in The X-Files. The particularly postmodern difficulty of maintaining categories of Otherness in the series is perhaps exemplified in the episode "Humbug" (2x20; March 31, 1995), which aired near the end of the second season. This episode, the first of several episodes to have been written by Darin Morgan, introduced an entirely new comic element into the show, but it is a sort of nervous comedy that suggests a basic discomfort with the show's own continual dramatization of Otherness as the site of evil. Mulder, from the beginning, had been wont to lighten the tension with wisecracks, but the series, by and large, had played it straight, treating its far-out subject matter with complete seriousness. "Humbug" was then the first of a number of ludic episodes to employ campy parody to satirize many of the themes pursued seriously in the other episodes. Then again, parody is a central strategy of the series as a whole, much in the way that Bakhtin sees parody as a key strategy through which the novel continually renews itself as a genre. Moreover, Bakhtin sees parody as a productive phenomenon, rather than mere mockery. Thus, by parodying earlier novel forms, novels do not reject the entire tradition of the novel, but engage in productive dialogues with it. Here, "every parody is an intentional dialogized hybrid. Within it, languages and styles actively and mutually illuminate one another" (Dialogic 76).

In particular, the novel is, for Bakhtin, the only genre that can parody itself and still belong to its genre. That is, a parody of a poem is not a poem at all, but a parody of a novel can still be a novel. But the same might be said for the self-parodic tendencies of much postmodern television. Thus, ludic episodes that parody The X-Files are still perfectly representative episodes of the series. In addition, by playing a number of in-games with the show's increasingly loyal audience of insiders, these ludic episodes act to increase the identification of these insiders with the series. After all, "Trust No one" is one of the show's mantras, and devoted fans like to think that they are far too skeptical and sophisticated to be taken in by a mere fiction, even a fiction of which they are devoted fans. Thus, the show's own self-conscious acknowledgement of its fictionality in the ludic episodes of self-parody congratulates these viewers on their sophistication by dropping all pretense that such viewers could ever suspend their disbelief and be taken in entirely — even by their most beloved TV program.

Congratulating viewers on their resistance to manipulation is a strategy that is also well known to advertisers, and any number of successful advertisements, especially on television, have employed this same strategy, as in the classic Isuzu liar ads or the Nike ads in which Michael Jordan repeatedly assured Spike Lee that his Nike shoes were not the key to his remarkable jumping ability.[11] Indeed, *The X-Files* employs this strategy in a number of ways. For example, one could argue that the representation of various conspiracies in the show is attractive (rather than disturbing) to audiences because it congratulates them on being sophisticated enough to know that such conspiracies do exist and that those in high places cannot be trusted. At the same time, to use these conspiracies for entertainment might serve to congratulate at least some viewers on being sophisticated enough not even to try to resist the sinister forces that surround them. As Robert Markley puts it, the conspiracy material exploits "our sense that we are too smart, to cool, to be conned into trying to resist the forces that manipulate us" (77).

As a crucial example of the reflexive ironization of the show's own treatment of the theme of Otherness, "Humbug" is a key *X-Files* episode. It begins with spooky music and a shot of an eerie-looking full moon, as two innocent children frolic at nighttime in a backyard pool, suddenly to be menaced by a strange-looking reptilian humanoid creature that stealthily creeps toward the pool, then dives in. But never fear: the threatening monster is just the boys' dad, Jerald Glazebrook (aka "The Alligator Man"), who is afflicted with a skin condition known as ichthyosis — which accounts for his strange appearance, but also allows him to make a living as a sideshow freak.

Glazebrook's show trailer is emblazoned with the question "Is he man or monster?" His ultimate harmlessness as a "normal" suburban dad then immediately asks us not to jump to conclusions about those who appear different. Meanwhile, this scene occurs in the real-life town of Gibsonton, Florida, which turns out to be the home base of numerous "freaks" such as Glazebrook, most all of whom are perfectly respectable citizens. However, danger does lurk in the town. As "Humbug" proceeds, Glazebrook sends the boys off to bed, then lounges in the pool. Then, just as all appears to be well after all, still another creature, this one unseen, attacks and kills Glazebrook, filling the pool with blood. The manner of Glazebrook's killing, meanwhile, echoes that recorded in numerous cases already recorded in the X-Files, bringing Mulder and Scully onto the scene. The episode thus begins like a typical *X-Files* episode, then suddenly becomes a parody of an *X-Files* episode, then returns once again to the *X-Files* norm, all before the show's distinctive open title sequence even begins.

Such reversals continue throughout the show, which tends radically to challenge the polar opposition between truth and fiction, normal and abnormal, investigative crime drama and campy comedy. Mulder and Scully travel to Gibsonton for the funeral, which is attended by an entourage of the other sideshow freaks who live in the town, then interrupted when one of the locals, Dr. Blockhead (played by Jim Rose, a real-life "body manipulator"), emerges from beneath the ground under the casket and proceeds to pound a metal spike into his chest as an "impromptu tribute" to Glazebrook, whom he did not know personally, but whose work as an escape artist he greatly admired. In this episode, which owes more than a little to Tod Browning's notorious 1932 film, *Freaks*, such bizarre events turn out to be par for the course. Indeed, the most normal inhabitant of the town seems to be Mr. Nutt (Michael Anderson, one of many *Twin Peaks* regulars to appear in *The X-Files*), the diminutive proprietor of Gulf Breeze Trailer Court, where Mulder and Scully rent trailers while staying in the town.

In this context, it is the ultra-normal FBI agents who are the real oddballs, while the difficulty in distinguishing between normal and abnormal in Gibsonton is highlighted when Mulder, noticing Mr. Nutt's small size, jumps to the conclusion that Nutt, too, is a sideshow performer, provoking an angry response on the part of the manager, who reminds Mulder that he is a trained professional with a degree in hotel management, not a freak. Meanwhile, Nutt turns the stereotyping tables by announcing that Mulder's "all-American features, dour demeanor, and unimaginative necktie design" have led him to surmise that Mulder works for the government.

Nutt's helper at the trailer court, however, is a freak indeed. In addition to being a prodigious drinker, Lanny (Vincent Schiavelli) has a partly-formed twin brother growing out of one side of his abdomen. Meanwhile, the strangest of all the locals is not a freak, but a geek, the Conundrum (played by the Enigma, a real-life geek who performs in Rose's sideshow circus), the distinction being that the Conundrum has no congenital abnormalities, but has simply imposed his own. In particular, his entire body is covered with a jigsaw puzzle of tattoos, while his "act" (which seems also to have become a lifestyle) consists of eating anything and everything that comes within his reach, including "live animals, dead animals, rocks, light bulbs, corkscrews, battery cables," and, we are told, "even cranberries." Dr. Blockhead, too, is not a natural freak, but (at least according to his own description) a skilled professional artist, who, after years of concentrated study, is able to perform feats such as incredible escapes and driving spikes into his chest or nails into his nostrils because of his carefully cultivated ability to endure great pain and to control and manipulate his body and its reactions.

In one highly comic, but thought-provoking, scene, the normal-abnormal distinction becomes particularly problematic when Scully and

Lanny confront each other, both wearing partly opened bathrobes. In a comment on the fascination of the difference of the Other, both try to be discreet, but Scully's eyes are irresistibly drawn to the partly exposed "twin" protruding from Lanny's abdomen, while Lanny cannot avoid gazing at the partly exposed twin protuberances coming from Scully's chest. Both quickly avert their eyes, adjusting their robes, but the point has been made.

The episode's title also involves a deconstruction of polar oppositions. "Humbug," in particular, is a reference to the machinations of P. T. Barnum, a founding figure of modern capitalist marketing practices and the most famous predecessor of the present-day employers of the freaks and geeks in Gibsonton. It was, in fact, performers in the Barnum and Bailey Circus who founded the town. Renowned as a promoter who played a bit fast and loose with the truth (and thus also an important predecessor of the entire American advertising industry), Barnum was, among other things, known to have exhibited a creature known as the "Fiji Mermaid," which supposedly had the head and torso of a monkey and the tail of a fish. Hepcat Helm (Gordon Tipple), proprietor of a local museum of oddities, tells Mulder and Scully the story of the mermaid, assuring them that it was really just a dead monkey with a fish's tail sewn on. In fact, the fakery was so obvious that Barnum decided to exhibit it not as a genuine freak of nature, but simply as a hoax, which turned out to draw even larger audiences — much in the way that this campy episode of *The X-Files* only increased its following among television viewers. "That's why Barnum was a genius," Helm explains. "You never know where the truth ends and the humbug begins." Maybe, Helms further speculates, the Fiji Mermaid was real, but Barnum merely marketed it as a fake to draw bigger crowds.

As the episode proceeds, Helm and Nutt are also murdered in a mysterious and gruesome fashion. Mulder and Scully continue their investigation, along with the Gibsonton's Sheriff Hamilton (Wayne Grace), though for a time suspicion falls on Hamilton after Scully discovers that he was once himself a freak billed as Jim-Jim the Dog-Faced Boy. In one crucial scene, Mulder and Scully snoop on the sheriff, secretly watching as he cuts something up with his pocket knife, then buries it in his yard under cover of darkness. After he goes back inside, Mulder and Scully rush to the spot and begin to dig up the object, though Mulder at one point pauses in a moment of guilt. "We're being highly discriminatory here," he tells Scully. "Just because a man was once affected with excessive hairiness, we have no reason to suspect him of aberrant behavior." "It's like assuming guilt based solely on skin color, isn't it?" she replies. They look at each other for a moment, as if to acknowledge that what they are doing is wrong. Then they resume digging. As they reach the object, the sheriff reappears and asks what they are doing. Mulder reaches for the object, saying, "We're exhuming ... your potato." He lifts a piece of a potato from the ground. Scully then tries to give a scientific explanation for their suspicions concerning the sheriff, but Mulder interrupts with the truth: "We found out you used to be a dog-faced boy." The sheriff then explains that burying a slice of potato under a full moon is a folk remedy for the warts he has on his hand, and is able to allay their other suspicions as well.

Chagrined at having jumped hastily to conclusions regarding the sheriff just because he once looked different, Mulder and Scully nevertheless continue their investigation. Suspicion for a time falls on Dr. Blockhead, but it eventually becomes apparent that the real culprit is Leonard, Lanny's partly-formed twin, who apparently has the ability periodically to exit Lanny's body, slithering about on the ground and committing gruesome murders. Mulder and Scully pursue Leonard through a funhouse, including one scene, reminiscent of the famous ending scene of Orson Welles's *The Lady from Shanghai* (1948), in which Scully attempts to shoot Leonard in a hall of mirrors. Here, of course, one cannot distinguish between the real target and his mirror images, just as the distinction between reality and illusion is challenged throughout the episode. The suspect thus escapes, then apparently attacks the Conundrum, who, in one final reversal of roles, responds by eating the attacker. With the suspect having thus disappeared, Sheriff Hamilton finds Scully's identification of the twin as the killer farfetched, mocking her and asking if she's sure it wasn't the Fiji Mermaid. Mulder, accustomed to having his theories scoffed at (including by Scully), then walks by and mumbles, "Now you know how I feel."

In one final scene, Dr. Blockhead and the Conundrum prepare to leave town. Meanwhile, Dr. Blockhead has suggested to Scully that unusual individuals like those inhabiting Gibsonton add a richness to life that will be sorely missed after twenty-first century genetic engineering has imposed a bland uniformity on everyone, extending capitalist routinization to our very DNA. "You see," he says, "I've seen the future, and the future looks just like ... him." He then points to Mulder, who strikes a comically statuesque pose in the distance, apparently trying to look like an ad from *GQ*. With no genetic freaks left, Blockhead concludes, it will be up to self-made freaks like himself and the Conundrum to remind people that all this normality just isn't normal. Then they drive away, with the Conundrum, who is feeling under the weather, explaining that it was "probably something I ate."

Blockhead, in a postmodern celebration of difference, presents the existence of freaks and geeks as a form of escape from mind-numbing conformity and routine, while "Humbug" as a whole takes a thoroughly ludic approach to the general fascination with Otherness that marks the entire series. The most radically Other resident of Gibsonton is the abject Leonard, and he is presented as a dangerous, blood-thirsty killer. Indeed, *The X-Files* as a whole is anything but a 1960s-style celebration of difference. Most of the Others in the series (many of whom come from the Third World) are dangerous and sinister, in the mode of Leonard. Still, the show's projection of the very existence of such Others addresses the desire of audiences to feel that the world is richer and stranger than it might first appear, that there is more to life than working from 9 to 5 in order to be able to consume an endless stream of unneeded commodities.

The "I Want to Believe" UFO poster that adorns Mulder's basement office addresses this same desire to find a richness to life that goes beyond the stultifying routine of the everyday. A more conventional version of this same desire is often dramatized in *The X-Files* through a treatment, unusually extensive for American television, of religious experience. Mulder, who wants so badly to believe in aliens, tends to be skeptical toward organized religion, while Scully, despite her scientific background, is continually portrayed as a reasonably faithful Catholic who remains on the margins of the church but still wants to believe in the validity of its doctrines. Several episodes, in fact, centrally concern the contrast between Scully's faith in science and her desire to believe in the church, as well as that between Mulder's religious skepticism and desire to believe that aliens are conspiring to colonize the earth.

In the early episode "Revelations" (3x11; December 15, 1995), Mulder and Scully investigate a series of murders of supposed "stigmatics," i.e., individuals who display symptoms of the wounds of Christ, apparently as a sign of a special relationship with God. St. Francis of Assisi, for example, was a reported stigmatic, and the phenomenon has an important place in Catholic mythology. It also seems to have gained an increasingly prominent place in the popular imagination at the end of the twentieth century, as evidenced by the release of the feature film, *Stigmata,* in 1999. As this episode proceeds, Scully investigates not only the murders, but her own religious faith, eventually coming to suspect that she has been ordained by God to protect a young stigmatic, Kevin Kryder (Kevin Zegers), from the killer, who turns out to be Simon Gates, a millenarian fanatic, played by none other than Kenneth Welsh, who had played the fanatical Windom Earle in *Twin Peaks.* In one of several attempts of *The X-Files* to cash in on millenarian fascination at the end of the twentieth century, Gates believes that he must kill stigmatics in order to enable the coming of the Apocalypse and the subsequent New Age. Mulder and Scully manage to stop him and to save the boy, who seems, within the context of the episode, to be a genuine stigmatic, despite Mulder's doubts.[12] Indeed, Scully complains in the episode of Mulder's willingness to draw all sorts of wild conclusions whenever he sees a "light in the sky," while remaining unwilling to accept "the possibility of a miracle." "I wait for a miracle every day," replies Mulder, "but what I've seen here has only tested my patience — not my faith."

The millennium motif in "Revelations" never really goes anywhere (except into another Carter-produced series, *Millennium*), just as the millenarian fears that Americans almost seemed to want to feel never really got off the ground, taking their strongest form in the routinized fear of a Y2K computer glitch, rather than genuine apocalyptic terror.[13] The episode ends with Scully attending confession for the first time in six years, her own faith in miracles apparently having been renewed. For Carter, this emphasis on faith made the episode a paradigm of the series as a whole. "To me," he stated in an interview, 'the idea of faith is really the backbone of the entire series — faith in your own beliefs, ideas about the truth, and so it has religious overtones always" (qtd. in Lowry, *Trust* 139). As a rule, *The X-Files* is quite respectful in its treatment of religion, especially of conventional Christian religion. Even cultish religions are often treated rather positively. A favorite motif, for example, involves small-town crimes in which cult members immediately become suspects because of their unusual beliefs — only to be exonerated in the investigations of Mulder and Scully, often turning out to be victims themselves. In "Red Museum" (2x10; December 9, 1994), a cult in rural Wisconsin is suspect because its members are vegetarians in the middle of cattle country. But the cult members, as it turns out, are not only innocent, but are apparently being used as a control group in a series of experiments (it is not clear by whom) to investigate the effect of tainting the local beef with alien DNA.

Other episodes, such as the later "All Souls" (5x17; April 26, 1998), would also center on Scully's Catholicism, but *The X-Files*, in keeping with its general exploration of the mysterious and the extraordinary, has usually involved more exotic forms of religion, often emanating from the dark places of the earth, which in *The X-Files* can mean either the Third World or the rural poor-white South. Thus, "Fresh Bones" (2x15; February 3, 1995) features voodoo, perhaps *the* stereotypical scary Third World religion, while "The Calusari" (2x21; April 14, 1995) followed soon afterward with a treatment of sinister Romanian mystic practices. "Genderbender" (1x13; January 21, 1994) involves an even more exotic cult, this time apparently from outer space. Meanwhile, perhaps the ultimate bizarre treatment of Third World mysticism comes in the late episode "Badlaa" (8x12; January 21, 2001), in which an Indian mystic, spurred by a chemical spill that earlier caused numerous deaths in India, goes on a rampage of murder by anal penetration against Americans. The episode thus dramatizes in a particularly direct way Western fears that the Third World might have access to magical powers that will allow it to seek revenge for the abuses visited upon it by First World science and capitalism.

Poor whites are also scary in *The X-Files,* as in "Theef" (7x14; March 12, 2000), which features a sinister Appalachian conjure man who performs revenge murders via backwoods black magic that is explicitly compared to voodoo. In at least one episode, "Our Town" (2x24; May 12, 1995), southern religiosity is directly linked to abject Third World practices. Here, Mulder and Scully travel to the small town of Dudley, Arkansas, to investigate the disappearance of a federal inspector who had gone there to check out the local chicken processing plant. They then discover that many of the locals are involved in a cannibalism cult that the founder of the processing company (whose slogan is "Good People, Good Food") apparently imported from New Guinea. In "Signs & Wonders" (7x09; January 23, 2000), Mulder and Scully run afoul of deep south snake handlers, not to mention Satan himself, or at least his minion. In "The Field Where I Died" (4x05; November 3, 1996), they encounter a mass suicide cult in Tennessee, while in the early "Miracle Man" (1x17; March 18, 1994) they investigate a Tennessee faith healer. The young healer turns out to be a victim, rather than a villain, but Mulder nevertheless dismisses his powers, concluding that "people are looking hard for miracles, so hard that they make themselves see what they want to see."

Mulder expresses a similar skepticism toward southern-style religion in "3" (November 4, 1994), after a group of vampire killers shows a penchant for leaving biblical allusions at the sites of their crimes, presumably to explain their motivation. "They have the same feeble, literal grasp on the bible as all those big-haired preachers do," Mulder explains. Meanwhile, the representation of poor southern whites in *The X-Files* sometimes goes well beyond their strange religious practices to include other cultural stereotypes, such as degeneracy, inbreeding, and a tendency toward abject violence. The series was thus able, in a politically correct way, to locate radical Otherness right here at home.

The episode that illustrates this motif best is actually entitled "Home" (4x03; October 11, 1996) and is set in the seemingly idyllic small town of Home, Pennsylvania. "Home" begins with a weird, sparsely lit opening scene in which a baby is born and then carried out into the night to be buried alive by a trio of misshapen humanoid figures. Having established this note of abjection, the episode then cuts to the dramatic contrast of kids playing baseball, beginning with a shot of them placing home plate to begin the game. It turns out, however, that they have placed home plate in exactly the spot of the shallow grave from the previous scene, leading to the discovery of the body. Abjection thus intrudes into small-town tranquility, much in the manner of *Twin Peaks*. In this case, though, the infant victim itself is weird, apparently being afflicted with virtually every birth defect known to medical science—or at least every one that can be caused by inbreeding.

The strange nature of the infant and the complete inexperience of the local authorities in dealing with such crimes lead Mulder and Scully to be called in to investigate the case. When they arrive, Scully begins a scientific examination of the burial scene, while Mulder plays with a baseball left by the kids in the earlier scene and dreams of returning to the simple days of childhood and living in such a peaceful small-town community, with "no modems, no faxes, no cell phones." Scully then re-minds Mulder that he would go nuts without a cell phone. She also sar-donically compares Mulder's vision to the legendary TV town of May-berry, at which point the local sheriff arrives and introduces himself, to Mulder's astonishment, as Andy Taylor (Tucker Smallwood).

"Home," in fact, features a number of such self-consciously ironic elements (Taylor's deputy is even named "Barney"), many of which refer specifically to the television tradition of idyllic small towns, of which Mayberry is the paradigm. But the town of Home is no Mayberry, as evidenced not only by the initial burial of the deformed baby, but by the fact that Taylor is black and both Taylor and Barney are brutally killed by the baby's family, the Peacocks, a veritable walking catalog of inbred white trash stereotypes. Of course, "Home" suggests that Mayberry, as presented on *The Andy Griffith Show*, was simply unrealistic. Mayberry, after all, is in the rural South, and the episode's parodic undermining of the television small-town tradition also participates in a denigration of the South that frequently occurs in *The X-Files*. The town of Home may be in the North, but the Peacocks, depicted as paragons of depravity and degeneracy, are originally from the South, and they still refer to the American Civil War as the "War of Northern Aggression." The horrible violence that disrupts the tranquility of Home, Pennsylvania, thus comes about because poor southern whites have invaded the North, bringing their degenerate habits with them.

I would argue, however, that the negative portrayal of poor southern whites in *The X-Files* is really a case more of class than geography and that the show tends to use poor southern whites as a stand-in for the lower classes as a whole.[14] This aspect of the show can thus be read as an attempt to recover the earlier ability, central to naturalism as described by Jameson, to imagine "the proletarian, the lumpen, and their cousins the urban criminal (male) and prostitute (female)" as "secure characters," firmly and irredeemably Other to respectable bourgeois society (*Seeds* 152). Meanwhile, this nostalgic yearning for naturalist antinomies par-ticipates in the general nostalgia for older forms and stabilities that un-derlies the entire conception of *The X-Files*, in which numerous hip, postmodernist gestures are held together by a basically realist aesthetic.

In terms of the portrayal of class in *The X-Files*, it is worth remember-ing that Mulder and Scully are portrayed as thoroughly bourgeois. They are both, in fact, classic bourgeois individuals, portrayed as opponents of conformism and routine, even as they battle against a variety of radically Other foes. The portrayal of Mulder and Scully as rebel FBI agents, bat-tling against their own government bureaucracy almost as much as against aliens, monsters, and criminals, is, in fact, another aspect of the show's exploration of various fantasies of escape from routinization. In terms of its treatment of the professional activities of Mulder and Scully, *The X-Files* recalls the entire tradition of detective fiction, one of the few cultural traditions in American literature that focuses on protagonists who are primarily engaged in the work of doing their jobs. This does not, however, mean that they are "working-class heroes," as Markley suggests (98). Both Mulder and Scully are highly educated individuals whose jobs with the FBI place them comfortably within the middle class, however much they may function as outsiders within the halls of government power. Indeed, this outsider status is part of their charm and part of what makes their jobs something like the fulfillment of fantasies of nonalienated labor—but these are thoroughly bourgeois fantasies, based on an ethic of individualism and creativity that is itself central to the ideology of capitalism. Most of the time, Mulder and Scully operate essentially on their own, with very little supervision. They certainly do not punch time clocks or work according to rigid schedules of any kind. For government employees, in fact, they come amazingly close to being free agents, making their own decisions and performing labor not to generate profits or please management, but simply because they believe what they are doing is valuable and important.

Along these same lines, another fantasy element of the portrayal of work in *The X-Files* is the seeming indifference of the protagonists to material rewards. They work not for pay, but because of devotion to the task at hand. We are repeatedly reminded that the two have forgone numerous opportunities for promotions and raises in salary because of their unconventional professional activities, but neither seems very concerned with this loss. Indeed, both have extremely modest lifestyles (out of all proportion to the salary level of FBI special agents), their devotion to their duty leaving them little time to enjoy anything else, anyway. Mulder, in particular, lives in a meager and sparsely furnished two-room apartment, sleeping on his worn couch because his unfurnished bedroom is used for storage, stacked full of files and other work-related materials (plus a few girlie magazines and adult videos). In the two-part episode "Dreamland" (6x04 and 6x05; November 29 and December 6, 1998), a UFO-induced timewarp causes Mulder to switch bodies with comically sinister government agent Morris Fletcher (Michael McKean). Fletcher, anxious to escape his own life, decides to assume Mulder's identity, but is first forced to redecorate the apartment, which he describes as looking like that of a frat boy.

This lack of concern for material things or upward mobility gives Mulder and Scully a certain apparent freedom from the rat race, but the free agency of Mulder and Scully is in fact rather limited, given their situation as government agents. The two are constantly in hot water with the bureau management, even including Assistant Director Walter Skinner (Mitch Pileggi), whose basic sympathy with their efforts is one of the few things that makes their work possible at all. In one late episode, "Requiem" (7x22; May 21, 2000), the two are admonished by Agent Chesty Short (Andy Umberger), the deputy chief auditor of the FBI, for the extravagant expenses they have incurred in investigating the X-Files. Meanwhile, in the sixth season, Skinner is replaced by a new supervisor, the rather sinister Assistant Director Kersh (James Pickens, Jr.), who is unremittingly hostile to their investigations, perhaps because he suspects that their work might eventually point to his own nefarious activities. And it is fairly common, throughout the course of the series, for Mulder, or Scully, or both, to be temporarily removed from the X-Files project — or from the bureau altogether.

Among other things, these difficulties show just how hard it is to fulfill fantasies of nonalienated labor amid the commodification of late capitalism and the routinization of a government bureaucracy. But, within the fantasy world of *The X-Files*, Mulder and Scully tend eventually to triumph over their bureaucratic antagonists, at least in small and local ways. They are repeatedly reinstated from their various suspensions (though Mulder is again out at the end of season eight due to Duchovny's departure from the series), and Mulder even gets direct vengeance by the end of "Requiem," when he literally punches out the obnoxious auditor (or at least tells Scully he did). Moreover, at the end of season eight, Special Agent John Doggett (Robert Patrick), who becomes Scully's new partner during an extended period when Mulder has been abducted by aliens (and Duchovny has bolted from the series), announces that Kersh himself is now a prime focus of the X-Files investigations.

If Mulder and Scully are thus, to a surprising extent, able to surmount the obstacles put in their path by the routinized government bureaucracy in which they work, it is also the case that their greatest triumphs are related to their ability to break through the impersonal bureaucracy of the FBI to establish a genuine interpersonal connection with each other, despite (or perhaps because of) the continual deferral of their obvious mutual sexual attraction. The romantic connection between Mulder and Scully may recall the tradition of screwball comedy (or *Moonlighting*), but it lacks the mock hostility between the partners that is typical of that tradition. Mulder and Scully pursue a relationship based not on sex but on mutual respect, trust, and caring — a fantasy of precisely the kind of genuine interpersonal connection that is virtually impossible within the context of the radical commodification of everything (including people and relationships) that constitutes late capitalism.[15] Indeed, the relationship between Mulder and Scully serves as a sort of anchor for both their identities, allowing them to maintain a certain amount of subjective integrity in the face of the psychic fragmentation of the postmodern world. In this sense, the Mulder-Scully dynamic is probably more reminiscent of the buddy movie tradition than of screwball comedy, particularly recalling the difference-spanning partnership of Crockett and Tubbs in *Miami Vice*, with ethnic and cultural difference replaced by a difference in gender and epistemological style.[16]

If the Mulder-Scully relationship can thus be taken as a protest against late capitalism, it is also surely the case that the bond between them is hardly an example of proletarian solidarity in the face of an oppressive capitalist system. Rather, it is based on a thoroughly bourgeois fantasy of two against the world — the same fantasy, in fact, on which bourgeois marriage is based. The portrayal of this relationship in the show is also a case of excellent marketing. The continual deferral of consummation helped to create a tension that kept many viewers interested in the show, much along the lines of *Moonlighting*, and it is significant that the two openly acknowledge their romantic attraction (with Scully's cute infant tucked between them) only at the end of the eighth season, by which time Duchovny had vowed that he would not be returning, though he did in fact return to the show (and Mulder, who turns out to be the father of the baby, returns to Scully) for the final episode of the ninth and last season.

The X-Files is quite self-conscious about the extent to which it plays on the deferred consummation of the attraction between Mulder and Scully. Thus, some of the show's most effective comic episodes play on precisely this motif. In "War of the Coprophages" (3x12; January 5, 1996), the series achieves some of its funniest moments via Mulder's open-mouthed reaction to the stunning beauty of entomologist Dr. Bambi Berenbaum (Bobbie Phillips), who clearly serves as a marker of what *The X-Files* might have been had they decided to make Scully a more conventional television sex object, but with courage and brains, somewhat along the lines of Max Guevara (Jessica Alba), the protagonist of *Dark Angel*, a later Fox cyberpunk science fiction series. Also humorous here is Scully's obvious jealousy as Mulder pursues an investigation aided by Dr. Berenbaum, while Scully stays home and performs various domestic chores, such as washing her dog and (being an FBI agent) cleaning her gun. For example, when Mulder explains the situation to Scully via his ever-present cell phone, she has only one question: "Her name is Bambi?"

In both "Small Potatoes" (4x20; April 20, 1997) and the two-part "Dreamland," Mulder in a sense gets to act out his desire for Scully vicariously. In both episodes, impostors assume Mulder's identity and then try (unsuccessfully) to take advantage of his relationship with Scully to get her into bed. This motif again leads to some high comic moments, especially Scully's amazed reactions to Mulder's sudden amorousness. "Hollywood A.D." (7x18; April 30, 2000), one of the pinnacles of *X-Files* self-consciousness, also plays on the Mulder-Scully relationship. Here, Hollywood writer/producer Wayne Federman (played by himself) follows Mulder and Scully on their investigations as part of his research for a movie based on their work. The movie itself then climaxes as "Mulder" (played by Duchovny's real-life friend, Gary Shandling) falls atop "Scully" (played by Duchovny's real-life wife, Tea Leoni) in a coffin after the two do battle in a graveyard with an army of zombies. Scully again has only one question: "Is that your flashlight, Mulder, or are you just happy to be lying on top of me?" It's the latter, and the two start to make love, while the TV Mulder and Scully look on from the front row of a celebrity-studded premiere audience. Unfortunately, the movie Scully quickly interrupts the lovemaking to announce that she is in love with A.D. Skinner, because "he has a bigger flashlight," sending the TV Mulder rushing from the theater in disgust.

If this proliferation of Mulders and Scullys sounds a bit confusing, it is also the case that a postmodern confusion of ontological boundaries is crucial to the entire episode. Thus, when Mulder and Federman observe some weird dancing bones, Federman explains that they must be either "mechanical or c.g.i. [computer generated images]." When Mulder responds that this is real life, not a movie, Federman merely asks, "The difference is?" Meanwhile, the actual case underlying this episode (and the one on which Federman's film will be based) involves forged copies of The Gospel According to Mary Magdalene, the original of which is a fake to begin with. Thus, the forgeries are copies of a nonexistent original, precisely matching Baudrillard's definition of the simulacrum. But this apocryphal gospel (in which Christ finally has sex with Mary Magdalen) is also an internal image of "Hollywood A.D," in which a film is made based on a fictionalization of the activities of Mulder and Scully, who are fictional characters to begin with—creating considerable irony when the film fails accurately to portray what "really" happened.

"Hollywood A.D." makes a joke of the interruption of sexual desire between Mulder and Scully.[17] But, the series often works to establish this desire, as a clear sexual connection is crucial to the effectiveness of the deferral of that connection. In the very early episode "The Jersey Devil" (1x04; October 8, 1993), we observe Scully dating a new suitor, who turns out to be so boring that she has to escape in the middle of a dinner to join Mulder on a case. The implication, presumably, is that she prefers her rewarding work to the banalities of dating, but is also clear that she prefers the company of Mulder to that of the would-be suitor. And, by the time of "Fire" (1x11; December 17, 1993), we see clear sparks of jealousy on the part of Scully when she meets Mulder's old college sweetheart. And, in "Home," which otherwise so thoroughly dismantles the myth of the ideal American TV family, we see the two agents discussing their families, while Mulder gazes tenderly at Scully and tells her (oddly anticipating the end of the eighth season) that this is the first time he has ever thought of her as a mother.

The X-Files, in fact, places a great deal of emphasis on Scully's maternal instincts, apparently seeking to give her a soft, feminine side that would make her scientific objectivity less threatening to television audiences. Thus, it is treated as a great tragedy when she apparently becomes barren as a result of her own alien abduction, while one heart-tugging two-part episode—"Christmas Carol" and "Emily" (5x05 and 5x07; December 7 and 14, 1997) — plays on the possibility that some strange experimental procedure might already have made Scully a mother without her knowledge. (The child, a little girl, dies of complications apparently related to her experimental nature.)

At times, the Mulder-Scully relationship seems to move toward romance — always at Mulder's instigation, and usually in some sort of strange circumstance. In "Triangle," for example, Mulder travels (or maybe dreams that he travels) back in time to the beginning of World War II, where he seeks to prevent the Nazis from developing atomic weapons and thus winning the war.[18] Back in 1939 (in a motif borrowed rather transparently from *The Wizard of Oz*), Mulder meets numerous characters who seem to be doubles of people he had known back in the 1990s. One of them is Scully, whom he passionately kisses, receiving a punch to the jaw in response. Eventually rescued by the "real' Scully and the Lone Gunmen (see below), Mulder awakes in a hospital bed in 1998, with Scully at his side. In "Millennium," meanwhile, Mulder and Scully celebrate the coming of the new millennium with a long kiss at midnight on New Year's Eve, 1999, after which Mulder looks around and notes that "the world didn't end," referring both to the coming of the year 2000 and to the long-anticipated kiss.

Mulder and Scully kiss at other times as well, but usually on the cheek or forehead, and usually when one of them is seriously ill or injured (due to job-related mishaps) and being tended by the other. Such moments are generally the most tender shared by the pair, whose dangerous work quite frequently leaves them in extremely bad condition. This is especially the case with Mulder, who often needs medical attention of a kind that Scully, who is both a trained physician and a nurturing female, is well equipped to provide. Indeed, though much has been made of the unconventional gender typing of the show (with Mulder the intuitive one and Scully the scientific one), the fact is that Mulder and Scully are ultimately very conventional representatives of their respective genders, a fact acknowledged in the show by Mulder's admiration for Scully's maternal instincts and by Scully's comic exasperation at Mulder's various boys-will-be-boys tendencies, such as his competitiveness and his penchant for pornography.

One could read the continual deferral of romance between Mulder and Scully as a progressive attempt to portray intergender relations based on respect and friendship, rather than sexual desire. But one could also read this deferral as a sign that both protagonists are simply too psychically damaged and fragmented to be able to act out their desire — or to feel a desire strong enough to spur them to action. After all, neither of them has a meaningful sexual relationship with anyone else, either. In addition, the Prufrockian fear of Mulder and Scully to commit to a sexual relationship is part of a very 1990s fear of sex that runs throughout the series. Sexual encounters, somewhat in the tradition of horror films, quite often place the participants in considerable danger. In "Avatar" (3x21; April 26, 1996), A. D. Skinner, in the midst of a divorce, has sex with a woman he picks up in a bar, only to awake to find her dead in his bed and himself suspected of her murder. In "Genderbender," a club-hopping alien cult member uses his/her strange powers to seduce and then murder sex partners. Able to change gender at will, the alien thus represents anxieties arising from both the uncertainty of gender roles in the 1990s and a basic fear of sexual contact, especially with strangers.

This fear has to do with making oneself vulnerable (both physically and emotionally) to the Other, and thus recalls such films as *Looking for Mr. Goodbar* (1977). Vampire stories are a classic expression of this fear, and *The X-Files* occasionally draws on this motif, as in the sexually charged vampire tale, "3." In the 1990s, vampirism, with its particularly overt exchange of bodily fluids, also allegorizes the fear of AIDS, a principal source of sexual fear in the decade. Not surprisingly, *The X-Files* (which gains so much of its energy from playing upon contemporary fears and anxieties) draws upon the fear of AIDS quite extensively, if indirectly. In particular, as the mytharc develops, it becomes more and more clear that the plans for alien colonization of the earth involve a central emphasis on infecting the earth's population with an alien virus that will convert them into obedient slaves of the aliens — or perhaps into human-alien hybrids.[19]

Vampire stories function as allegories about not only sex, but capitalism as well, as Marx himself indicated when he wrote, in the first volume of *Capital*, that "capitalism is dead labour, that, vampire-like, only lives by sucking living labour, and lives the more, the more labour it sucks" (Marx and Engels 362–63). Remarking on the resurgence of interest in vampires in the popular culture of the 1990s, Julian Stallabrass builds upon this Marxian metaphor, arguing that "the modern cult of the vampire, which has recently undergone a revival, is not merely a pale reflection of the concern about AIDS but a fitting metaphor for the relation between rich and poor, the former extending their lives and good looks ever further in search of eternal youth, the latter having theirs ever more abbreviated and impoverished, not just in terms of money but also environment and education" (226). From this point of view, it is also worth pointing out that the libidinal economy of *The X-Files* operates very much like consumer capitalism itself, which relies on the creation of a commodified desire for consumption that can never be fulfilled, thus leading to more and more consumption. The lack of closure in the relationship between Mulder and Scully is also perfectly consistent with the show's avoidance of closure in general, a commercially successful gesture that allowed the show to continue year after year, but also a gesture that many have taken as a key sign of the show's postmodernity.

In Mulder's case, the crucial desire underlying *The X-Files* is epistemological. Despite the poster in his office, Mulder doesn't really want to believe: he wants to *know* – the truth about his sister, the truth about aliens, the truth about our government, however unpleasant these truths. Mulder's seeming desire to find out the worst about the world in which he lives indicates the paradoxical appeal of the conspiracy motif in *The X-Files*, in which audiences seem to find pleasure in the notion that sinister forces are involved in massive behind-the-scenes maneuvering to determine the course of events on a global scale. This particular form of paranoia is, I think, a peculiarly postmodern phenomenon, suggesting a yearning for any kind of order in a world so seemingly random and fragmented that it is devoid of meaningful patterns of any kind. A similar idea occurs in the work of Thomas Pynchon, perhaps the postmodernist author best known for his paranoid projection of conspiracies afoot in the world. In *Gravity's Rainbow*, his central work, Pynchon, via his narrator, explains the phenomenon quite clearly and in a way that seems highly relevant to *The X-Files*. "There is," the narrator points out, "something comforting – religious, if you want – about paranoia," which is elsewhere defined in the same text as the "discovery that *everything is connected*" (434, 703). However, the narrator goes on in the first passage to note that there is something particularly frightening in the disorientation of the opposed condition of "anti-paranoia," or the sense that "nothing is connected to anything."

This feeling of disconnectedness would surely make any sort of stable cognitive mapping impossible, perhaps accounting for the pleasure (and even reassurance) that audiences seem to find in the portrayal of sinister conspiracies in *The X-Files*. In any case, the epistemological orientation of *The X-Files*, which is all about finding patterns through inquiry into the unknown, seems to have spilled over into both the popular and the critical reception of the show. Fans of *The X-Files* (widely known as X-Philes) seem to have an unquenchable thirst for knowledge about the show and its participants, which has spawned an entire industry of fan-based commentary, including a panoply of websites and a variety of books providing supplemental information about the show.[20] In addition, *The X-Files* has received more serious critical attention than any other TV series from the 1990s. Articles about the show regularly appear in academic journals, there is a least one published collection of scholarly essays (*"Deny All Knowledge": Reading* The X-Files) about the show, and at least one full-length monograph (Jan Delasara's *PopLit, PopCult, and* The X-Files) has been devoted to the show.

Each episode of *The X-Files* concerns an investigation, usually one in which numerous questions remain unanswered. But the most striking examples of lack of epistemological closure reside in the ongoing story of the mytharc episodes, in which new questions continually arise, old questions often remain unanswered, and even old answers are continually challenged and revised. Much of this open-endedness, reminiscent of the never-ending dialogues of Bakhtin, probably comes from the fact that the show's producers have no absolute idea where the mytharc is going at any particular moment. It is certainly clear, in re-viewing the episodes from the first season, that Carter and the other creative forces behind the series were feeling their way toward what the series would eventually become. Still, by the sixteenth episode, "E.B.E." (1x16; February 18, 1994), many of the standard features of the mytharc were already in place, as Mulder and Scully, aided (and sometimes hampered) by hints provided them by "Deep Throat" (a highly-placed member of the conspiracy, played by Jerry Hardin) learn of a top-secret international pact in which the world's governments have agreed to try to cover up the fact of an alien presence on earth and to exterminate any aliens that might be captured alive. The episode also introduces a group of three paranoid computer-geek conspiracy theorists known as the Lone Gunmen—who would eventually become popular recurring characters on the show and even star in their own self-titled spinoff series in early 2001. Meanwhile, by the end of the first season, the important motif of genetic experiments to produce human-alien hybrids (for whatever reason) had also been introduced, and the mytharc was off and running.

The second season proceeded in much the same manner as the first, with the ever-evolving mytharc episodes playing an increasingly important role, including the crucial two-part sequence, "Duane Barry" (October 14, 1994) and "Ascension" (October 21, 1994), in which Scully herself is apparently kidnapped by aliens, who perform strange experiments on her, place a metal implant in her neck, and eventually cause her to contract cancer and become (seemingly) sterile. As the mytharc proceeds, numerous motifs, such as good and bad aliens, shape-changing alien bounty hunters, and alien corpses that dissolve into green goo, add details that tend to raise more questions than they answer, with periodic plot twists appearing to undermine all that seems to have gone before. Sometimes, for example, there appear to be no aliens after all, the alien invasion itself simply being a government-engineered hoax. At times, meanwhile, the international conspirators, led by the almost Satanic Cigarette-Smoking Man (aka Cancer Man, played by William B. Davis) seem actually to be working to save humanity from the sinister aliens, while at other times the conspirators seem to be working in league with the aliens.[21]

The complexity and confusion of the mytharc episodes can be so extreme that it almost invites parody. Indeed, at least one ludic episode, "Jose Chung's *From Outer Space*" (April 12, 1996), is an open parody of a variety of mytharc elements. Like "Humbug" and the intervening ludic episodes, "Clyde Bruckman's Final Repose" (3x04; October 12, 1995) and "War of the Coprophages," the Jose Chung episode was written by Darin Morgan, making the third season the pinnacle of his contributions to the show.[22] The Chung episode, much discussed and admired by critics, is a veritable collection of in-jokes and reflexive ironies, though it also revolves around a relatively serious core of mytharc motifs, making the episode perhaps the single most representative of the series as a whole.[23] Indeed, the episode well illustrates the relationship between *The X-Files* and postmodernist television and is therefore worth looking at in some detail here.

Like most of the ludic episodes, "Jose Chung" begins very much like a typical *X-Files* episode, as two teenagers, out on a date, drive along a se-cluded road in Klass County, Washington. The car suddenly stalls and the two are dragged from it by two gray aliens,[24] apparently bent on ab-duction, as their flying saucer hovers overheard. Then, however, another saucer appears, beaming down a Ray Harryhausen-style alien monster, which then confronts the startled grays. This alien abduction within an alien abduction announces the complex nesting and layering of levels that will mark the entire episode, while the overtly allusive Harryhausen creature, harking back to the classic science fiction films of the 1950s, suggests the campy self-conscious fictionality of the episode.

The rest of the plot revolves around the apparent abduction of the teenagers and the investigation of this abduction by Mulder and Scully, though most of the subsequent events are presented retrospectively through the optic of popular writer Jose Chung (Charles Nelson Reilly), who is writing a book on the UFO phenomenon and who interviews Scully seeking material for his book. Chung's research on the Klass County incident is made difficult by the fact that different witnesses give widely varying accounts of the same events. This case proves that "truth is as subjective as reality," Chung tells Scully. On the other hand, Chung himself is interested less in determining the truth than in telling an inter-esting—and marketable—story. Scully, a great admirer of Chung's pre-vious books, is willing to provide what information she can, but Mulder, fearing that Chung will merely sensationalize or make a joke of the events and thus discredit serious investigations such as his own, refuses to speak to the author. Of course, this episode of *The X-Files* does pre-cisely what Mulder fears. Indeed, the episode, as its title indicates, in-cludes Chung's book as a reflexive image of itself.[25]

Within this basic framework, "Jose Chung" constructs, in piecemeal fashion, a serious narrative suggesting that the U. S. Air Force is involved in staging fake UFO phenomena in order to draw attention away from other top-secret government programs, but also suggesting there may be real aliens (represented by the Harryhausen creature) who are fed up with the Air Force project. Otherwise, the episode is largely a series of comic fragments, the bits and pieces of which Mulder and Scully, then Chung, try to piece together into a coherent narrative. Much of the hu-mor is aimed at *The X-Files* itself, as well as at the entire UFO phenome-non.[26] For example, one series of fragments involves the discovery of the body of one of the gray aliens, a sort of holy grail of UFO investigators. When Mulder is brought to the scene and sees the body (which seemingly represents precisely the proof of alien life forms that he has sought for so long), he is so surprised that he lets out a girlish scream. The moment is funny in itself, but it is much funnier if one appreciates the in-joke of the reference to the moment in "War of the Coprophages" when Mulder confesses to Scully that, as a child, he once screamed when he suddenly came upon a praying mantis while climbing in a tree. He assures his partner that it wasn't a "girly scream," but Scully isn't so sure.

Such self-referential moments clearly serve to give satisfaction to dedicated viewers. By recognizing such allusions, viewers can feel that, like Mulder and Scully, they are gradually accumulating information that helps them to interpret what they see. Further, such viewers can feel like they belong to a community of insiders, that they are true X-Philes. Other scenes in "Jose Chung" also offer considerable opportunities for viewers to congratulate themselves on their knowledge of the series. For example, after the body is collected, it is taken back to Scully for an autopsy, autopsies being one of her specialties throughout the series. Scully's skills here seem a little questionable, however: she is well into the autopsy before she realizes that the "alien" is really just a human (an Air Force major, in fact) wearing an alien costume. Meanwhile, local teenage slacker Blaine Faulkner (Allan Zinyk) makes a videotape of the autopsy, which is then turned into a television program (parodying the taped alien autopsy that had recently aired on Fox, as well as the one featured in "Nisei" on *The X-Files*). Meanwhile, the program (which omits the minor detail that the alien is a fake) is hosted by The Stupendous Yappi (played by Yaap Broeker, Duchovny's stand-in on the series), a professional psychic who had also been featured in "Clyde Bruckman's Final Repose."

Other television allusions in the episode go beyond the bounds of *The X-Files*, allowing viewers to exercise even wider knowledge. In one scene (or at least in one account of one scene), Mulder consumes large quantities of pie in a local diner, recalling the pie-eating Dale Cooper of *Twin Peaks*, but also thereby recalling Mulder's infamous role as a tranvestite DEA agent on that series. In a more general television allusion, the transparency of the censorship involved in the practice of bleeping is lampooned through the colorful language of a local policeman, Detective Manners (Larry Musser), for whom virtually every other word is "bleep" or a variation thereof.[27]

Moving beyond the world of television, we learn that Chung is the author of *The Caligarian Candidate*, a thriller that deals with mind control and whose title links it to the classic 1962 film, *The Manchurian Candidate*, an important predecessor to the paranoid world view of *The X-Files*, with a dash of *The Cabinet of Dr. Caligari* thrown in for good measure.[28] Other allusions are not to specific texts but to UFO lore in general. For example, some witnesses of the events in Klass County are visited by "men in black," who attempt to intimidate them into testifying that they saw nothing. But this motif, part of UFO lore since the 1950s, is treated in a mode of high camp.[29] The principal man in black is played by Jesse Ventura, an over-the-top performer if there ever was one. In another television allusion, meanwhile, one of the men in black is none other than Alex Trebek, well known host of the *Jeopardy* game show, on which Duchovny once appeared as a celebrity contestant. In addition, Mulder and Scully themselves are described to Chung by Faulkner as men in black, one of whom was "disguised as a woman, but wasn't pulling it off," while the other didn't seem human because "his face was so blank and expressionless." According to Faulkner, Scully threatened him with death if he talked, though Scully vehemently denies the charge when told about it later by Chung. The central target of the men in black, meanwhile, is one Roky Crikenson (William Lucking), a parodic version of the typical UFO "nut." Other references to the world of UFO sightings are more specific (and esoteric), as when the names of several well known UFO researchers. For example, Klass County itself is named for Philip Klass, a prominent UFO debunker (Lowry, *Trust* 196).

The densely allusive texture of "Jose Chung" seems, at first glance, to resemble the allusiveness of such modernist classics as Joyce's *Ulysses*. However, the allusions of *Ulysses*, when pursued, tend to produce dialogic interactions that extend and enrich the meaning of Joyce's text. The allusions in "Jose Chung" are much jokier and tend to add little to the meaning of the text, even though they do form an important part of the experience of viewing the episodes. The various allusions essentially stand as fragments, never connecting up into any sort of coherent whole. In this sense, they resemble the rest of the episode, in which the various bits and pieces never quite fit together. This postmodernist lack of coherence can also be taken as a comment on the famous lack of epistemological closure that underlies the entire series. As Scully tells Chung, finishing their interview, "I know it probably doesn't have the sense of closure that you want, but it has more than some of our other cases."

If the conflicting testimonies of "Jose Chung" are reminiscent of the classic 1951 Akira Kurosawa film *Rashomon*, the problematic epistemology of the *X-Files* episode is actually far more radical (and postmodern) than that of the (modernist) film. In particular, the varying accounts of the crime that occurs in *Rashomon* seem primarily intended as a comment on the way different observers may perceive and report the same events in different (generally self-interested) ways. Much of *The X-Files*, with different observers interpreting events in different ways depending on their particular points of view, seems to operate in the same way.[30] In "Jose Chung," however, there are suggestions that the conflicting testimonies may actually arise from the intersection of alternative, conflicting realities, more in the postmodern mode of Jorge Luis Borges's "The Garden of Forking Paths" than *Rashomon*.[31] Thus, Mulder, late in the episode, pleads with Chung to abandon his book because it cannot possibly do justice to the complexity of these conflicting realities and will therefore not only discredit the work of serious investigators such as himself, but also directly serve the interests of the corporate conglomerate that owns Chung's publisher and the "military-industrial-entertainment complex" of which that conglomerate (like the particularly right-wing one that owns the Fox network) is a part.[32]

Mulder's pleas go unheeded, serving merely to cause Chung to describe his character Reynard Muldrake (transparently based on Mulder) as a "ticking time bomb of insanity." Nevertheless, Mulder's suggestion that there is no single authoritative "true" account of the events in Klass County is one of the surest signs in all of *The X-Files* of a postmodernist vision in which the truth is not, in fact, out there at all. "Jose Chung" also includes some of the most overt charges of conspiracy (and even murder) on the part of the U.S. government and military. However, the contradictory nature of the episode tends to mitigate these charges, while the ludic framework in which all of the episode's contents are presented undermines the most troubling implications of the contents. The episode is thus again representative of the entire series, which consistently pulls back from truly radical positions, ultimately remaining safely within the bounds of mainstream commercial television.

Of course, *The X-Files* could not have achieved its long-term commercial success (which goes well beyond that of any of the other strange programs discussed in this study) without remaining within these bounds. Thus, those who see the series as subversive (because of its dramatization of government conspiracies, its eclectic mix of genres, or its avoidance of traditional closure) are probably underestimating the ease with which the style and content of *The X-Files* can be absorbed by the commercial television context in which it exists.[33] There are, after all, reasons why large corporate sponsors (more worried about demographics than democracy) have long paid handsomely for the right to advertise on this "subversive" series. Ultimately, the logic of *The X-Files* is perfectly attuned to the logic of late consumer capitalism. Thus, the thematization of desire in the series is part of an ongoing tease in which the series assures viewers that "the truth is out there," that all of their questions will be answered if they only keep watching. The series then continually defers the fulfillment of this desire (just as it defers the consummation of the desire of Mulder and Scully for each other), knowing that audiences will not be put off by this deferral, because they are accustomed to a never-ending postponement of the ultimate fulfillment of the desires that are continually produced by the never-ending barrage of consumerist images with which the population of the late capitalist world is bombarded. Indeed, the conformity of *The X-Files* with the logic of consumerism serves as strong confirmation of Jameson's vision of postmodernism as the cultural logic of late capitalism. It also raises the question of whether it is possible for any commercial television series to be truly subversive of late capitalism, a question I will pursue in more detail in the conclusion.

Conclusion:
Television, Capitalism, and Postmodernism

In her book-length study of *The X-Files*, Jan Delasara observes that, in general, "popular television shows and novels project action, ideas and images of reality that are hegemonic in representing the interests of the ruling class and market system. These mass-produced stories are one way those in control convince the rest of us that their truth is our truth and that our cultural situation is natural, incapable of being questioned or changed" (31). This observation is hardly remarkable. What may seem more remarkable, however, is that, though Delasara goes on to admit that "even" *The X-Files* functions in this way to a certain extent, she spends most of her time arguing the subversive potential of the series via its challenge to authoritative truth systems.

This equation of truth with authoritarian repression and of challenges to truth systems with resistance to that repression is central to much of the rhetoric of postmodernist theory. On the other hand, capitalism requires a certain multiplicity and fluidity in order to operate, so that capitalism is already itself opposed to authoritarian and monological versions of truth. Thus, it is difficult to see how a simple challenge to such notions of truth could be a threat to the capitalist order. Here, we might take heed of Terry Eagleton's suggestion that the central tool of capitalist domination is not truth, but "gross deception, whitewash, cover-up, and lying through one's teeth" (*Ideology* 379). Under these circumstances, a dogged insistence on telling the truth, however seemingly old-fashioned, might just be the most subversive stance of all. "In such conditions," Eagleton goes on, "the true facts — concealed, suppressed, distorted — can be in themselves politically explosive. ... The beginning of the good life is to try as far as possible to see the situation as it really is. It is unwise to assume that ambiguity, indeterminacy, undecidability are always subversive strikes against an arrogantly monological certitude" (379–80).

If the notion of challenging authoritarian truth is itself perfectly consistent with the ideology of capitalism, it is also the case that Delasara's assumption that subversion is a positive virtue falls very much in line with capitalist ideology, in which the ever-present drive for innovation requires constant challenges to the existing order (as long as they do not threaten its fundamental structure). Of course, it is not really clear exactly what *The X-Files* is supposed to subvert, though to a large extent its subversive energies, in Delasara's view, seem directed at the bulk of commercial television programming, which presumably reflects the ideology of capitalism in direct and formulaic ways. Indeed, Delasara here is in very much the same position as any number of academic critics of television, who seem to feel that television programming is typically so baleful that specific television programs are worth discussing in detail only if they can be shown to go against the grain of most other television programming. Frankly, I have to some extent followed that same strategy in this book, singling out for detailed discussion four series that seem "strange" when compared with the bulk of commercial television. I have also attempted to explore some of the ways in which these strange series might be subversive, though I have ultimately found that each of the series is gravely lacking in genuine subversive power.

More specifically, the preceding chapters have demonstrated that commercial television series such as *The Twilight Zone, The Prisoner, Twin Peaks,* and *The X-Files* display many of the central characteristics that critics and theorists have associated with postmodernism, including fragmentation of narratives and characters, multiplicity in style and genre, and the collapse of traditional categorical boundaries of all kinds. Commercial television series are inherently fragmented, given the fact that each series is composed of discrete episodes, while each episode is punctuated by commercial interruptions. Indeed, this sort of inherent fragmentation represents one of the clearest ways in which all commercial television series can be regarded as postmodern. The series discussed here display other forms of postmodern fragmentation as well, including the use of discontinuous and inconclusive narrative structures and the portrayal of individual characters as unstable. This sort of fragmentation is closely aligned with the postmodern plurality of these programs, which tend to participate in multiple genres and to display a multiplicity of styles and moods, drawing upon a diverse array of materials from both low and high culture. This collapse of genre boundaries and of the traditional distinction between high and low culture is part of a more general postmodern collapse of boundaries of all kinds, including a challenge to the logic of polar oppositions and a refusal to accept traditional boundaries between different ontological levels, such as the fundamental distinctions between truth and fiction, good and evil, life and death.

Such characteristics seem, at first glance, to be anti-authoritarian and potentially subversive, much in the way that Mikhail Bakhtin's association of similar characteristics with the genre of the novel has often been seen by critics as verification of the subversive potential of the novel. Thus, the postmodern collapse of boundaries and hierarchies in commercial television closely resembles a similar collapse in the novel that, for Bakhtin, is crucial to the carnivalesque impulse that gives that genre much of its dynamic power. Similarly, the postmodern fragmentation of commercial television is reminiscent of Bakhtin's emphasis on the centrifugal nature of the novel as a genre, a characteristic he sees as assuring that the novel will maintain a multiplicity of points of view, rather than subordinating different views to a single authoritative one, in the manner of more centripetal genres, such as poetry. This ability to maintain a multiplicity of points of view, often emanating from different generic traditions, is crucial to the special dialogism that Bakhtin associates with the novel, but it is also similar to the postmodern plurality of commercial television.

Such continuities between the novel and postmodern television suggest that the postmodern era is not a radically new historical departure in which the old rules of the Enlightenment no longer hold sway. It also suggests that postmodernism as an aesthetic and cultural phenomenon does not represent a total rejection of the earlier cultural traditions of the modern, capitalist era, including realism and modernism. My readings of postmodern television series from the 1950s to the end of the twentieth century indicate that, as a rule, new assumptions and techniques that one might describe as postmodern become increasingly important over that period. Nevertheless, basic techniques inherited from modernism and basic assumptions about character and plot inherited from realism remain extremely strong and constitute a sort of baseline against which the newer postmodern techniques define themselves. Indeed, my conclusion is that the cultural phenomenon we typically describe as "postmodernism" is best understood not as a new, independent departure, but as a historical accumulation that incorporates earlier traditions, such as realism and modernism, while also adding new elements that arise in Western culture after World War II.

The status of realism and modernism as ongoing components of postmodernism supports Teresa Ebert's insistence on the continuity of Western history throughout the capitalist era, while also pointing toward Terry Eagleton's argument that the "post" in "postmodern" may simply mean "business as usual, only *more so*" (*Ideology* 381, Eagleton's emphasis). In short, the postmodern era is one in which the capitalist drive for profit, with the requisite class inequalities and consequent phenomena such as alienation, reification, routinization, and commodification, remains the dominant force in Western society, except that each of these phenomena reaches new levels as the capitalist system achieves unprecedented penetration into every aspect of daily life. Television is a key carrier of this new penetration, both because of its unparalleled ability to reach and hold audiences and because of the basic consumerist message that is built into television, especially American commercial television, in which it would not be at all inaccurate to say that the real show is the advertising, while programs such as those discussed in this volume serve merely to attract audiences to the commercials, somewhat in the mode of a carnival barker.

This image, of course, seriously calls into question the notion that commercial television can ever be truly subversive of the capitalist order, however much its style and content might seem to challenge the verities of the Enlightenment. Indeed, capitalism itself constantly challenges its own assumptions in a relentless drive for innovation (and new profits), as long as that innovation does not challenge certain fundamental necessities of the capitalist system, such as the exploitation of the surplus labor of workers in order to produce profits for capitalists. It is not for nothing that Marshall Berman selects Marx's and Engel's description of this drive for change as a sort of unofficial slogan of capitalist modernity. For Marx and Engels,

constant revolutionizing of production, uninterrupted disturbance of all social conditions, everlasting uncertainty and agitation distinguish the bourgeois epoch from all earlier ones. All fixed, fast-frozen relations, with their train of ancient and venerable prejudices and opinions, are swept away, all new-formed ones become antiquated before they can ossify. All that is solid melts into air, all that is holy is profaned, and man is at last compelled to face with sober senses, his real conditions of life, and his relations with his kind. (476)

Marx and Engels go on in the very next passage of *The Communist Manifesto* to argue that this constant demand for innovation includes an expansionist drive that makes eventual capitalist domination of the globe historically inevitable. Thus, the post–World War II era of global capitalist expansion, which theorists such as Fredric Jameson and David Harvey have associated with the growth of postmodernism in the cultural realm, appears not as a dramatic departure from the classic capitalism of Marx's day but as a logical, and even inevitable, extension of that same capitalism.

Looked at through the optic of Marxist critiques of capitalism, the plurality, fragmentation, and boundary crossing of neither television nor the novel are inherently subversive, because they function within a capitalist system in which such characteristics are fundamental to the dominant economic system and the prevailing ideology. Meanwhile, Eagleton's reminders of the inherent multiplicity of capitalist ideology cast considerable doubt on the vision of critics such as Hassan and Hutcheon that postmodernism is somehow subversive of existing authority through the sheer multiplicity of its styles and modes (*Illusions* 133).

Elsewhere, Eagleton also challenges the assumption that postmodern fragmentation, with its inherent challenge to the presumably authoritarian notion of totality, is necessarily subversive. Further, he notes that postmodernist thinkers such as Foucault often appear suspiciously totalizing in their sweeping rejection of totality (*Ideology* 380). Politically, the postmodern celebration of fragmentation (which, in the political realm, translates into the recent popularity of "identity politics") renders very difficult any viable notion of the kind of collective action that could bring about genuine systemic change. Moreover, when one views postmodern fragmentation in the context of Jameson's reminders of the potentially crippling consequences of the psychic fragmentation of the postmodern subject, then the glories of centrifugal plurality seem suspect, indeed.

Again, however, this kind of social and psychic fragmentation is not new to postmodernism or late capitalism but is simply taken to new heights in the postmodern era. After all, such fragmentation (and consequent rejection of the notion of totality) was diagnosed by Georg Lukács as a crucial symptom of the reification of the social world under capitalism as long ago as the 1920s. For Lukács,

the capitalist separation of the producer from the total process of production, the division of the process of labour into parts at the cost of the individual humanity of the worker, the atomization of society into individuals who simply go on producing without rhyme or reason, must all have a profound influence on the thought, the science and the philosophy of capitalism. (*History* 27)

The process of reification removes all traces of the actual activity of production from finished goods, making them appear as finished units without history. In this way, reification contributes to an overall loss in historical sense.

Especially as formulated by Lukács, the process of reification is closely associated with the phenomenon of alienation, the reification of individuals and of social relations producing free-floating subjects with no sense of connection to the world around them or to other subjects. But this process, in which subjects become objects, is a dialectical one, and the other side of this process of distinction and separation is the phenomenon of commodification, which tends to collapse boundaries and to reduce all objects to the same level of interchangeability. Thus, the collapse of categorical boundaries in postmodernism can be seen largely as an aspect of the commodification of everything under capitalism, reaching new heights in the post–World War II era when consumerism takes commodification to unprecedented levels.

In short, postmodern plurality, fragmentation, and boundary crossing can be seen as the consequence of an extension of the basic characteristics of capitalism as described via the traditional Marxist mediatory codes of alienation, reification, and commodification. This being the case, my conclusion that the programs I discuss here are not particularly subversive is not a surprising one. However, given the thorough embeddedness of commercial television within the system of late consumer capitalism, one could also argue that it *is* surprising that series such as those discussed here, which at least raise the question of potential subversion in a serious way, ever got on the air in the first place.

I would certainly argue that the ultimate failure of these television series to be truly subversive does not make them unworthy of serious critical attention. For one thing, the tendency of such strange series to deviate from the televisual norm in ways that seem potentially subversive reminds us that capitalist power is not total, but merely hegemonic, so that effective resistance to that power is still possible. After all, series such as *The Prisoner* and *Twin Peaks* (from the right) and *The Twilight Zone* and *The X-Files* (from the relative left) seem to take ideological positions outside the mainstream of consumer capitalism. In addition, these strange television series are formally and thematically inventive in relation to mainstream television, thus indicating that commercial television need not be as formulaic and predictable as it has generally been seen to be.

However, diversity and innovation are crucial values of consumer capitalism, so it is certainly not the case that such characteristics are, in themselves, subversive of the capitalist order. Indeed, the failure of series such as *The Twilight Zone, The Prisoner, Twin Peaks,* and *The X-Files* to strike telling blows against the capitalist order can serve as a case study in the workings of capitalist hegemony and of the ways in which the celebration of diversity and innovation in much recent critical discourse on postmodernism merely reinscribes the prevailing dominant ideology of consumer capitalism. Thus, the failure of strange television to be truly subversive can teach us important lessons, not only about television and postmodernism, but about criticism as a whole.

The most important of these lessons, I think, is that critics who celebrate subversion, but refuse to speak the unspeakable name of socialism, are providing support for, not resistance to, the prevailing order of late capitalism. Mere criticism of the negative consequences of capitalism cannot strike telling blows against capitalism, because such criticism is already built into capitalism itself. To be truly effective, any critique of capitalism must also contain a utopian dimension that gets beyond the capitalist order and thinks thoughts that are, within the confines of capitalism, unthinkable. Aesthetic innovation, in itself, can certainly never do this. Nor can cries for equality of the races or genders by themselves get beyond capitalism, because oppression on the basis of race and gender, however convenient as a tool of domination, is not crucial to the workings of the capitalist system. Indeed, the only form of oppression or inequality that is crucial to capitalism is that based on class, with the consequent emphasis on competition, class conflict, and antagonistic social relations. Thus, capitalism can be effectively challenged only through a critical focus on the category of class and through a dogged and stubborn pursuit of the idea, however unpopular and seemingly old-fashioned in the postmodern age, that it is fundamentally unjust (and unnecessary) for one group of persons, as a class, to profit from the exploitation of the labor of another group of persons, as a class.

I am, therefore, skeptical of the claims of critics such as John Fiske that commercial television is inherently subversive simply because it has a diverse audience that is likely to respond to it in a variety of ways. Most of these responses can be easily accommodated by the astonishingly flexible and resilient system that is late consumer capitalism. However, I entirely agree with Raymond Williams's warnings against the technological determinism of assuming that all television programming is by its very nature supportive of bourgeois ideology. Certainly, the system of commercial programming, which requires substantial support from major corporate sponsors, is inherently inclined toward support of the existing capitalist order, but other systems, in some as yet unforeseeable future, are clearly possible. Meanwhile, the programs I have discussed in this study show glimmers of an ability to project alternative views of the world even within the current system of commercial programming.

Indeed, I might close by pointing out that even more subversive programming has occasionally appeared, especially on British television, no doubt largely because networks such as the BBC do not depend on commercial sponsors in the way that American commercial networks do. I am thinking especially of the body of work associated with legendary screenwriter and television writer Dennis Potter, who practically made the television miniseries into his own personal art form. Potter's best known and most respected miniseries, *The Singing Detective* (1986), is a profound work of modernist art that directly engages a number of crucial social and political issues, though it does tend, ultimately to become a bit bogged own in personal, essentially psychoanalytic, explanations for the behavior of its protagonist. For that reason, I am more interested here in Potter's later *Lipstick on Your Collar* (1993), a work that has received far less critical praise, partly, I think, because it bears a more genuinely socialist message.

In fact, *Lipstick on Your Collar* is, as Rick Wallach has argued, a "socialist allegory." Like *The Singing Detective*, it often focuses on personal issues; it is, in fact, essentially a love story that focuses on the efforts of two young couples to get together (they eventually do) despite the numerous obstacles they find in their path. But the series is also firmly rooted in historical reality. For one thing, many of the difficulties experienced by the young characters are related to their class positions. For another, all of the action occurs against the backdrop of the 1956 Suez Crisis, depicted here as the moment in history when it became clear that Great Britain had been supplanted by the United States as the major Western global power.

In *Lipstick on Your Collar*, the inability of the British military to deal swiftly and decisively with the crisis (brought about largely by American demands that they proceed cautiously) is seen as a marker of the decline in British power and prestige after World War II. Meanwhile, as the British Empire loses its colonial clout abroad, the consciousnesses of the British characters are colonized by American popular culture, dramatized by the way in which American rock 'n' roll music continually disrupts the narrative in the form of Brechtian intrusions in which the characters enact their fantasies by lip synching to recordings of popular American music of the period (featuring such artists as Elvis Presley and Buddy Holly), often accompanied by elaborate stage productions. Meanwhile, the major official British response to the announced Egyptian nationalization of the Suez Canal consists of little more than American-inspired posturing, as Prime Minister Anthony Eden belts out a blustery warning by lip-synching to Carl Perkins's "Blue Suede Shoes."

To an extent, Glen Creeber is correct when he argues that Potter, in general, "longs to remember England before its 'Cultural Fall', a time before it had been soiled and corrupted by an American mass society which had destroyed Britain's own organic and vibrant folk communities" (196). However, *Lipstick on Your Collar*, which contains Potter's most bitter denunciation of American culture, also contains his least nostalgic vision of the British past. In particular, it depicts the decline of British imperial power absolutely without nostalgia. The series's main marker of traditional British culture, before Americanization, is once-famous organist Harold Atterbow (Roy Hudd), now a crazed and pathetic old pervert, though he is treated with a certain sympathy. Meanwhile, the "grandeur" of the empire is converted to ordure in the riotously carnivalesque production scene in which bureaucrats in the British War Office perform "I See the Moon" in elaborate Orientalist costumes amid a rain of flying shit, punctuated as a camel squirts a stream of liquid dung directly into the camera. Such scenes openly mock the bullshit rhetoric of colonialism, making clear that Potter's vision of American ascendancy does not involve a longing for the grand old days of empire. Rather, Potter depicts the rise of America and concomitant fall of Britain as part of the natural historical flow of capitalism, of the movement of capitalism from its imperial stage to the late stage of global consumerism. The British, by accepting capitalism, have made their historical bed, and now it is time to lie in it.

The love stories of *Lipstick on Your Collar* carry a similar historical (rather than merely personal) message. Through much of the series, naïve Welsh scholarship boy Francis Francis (Giles Thomas) pines for the ravishing Sylvia Berry (Louise Germaine), a young working-class woman who dreams of love but knows what it takes to survive on the street.

Meanwhile, Francis's co-worker, Mick Hopper (Ewan McGregor), is smitten by a beautiful young American woman, Lisa Trekker (Kymberly Huffman).[1] The resulting attempts at courtship are ironized by the way in which the series makes it apparent that the couples are crossed: the earthy and vulgar Hopper is better suited to Sylvia than to Lisa (a dreamy romantic immersed in literary fantasies), while Lisa is better suited to Francis, who is similarly enthralled by romantic literature. In the end, all seems well: Hopper and Sylvia are in love and ready to pursue life together. Francis and Lisa are together as well. The only problem is that Hopper's mind consists almost entirely of fantasies inspired by American rock music; he has essentially no career prospects and does not seem likely to make Sylvia's hard life any easier. Francis, meanwhile, is held in thrall by the Texas oil money of Lisa's American family, wealth that may well serve his aspirations to upward mobility but that is not likely to lead to the life of beauty and poetry that he envisions for himself.

The "proper" matching of the couples at the end of *Lipstick on Your Collar* is thus hardly unequivocally good news for those involved. Then again, few things are unequivocal in the series, which treats both American popular culture and British tradition in a subtle and dialectical fashion. Thus, while the intrusion of American culture into British society is depicted as a movement toward more commercialized and less genuine cultural life, Potter also grants that American culture contains certain demotic aspects that might actually have a positive impact in Britain. As John Baxendale and Chris Pawling note, Potter seems to have been appalled by many aspects of American popular culture but also to have seen this culture as "an important alternative to a class-ridden, establishment English culture" and as "the repository of alternative values to those of a staid, hidebound prewar English establishment" (186). Potter shows this side of his view of American rock music near the end of the final episode of *Lipstick*, when Hopper explains to Sylvia the centrality of the new American rock music to his personal dreams for the future. He is inspired by music that challenges tradition and authority, he tells her, "songs that aren't about your mom and dad, a bit rough, a beat that busts up the old way, the old stodge, the empire, and knowing your place, and excuse me and dressing up and doing what you're told."

Hopper, of course, is not sophisticated enough to realize that the "subversive" attitude of these songs goes only so far. In particular, it stops short of depicting a socialist alternative that might serve as a genuine threat to the capitalist order of which popular music is, in fact, a key part. Indeed, such music keeps subversive impulses contained within a safe sphere, allowing young people like Hopper to feel that they are challenging authority, when in fact they are not—much in the mode of the strange television series discussed in this volume. Thus, the participation of Hopper's stuffy bosses at the War Office in various rock music production numbers in *Lipstick* may be highly comical because so seemingly incongruous, but it also makes the serious point that this music can very easily coexist with the official power that these bosses represent.

Meanwhile, Potter's work, despite its lack of nostalgia for empire, also provides occasional glimpses of a genuine British working-class communal cultural tradition that might provide a real alternative to the advancing order of global capitalism. If there is nostalgia in Potter's work, it is nostalgia not for the glory days of empire but for the days when the working-class culture described by E. P. Thompson in *The Making of the English Working Class* was still a powerful element of British cultural life. But this is a positive and genuinely utopian form of nostalgia that points toward a possible future rather than simply longing for a lost past. In particular, Potter dialectically suggests that the populist energies of American rock music might help to revitalize British working-class culture, even as American popular culture in general has historically been one of the most important sources of the destruction of British working-class cultural traditions.[2]

The "happy" ending of *Lipstick on Your Collar* is similarly dialectical. In some ways, it is a genuinely happy ending, so much so that many critics complained at the time that the series collapsed at its close into complete conventionality. But, given the troubles that still loom for the characters, the ending is largely a burlesque of the happy endings so often found on American television and in American film. Indeed, the series ends (and, for that matter, begins) in the movie theater in which Sylvia works as an usherette, emphasizing the way in which the contrived ending of the series seems derived from film. After a performance in which most of the major characters participate in dancing and lip-synching to Ann Shelton singing "Lay Down Your Arms," the movie screen shows an Egyptian desert scene in which the Union Jack is projected onto the face of the sphinx. Then the projector flickers off and the screen goes dark, the sun having set on the British Empire at last.

This ending also essentially brought to a close the career of Potter, who died in 1994, though the posthumous broadcast of his last works for television, *Karaoke* and *Cold Lazarus*, would not occur until 1995. His works are still occasionally rebroadcast today, and both *The Singing Detective* and *Lipstick on Your Collar* are commercially available on video (even in the United States).[3] It is, in short, possible for such works to be commercially viable, if in a minor key. In any case, such aesthetically sophisticated and politically engaged works stand as evidence of the artistic and critical potential of television, which is, we should remember, still a very young medium, only halfway through its first century. In the next fifty years, the proliferation of cable and satellite networks, combined with the gradual merger of television and the Internet, will create vast new opportunities for access to the cultural distribution system. The time is ripe for cultural critics to do what they can to contribute to the evolution of future television programming by giving close and careful attention to the strengths and weakness of the programming of the past.

Notes

INTRODUCTION

1. For a cogent discussion of Cody's staging of reality as spectacle, see Slotkin (69–79). For a superb dramatization of this phenomenon, see the Robert Altman film *Buffalo Bill and the Indians* (1976).

2. Compare John Caughie's suggestion that television critics tend to focus on audience response rather than the programs themselves, at least partly due to "a lack of fascination with the texts" (54).

3. Postman similarly finds preferable alternatives in the past, particularly in the good old days of the eighteenth-century Enlightenment. His most recent book, *Building a Bridge to the 18th Century*, thus suggests that we might find answers to many of our contemporary problems in the High Enlightenment past.

4. For an argument that the content (and not just the structure) of the program may be more interesting and complex than it appears, see Kellner (*Media Culture* 143–52). Kellner may, however, exaggerate the seriousness of this thoroughly ludic series, which seems to mock in advance any such serious critical treatment via its characterization of Beavis and Butt-head as parodies of critics in their own right.

5. Ann Kaplan's *Rock around the Clock* remains the standard study of MTV as a postmodern cultural phenomenon, though the network (largely through the institution of more "conventional" programs such as *Beavis and Butt-head*) has in the meantime evolved considerably beyond the early all-music-video format addressed by Kaplan. Among other things, programs such as *The Real World* pioneered the end-of-the-century move toward "reality-based" programming.

6. One might also note the outrageous male chauvinism of the protagonists, which seems to mock the frequent critique of MTV (and music videos in general) as misogynist.

7. For a different take on the novel's close contact with contemporary reality, see Davis's *Factual Fictions*, which emphasizes that new printing technologies allowed the emergent novel of the eighteenth century to be produced rapidly

and thus "to embody recentness," much in the mode of journalism (48). This phenomenon continued through the nineteenth century, especially via the serial publication of many novels.

8. At the beginning of the twenty-first century, new recording technologies continue to complicate this opposition. Thus, hard-disk devices such as "TiVo" continually record television broadcasts, allowing viewers to pause or replay even "live" television.

9. My thanks to Peggy Maddox for loaning me these tapes, as well as the tapes of several episodes from earlier seasons.

CHAPTER 1

1. Jameson's approach here is also reminiscent of Theodor Adorno's rather elitist dismissal of works of art that engage in direct dialogue with social reality, arguing that this reality was so saturated by capitalist ideology that the works themselves would thereby be contaminated.

2. For Browne, the supertext includes the entire programming schedule, plus advertising and other "intersticial materials," plus "the relation of the schedule to the structure and economics of the workweek of the general population." Browne also defines a relevant "megatext," which consists of everything that has ever appeared on television (588–89).

3. Both Fiske and Collins cite the work of Horace Newcomb, who may have been the first to apply Bakhtin's theories of dialogism to television multivocality.

4. I survey a number of attempts to characterize postmodernism in the appendix to *Vargas Llosa among the Postmodernists*.

5. One might compare here a similar characterization by Best and Kellner, who see postmodernism as "organized around a family of concepts, shared methodological assumptions, and a general sensibility that attack modern methods and concepts as overly totalizing and reductionistic; that decry utopian and humanistic values as dystopian and dehumanizing; that abandon mechanical and deterministic schemes in favor of new principles of chaos, contingency, spontaneity, and organism; that challenge all beliefs in foundations, absolutes, truth, and objectivity, often to embrace a radical skepticism, relativism, and nihilism; and that subvert boundaries of all kinds" (19).

6. See *The Postmodern Condition* (xxiv).

7. A significant number of bourgeois critics have also doubted the reality of postmodernism as a cultural phenomenon, seeing it instead as the invention of critics and theorists. For example, Gerald Graff suggests that "postmodernism should be seen not as a break with romantic and modernist assumptions but rather as a logical culmination of the premises of these earlier movements" (32). Frank Kermode similarly sees postmodernism as a continuation (in a depleted form) of the impulses of romanticism and modernism. He thus argues that what has been called postmodernism is really just a sort of weakened neo-modernism that cannot really be expected to match the revolutionary achievements of modernism (26).

8. Zavarzadeh and Morton suggest that the "ludic" mode of postmodernism, which they associate largely with French poststructuralism, derives largely from the work of Nietzsche; they argue that the "resistance" mode of postmodernism, on the other hand, traces its genealogy to the work of Marx (107).

9. Here, Huyssen agrees with Matei Calinescu, who argues that postmodernism, especially as conceived by Hassan, is in fact an "extension and diversification of the pre–World-War II avant-garde" (143).

CHAPTER 2

1. For this program scheduling information, I am indebted to Alex McNeil's *Total Television*, which includes, in an invaluable appendix, network primetime schedules for the years 1948–96.

2. Both teleplays were remade into feature films of the same title, both with screenplays by Serling. They thus became two of the earliest examples of that quintessential postmodernist phenomenon, the making of films based on television programming

3. Unless otherwise indicated, all *Twilight Zone* episodes discussed were written by Serling.

4. For accounts of Serling's battles with censors, see Cochran and Engel.

5. See, for example, "Probe 7—Over and Out" (November 29, 1963) and "Third from the Sun" (January 8, 1960), a thematically rich episode that also deals with nuclear fear and McCarthyism.

6. Appropriately, the woman is played by Donna Douglas, later, in a nice bit of serendipitous intertextuality, to achieve fame on *The Beverly Hillbillies* as Ellie Mae Clampett, whose backwoods family regards her as rather plain because she does not match their ideal of rough-hewn hillbilly beauty.

7. The episode "Number Twelve Looks Just Like You" (January 24, 1964, written by John Tomerlin) presents a variation on this same theme, showing a future society in which nineteen-year-olds all undergo surgery to give them a standardized beauty—whether they like it or not.

CHAPTER 3

1. *Society of the Spectacle* is arranged as a series of numbered theses, without pagination.

2. Still another way of distinguishing between Debord and Baudrillard, for Best and Kellner, is to see Debord as working in the tradition of Marx and Baudrillard more in the tradition of Weber (99).

3. Like most simple polar oppositions, this one has its exceptions. Note, for example, the notorious pessimism of the Marxist Theodor Adorno and the exuberance of the French poststructuralists Deleuze and Guattari.

4. This phenomenon in the Soviet Union is well captured in the early fiction of Vassily Aksyonov, including his central novel, *The Burn* (written in 1969–75, though not published until 1980).

5. Thanks to Patrick Ducher, who heads up the French *Prisoner* fan group, le Rôdeur, for information concerning the broadcast and reception of the series in France.

6. On this phenomenon, see J. Fred MacDonald.

7. There are numerous hints that John Drake may, in fact, be the Prisoner, though that connection is never made explicit.

8. Actually, *Danger Man* had an initial run as a half-hour series in 1961 (thus predating the Bond films), then reappeared in an hour-long format in 1965.

9. According to Alexis Kanner, an actor who sometimes appeared on *The Prisoner*, McGoohan was actually offered the part of Bond, but turned it down (qtd. in Rakoff 172).

10. For a fuller discussion of this phenomenon from a different point of view (that nevertheless still attributes the loss of place in America to the impact of consumer capitalism), see Leach, *Country of Exiles*.

11. Identifying Gibson as a central instance, Jameson declares cyberpunk "the supreme *literary* expression if not of postmodernism, then of late capitalism itself" (*Postmodernism* 419). On cyberpunk and postmodernism, see also McCaffery and Bukatman.

12. This sort of reversal underlies the entire episode of "Hammer and Anvil," in which Number Six uses psychological warfare to break Number Two, just as Number Two typically attempts to destabilize the psyche of Number Six.

13. The idea behind this episode was originally conceived by Ian Rakoff, whose *Inside* The Prisoner provides an extended memoir of the development of this episode and of the series as a whole.

14. Compare the *Twilight Zone* episode "The Old Man in the Cave," in which a post-apocalyptic community survives with the guidance of a reclusive "old man," who turns out to be a computer.

15. In *The Post-Utopian Imagination*, I note that, in the long 1950s, American writers such as Norman Mailer and (more subtly) Vladimir Nabokov tended similarly to suggest a basic similarity between the American and Soviet alternatives in the Cold War.

16. The seventeen episodes feature exactly seventeen different Number Twos, though some Number Twos appear in more than one episode and some episodes have more than one Number Two. There are signs, incidentally, that the Number Twos are being replaced precisely because of their failure to break Number Six.

17. *Rabelais and His World* had been Bakhtin's doctoral dissertation, written in the early 1940s, but it is also connected with the French structuralist/poststructuralist explosion of the 1960s. The book, along with much of Bakhtin's other work, had been discovered in the 1960s by Tzvetan Todorov and Julia Kristeva, East European intellectuals who had migrated to Paris, where they became important structuralists, then poststructuralists. Thus, despite his Soviet background, Bakhtin's work can be taken as part of the wave of French thought that broke on the shores of American academia in the late 1960s. *Rabelais and His World*, in fact, was first published in English in the crucial year of 1968, when its portrayal of subversive carnivalesque exuberance could not help but resonate with the temper of the time.

CHAPTER 4

1. Here Connor draws upon the work of Umberto Eco, who sees the self-referentiality of television by the 1980s as important enough to mark an entirely new phase in television history, which he calls "neo-television."

2. Michael Carroll probably overstates the case when he simply states that "*Twin Peaks* is *Blue Velvet* modified for the purpose of network television," but the relationship between the two works is certainly strong (293).

3. Presumably, this look is intended to create a dark atmosphere, in the manner of film noir. However, I would agree with Rosenbaum that the technical artifice of *Twin Peaks* is often "more fancy than artistic," frequently tending toward the "formulaic and goofy" (26–27).

4. Note that the detective story plot of *Blue Velvet* is actuated when Jeffrey Beaumont (MacLachlan) finds a severed human ear while throwing rocks at a glass bottle in a garbage dump.

5. In such endorsements of the local products (especially the cherry pie at the Double R Diner), Cooper sounds more like a commercial spokesman than an FBI agent. Thus, Eagle notes that television commercials should be added to the list of genres that are incorporated into the series (Reeves et al. 179–80).

6. Such choreographed character movements frequently occur in the series, serving as a Brechtian reminder of the artificiality of the action.

7. Of course, the soap opera *Invitation to Love*, presumably emanating from New York or Los Angeles, also represents such an intrusion from the outside world, though, again, this motif is not developed in the series.

8. The town actually seems smaller than this figure would indicate. Indeed, a mock visitors' guide published for fans of the show reveals that the population of the town is actually 5,120.1 (Lynch, Frost, and Wurman 2).

9. *Welcome to Twin Peaks: Access Guide to the Town* (attributed to Lynch, Frost, and Richard Saul Wurman) includes maps as well as other conventional bits of information that one might find in a visitors' guide. The hunger of *Twin Peaks* audiences for information about the show, its setting, and its characters triggered the publication of a number of such guides, including Mark Altman's Twin Peaks *Behind the Scenes*, as well as mock diaries of Laura Palmer (written by Jennifer Lynch, daughter of David Lynch) and Dale Cooper (written by Scott Frost).

10. Jameson specifically discusses *Blue Velvet* as a "call for a return to the fifties" (295).

11. In the final episodes, it is suggested, though never absolutely stated, that Horne is actually Donna's biological father. Paternity, like most other things, is often uncertain in *Twin Peaks*, most notably in the extended comic motif in which Lucy seeks to determine which of her lovers, Andy or the comically pompous Dick Tremayne (Ian Buchanan), is the father of her forthcoming baby.

12. The palindrome motif also resides in the fact that the distorted voices in the Red Room were produced by having the actors speak their lines backward, then playing the resultant recording in reverse.

13. Here see also my earlier argument in *Vargas Llosa among the Postmodernists* that a crucial distinction between modernism and postmodernism is that mod-

ernist works tend to take their own formal techniques seriously as art, while postmodernist works do not, employing technique in a more playful and parodic manner (17).

14. The surrealistic element in Lynch's work has often been noted. Thus, Mark Frost has called Lynch "the first surrealist director," while Lynch himself has argued that "the American public is so surreal, and they understand surrealism" (qtd. in Woods 91).

15. Scott Knicklebine thus describes the music of *Twin Peaks* as being like a "soap opera score on Percodan" (120).

16. At one point, the music intrudes directly into the action as Donna Hayward expresses her affection for James Hurley by lip-synching as Cruise sings "Rockin' Back inside My Heart."

CHAPTER 5

1. Episodes of *The X-Files* are cited according to episode number and date of first broadcast.

2. The show's final episode, at the end of the ninth season, answered a few of these questions, providing a few verifying details concerning the conspiracy arc involving the Syndicate and aliens. However, little real closure was achieved even in this final episode, which leaves Mulder and Scully together but on the run from a sinister U. S. government.

3. On the phenomenon of the sequential series, see Dolan.

4. These numbers are approximate and require judgment, as some episodes are poised on the boundary between different categories.

5. In "Shapes" (1x18; April 1, 1994), Mulder states that J. Edgar Hoover himself started the first X-File in 1946. Dales, however, seems to have been the first to think of the project as an extended one.

6. Dales also appears in "The Unnatural" (6x20; April 25, 1999). However, McGavin suffered a stroke early in the filming of that episode and had to be replaced by M. Emmett Walsh. Incidentally, Carter had originally hoped to cast McGavin in the role of Bill Mulder, Fox Mulder's father. Failing that, he did the next best thing and cast him as the father of the X-Files project. Note that McGavin did, in fact, later appear as Henry Black, the father of protagonist Frank Black (Lance Henriksen), in the *X-Files* knockoff, *Millennium*, which aired on Fox for three seasons from 1996 to 1999.

7. Spurred by the early popularity of *The X-Files*, *The Invaders* returned (on Fox, of course) as a four-hour miniseries in 1995. Thinnes, as Vincent, played a minor role in the miniseries, which focused on the tribulations of Nolan Wood (Scott Bakula), whose former infant autism seems to render him uncontrollable by the implants with which the aliens are gradually taking over the population of the earth.

8. For example, Richard Matheson, who had scripted numerous episodes of *The Twilight Zone*, also wrote the scripts for both *Night Stalker* TV movies. *The X-Files* acknowledges Matheson as an influence in the naming of Senator Richard

Matheson (Raymond J. Barry), who appears in several episodes as a supporter (maybe) of the efforts of Mulder and Scully.

9. In one episode, Mulder openly identifies his three greatest heroes as Willie Mays, Frank Serpico, and 1960s countercultural activist Micah Hoffman (a fictional character obviously based on real figures, such as Abbie Hoffman).

10. For Jameson, however, this motif also represents a perfectly typical postmodernist gesture. Noting that the postmodernist "war on totality" is centrally informed by an attack on targets "it claims to identify with state power," Jameson argues that these attacks are simply more evidence of postmodernist anti-Marxism and that they are really aimed at socialism, at "the now disorganized forces of a repudiation of late capitalism and of a Utopian intent to continue to imagine radical alternatives" (*Seeds* 149).

11. On this phenomenon of meta-advertising (especially prominent in the 1990s), see Rothenberg (211) and Twitchell (*Adcult* 238–42).

12. At the same time, the other supposed stigmatics killed by Gates appear to be fakes.

13. The *X-Files* episode "Millennium" (7x05; November 28, 1999) reprised this motif at the end of the 1990s. It features Frank Black, the protagonist of the *Millennium* series, who comes out of retirement to save Mulder from a gang of millennial zombies.

14. See Jim Goad for a spirited exploration of the way in which "rednecks" and "white trash" have come to be the last remaining American social group against whom it is acceptable to employ sweeping negative stereotypes, making clear that "racism" in America is quite often actually a case of classism.

15. Some have seen this relationship as an effective challenge to conventional gender roles. See Bellon (149). For a broader discussion of gender in *The X-Files*, see Wilcox and Williams.

16. See Ross for a discussion of the way the relationship between Crockett and Tubbs contributes to the development of a postmodern notion of masculinity in which the fragmented identities of the two characters are stabilized through the bond between them.

17. The episode self-consciously lampoons a number of other familiar *X-Files* motifs, as well. For example, Scully is often compared with Jodie Foster's Clarice Starling, the FBI-agent protagonist of *Silence of the Lambs* (1991); Federman, making notes for his film, describes Scully as "Jodie Foster's foster child on a Pay-Less budget."

18. *The X-Files* is, to an extent, haunted by the legacy of World War II, and there are frequent hints in the series that the activities of the Syndicate are rooted in the grisly scientific experiments performed by German and Japanese scientists on human subjects during the war, as well as the attempts of the United States and Soviet Union to continue those experiments using appropriated Japanese and German scientists.

19. Like everything else about the mytharc, the exact nature of this virus seems to change from time to time. In addition, there sometimes appear to be different viruses with different functions. For a fuller discussion of the viral motif in *The X-Files*, see the dissertation by Anne-Marie Thomas.

20. Central to this phenomenon is the series of "official guides" to the show, published by Harper Prism and, at this writing extending to five volumes covering the first six seasons, but there are any number of other examples as well, including such titles as *The Nitpicker's Guide for X-Philes*, *The Unauthorized X-Cyclopedia*, and The X-Files *Book of the Unexplained*.

21. In one of the show's many twists, the Cigarette-Smoking Man is eventually revealed to be Mulder's biological father, though this fact is made unequivocal only late in the ninth and final season.

22. The character of Jose Chung was also featured in a Morgan-scripted ludic episode of the otherwise extremely dark *Millennium* series—"Jose Chung's *Doomsday Defense*."

23. See Meehan for a detailed scene-by-scene account of the episode.

24. "Grays" (with gray skin and bulging heads) represent a classic type of alien in UFO lore. The alien supposedly discovered at Roswell, New Mexico, in 1947 was a prototype.

25. Emphasizing this fact, the manuscript of Chung's book is represented in the episode by a copy of the episode's own script (Lowry, *Trust* 195).

26. For discussions of *The X-Files* within the context of UFO discourse, see Dean and Delasara (177–213).

27. There is also an in-joke here: Kim Manners, who directed "Humbug" and "War of the Coprophages," is apparently notorious for his use of colorful bleeping language (Lowry, *Trust No One* 197).

28. Of course, *The Manchurian Candidate* was also a 1959 novel by Richard Condon, though the film is much better known. Indeed, when *The X-Files* alludes to novels, it almost always alludes to ones that are better known as films, thus making the allusions easier for postmodern audiences to recognized. For example, "The Post-Modern Prometheus" (5x06; November 30, 1997) reworks the Frankenstein story, but in ways that (especially visually) refer much more directly to the classic films than to the Mary Shelley novel.

29. The motif is also treated comically in the 1997 film *Men in Black*, which was a major box-office success, grossing over $250 million in the U.S. In comparison, the gross of the 1998 theatrical film of *The X-Files* was a more modestly successful $83 million.

30. Leslie Jones thus notes that the series "offers a vision of competing, parallel, but equally real worlds; which world you inhabit, which rules you are subject to, is determined by your beliefs" (80).

31. Other *X-Files* episodes deal with the motif of alternative realities, but usually in relatively conservative ways that allow for recuperation of the alternatives as a single "real" reality, opposed by a number of illusions. For example, the alternative versions of events in "Field Trip" (6x21; May 9, 1999) can be attributed to drug-induced hallucinations, while the hallucinations in "How the Ghosts Stole Christmas" (6x08; December 13, 1998) are induced by comically prankish ghosts.

32. That the entertainment industry might be a part of the various conspiracies uncovered by the X-Files project is also suggested in the episode "Wetwired" (3x23; May 10, 1996), which features mind control through television signals, somewhat in the mode of the David Cronenberg film *Videodrome* (1982).

33. In an on-line essay, Charles Taylor calls *The X-Files* "the most subversive show to hit American television since *Wiseguy*," largely for what he sees as its opposition to the legacy of Reaganism. Bellon characterizes the series as "an act of rebellion against authority" (151).

CONCLUSION

1. McGregor, in his first important role, proves that he can do a mean Elvis, perhaps foreshadowing his later development into a major star of American films.

2. In addition, Potter posits at least one icon of American music, Hank Williams, Sr., as a representative of a more genuine, folk-based culture. Thus, Williams's "Your Cheatin' Heart" plays in the background when characters commit various infidelities, though it is not lip-synched and functions strictly as a nondiegetic commentary.

3. Then again, more overtly radical British programming, such as Jim Allen's *Days of Hope* is not available in the U. S.

Works Cited

BOOKS AND ARTICLES

Aksyonov, Vassily. *The Burn.* Trans. Michael Glenny. New York: Vintage, 1985.

Althusser, Louis. *Lenin and Philosophy and Other Essays.* Trans. Ben Brewster. London: Monthly Review P, 1971. 170–83.

Altman, Mark. Twin Peaks *Behind the Scenes: An Unofficial Visitors Guide to* Twin Peaks. Las Vegas: Pioneer Books, 1990.

Anderson, Perry. *The Origins of Postmodernity.* London: Verso, 1998.

Bakhtin, Mikhail M. *The Dialogic Imagination.* Ed. Michael Holquist. Trans. Caryl Emerson and Michael Holquist. Austin: U of Texas P, 1981.

———. *Problems of Dostoevsky's Poetics.* Trans. Caryl Emerson. Minneapolis: U of Minnesota P, 1984.

———. *Rabelais and His World.* Trans. Helene Iswolsky. Bloomington: Indiana UP, 1984.

———. *Speech Genres and Other Late Essays.* Trans. Vern W. McGee. Ed. Caryl Emerson and Michael Holquist. Austin, U of Texas P, 1986.

Balzac, Honoré de. *Lost Illusions.* 1837–1843. Trans. Herbert J. Hunt. New York: Penguin, 1971.

Barnouw, Erik. *Tube of Plenty: The Evolution of American Television.* 2nd ed. New York: Oxford UP, 1990.

Baudrillard, Jean. *Selected Writings.* Ed. Mark Poster. Stanford, CA: Stanford UP, 1988.

Baxendale, John, and Chris Pawling. *Narrating the Thirties: A Decade in the Making, 1930 to the Present.* New York: St. Martin's, 1996.

Bellon, Joe. "The Strange Discourse of *The X-Files*: What It Is, What It Does, and What Is at Stake." *Critical Studies in Mass Communication* 16 (1999): 136–54.

Benjamin, Walter. *Illuminations.* Trans. Harry Zohn. Ed. Hannah Arendt. New York: Harcourt, Brace and World, 1955.

Berman, Marshall. *All That Is Solid Melts into Air: The Experience of Modernity.* New York: Simon and Schuster, 1982.

Bernstein, Michael André. *Bitter Carnival: Ressentiment and the Abject Hero.* Princeton, NJ: Princeton UP, 1992.

Best, Steven, and Douglas Kellner. *The Postmodern Turn.* New York: Guilford P, 1997.

Booker, M. Keith. *The Dystopian Impulse in Modern Literature: Fiction as Social Criticism.* Westport, CT: Greenwood P, 1994.

———. *Flann O'Brien, Bakhtin, and Menippean Satire.* Syracuse, NY: Syracuse UP, 1995.

———. *Monsters, Mushroom Clouds, and the Cold War: American Science Fiction and the Roots of Postmodernism, 1946–1964.* Westport, CT: Greenwood P, 2001.

———. *The Post-Utopian Imagination: American Culture in the Long 1950s.* Westport, CT: Greenwood P, 2002.

———. *Vargas Llosa among the Postmodernists.* Gainesville, UP of Florida, 1994.

Borges, Jorge Luis. "The Garden of Forking Paths." *Ficciones.* Ed. Anthony Kerrigan. New York: Grove, 1962. 89–101.

Brecht, Bertolt. *The Threepenny Opera.* 1928. Trans. Desmond Vesey and Eric Bentley. New York: Grove Weidenfeld, 1960.

Browne, Nick. "The Political Economy of the Television (Super)Text." *Television: The Critical View.* Ed. Horace Newcomb. 4th ed. New York: Oxford UP, 1976. 585–99.

Bukatman, Scott. *Terminal Identity: The Virtual Subject in Postmodern Science Fiction.* Durham, NC: Duke UP, 1993.

Buxton, David. *From* The Avengers *to* Miami Vice*: Form and Ideology in Television Series.*   Manchester: Manchester UP, 1990.

Calinescu, Matei. *Five Faces of Modernity.* Durham, NC: Duke UP, 1987.

Callinicos, Alex. *Against Postmodernism: A Marxist Critique.* New York: St. Martin's, 1989.

Carrazé, Alain, and Hélène Oswald. *The Prisoner: A Televisionary Masterpiece.* Trans. Christine Donougher. London: Virgin Publishing, 1995.

Carrión, María. "*Twin Peaks* and the Circular Ruins of Fiction: Figuring (Out) the Acts of Reading." *Film/Literature Quarterly* 21.4 (1993): 240–47.

Carroll, Michael. "Agent Cooper's Errand in the Wilderness: *Twin Peaks* and American Mythology." *Film/Literature Quarterly* 21.4 (1993): 287–95.

Caughie, John. "Playing at Being American: Games and Tactics." *Logics of Television: Essays in Cultural Criticism.* Bloomington: Indiana UP, 1990. 44–58.

Cochran, David. *America Noir: Underground Writers and Filmmakers of the Postwar Era.* Washington, DC: Smithsonian Institution P, 2000.

Collins, Jim. *Uncommon Cultures: Popular Culture and Post-Modernism.* New York: Routledge, 1989.

Condon, Richard. *The Manchurian Candidate.* New York: Random House, 1959.

Connor, Steven. *Postmodernist Culture: An Introduction to Theories of the Contemporary.* 2nd ed. Oxford: Blackwell, 1997.

Corber, Robert J. *In the Name of National Security: Hitchcock, Homophobia, and the Political Construction of Gender in Postwar America.* Durham, NC: Duke UP, 1993.

Creeber, Glen. *Dennis Potter: Between Two Worlds.* London: Macmillan, 1998.

Davis, Lennard J. *Factual Fictions: Origins of the English Novel.* New York: Columbia UP, 1983.

———. *Resisting Novels: Ideology and Fiction.* New York: Methuen, 1987.

Dean, Jodi. "The Truth Is Out There: Aliens and the Fugitivity of Postmodern Truth." *Camera Obscura* 40–41 (May 1997): 43–76.

Debord, Guy. *Society of the Spectacle*. 1967. Trans. anon. Detroit: Black and Red, 1983.

Delasara, Jan. *PopLit, PopCult and* The X-Files: *A Critical Exploration*. Jefferson, NC: MacFarland, 2000.

Deleuze, Gilles, and Félix Guattari. *Anti-Oedipus: Capitalism and Schizophrenia*. 1972. Trans. Robert Hurley, Mark Seem, and Helen R. Lane. Minneapolis: U of Minnesota P, 1983.

Denzin, Norman. "*Blue Velvet*: Postmodern Contradictions." *Theory, Culture and Society* 5.2–3 (1988): 461–73.

Dixon, Wheeler Winston. "*The Invisible Man, Secret Agent*, and *The Prisoner*: Three British Teleseries of the 1950s and 1960s." *Classic Images* 282 (December 1998): C-8–C-9.

Dolan, Marc. "The Peaks and Valleys of Serial Creativity: What Happened to/on *Twin Peaks*." *Full of Secrets: Critical Approaches to* Twin Peaks. Ed. David Lavery. Detroit: Wayne State UP, 1995.

Durante, Christian. "We Are Living in the Village." Carrazé and Oswald 20–22.

Eagleton, Terry. *The Ideology of the Aesthetic*. Oxford: Basil Blackwell, 1990.

———. *The Illusions of Postmodernism*. Oxford: Blackwell, 1996.

———. *Walter Benjamin: Towards a Revolutionary Criticism*. London: Verso, 1981.

Ebert, Teresa L. *Ludic Feminism and After: Postmodernism, Desire, and Labor in Late Capitalism*. Ann Arbor: U of Michigan P, 1996.

Eco, Umberto. "A Guide to the Neo-Television of the 1980s." *Framework* 25 (1984): 18–25.

Engel, Joel. *Rod Serling: The Dreams and Nightmares of Life in the Twilight* Zone. Chicago: Contemporary Books, 1989.

Farrand, Phil. *The Nitpicker's Guide for X-Philes*. New York: Dell, 1997.

Fiske, John. *Television Culture*. London: Routledge, 1999.

Flaubert, Gustave. *Madame Bovary*. 1857. Trans. Paul De Man. New York: Norton, 1965.

Foster, Hal. "Postmodernism: A Preface." *The Anti-Aesthetic: Essays on Postmodern Culture*. Ed. Hal Foster. Port Townsend, WA: Bay P, 1983. ix–xvi.

Foucault, Michel. *Discipline and Punish: The Birth of the Prison*. Trans. Alan Sheridan. New York: Vintage-Random House, 1979.

———. *Madness and Civilization*. Trans. Richard Howard. New York: Vintage, 1973.

Frank, Thomas. *The Conquest of Cool: Business Culture, Counterculture, and the Rise of Hip Consumerism*. Chicago: U of Chicago P, 1997.

Frost, Scott. *The Autobiography of F.B.I. Special Agent, Dale Cooper: My Life, My Tapes*. New York: Pocket Books-Simon and Schuster, 1991.

Fukuyama, Francis. *The End of History and the Last Man*. New York: Free P, 1992.

Gibson, William. *Mona Lisa Overdrive*. New York: Bantam Books, 1988.

Gitlin, Todd. *Inside Prime Time*. Berkeley: U of California P, 2000.

Goad, Jim. *The Redneck Manifesto: How Hillbillies, Hicks, and White Trash Became America's Scapegoats*. New York: Simon and Schuster, 1997.

Goldman, Jane. The X-Files *Book of the Unexplained*. Vol. 1. New York: Harper-Prism, 1996.

Graff, Gerald. *Literature Against Itself: Literary Ideas in Modern Society*. Chicago: U of Chicago P, 1979.

Gramsci, Antonio. *Selections from the Prison Notebooks*. Ed. Quintin Hoare and Geoffrey Nowell Smith. New York: International, 1971.

Habermas, Jürgen. "Modernity — An Incomplete Project." *The Anti-Aesthetic: Essays on Postmodern Culture*. Ed. Hal Foster. Port Townsend, WA: Bay P, 1983. 3–15.

Halberstam, David. *The Fifties*. New York: Villard, 1993.

Harvey, David. *The Condition of Postmodernity: An Enquiry into the Origins of Cultural Change*. Cambridge, MA: Blackwell, 1990.

Hassan, Ihab. "POSTmodernISM." *New Literary History* 3 (1971): 5–30.

Hatfield, James, and George "Doc" Burt. *The Unauthorized X-Cyclopedia: The Definitive Reference Guide to* The X-Files. New York: MJF Books, 1997.

Hendler, Glenn. "Channel Surfing: Postmodernism on Television." *Postmodern Times: A Critical Guide to the Contemporary*. Ed. Thomas Carmichael and Alison Lee. Dekalb: Northern Illinois UP. 173–98.

Holquist, Michael. "Whodunit and Other Questions: Metaphysical Detective Stories in Post-War Fiction." *New Literary History* 3 (1971): 135–56.

Horkheimer, Max, and Theodor W. Adorno. *Dialectic of Enlightenment*. Trans. John Cumming. New York: Seabury P, 1972.

Huskey, Melinda. "*Twin Peaks:* Rewriting the Sensation Novel." *Film/Literature Quarterly* 21.4 (1993): 248–54.

Hutcheon, Linda. *A Poetics of Postmodernism: History, Theory, Fiction*. New York: Routledge, 1988.

———. *The Politics of Postmodernism*. New York: Routledge, 1989.

Huxley, Aldous. *Brave New World*. 1932. New York: Harperperennial, 1998.

Huyssen, Andreas. *After the Great Divide: Modernism, Mass Culture, Postmodernism*. Bloomington: Indiana UP, 1986.

Jameson, Fredric. *The Political Unconscious: Narrative as a Socially Symbolic Act*. Ithaca, NY: Cornell UP, 1981.

———. *Postmodernism, or, The Cultural Logic of Late Capitalism*. Durham, NC: Duke UP, 1991.

———. "Postmodernism and Consumer Society." *The Anti-Aesthetic: Essays on Postmodern Culture*. Ed. Hal Foster. Port Townsend, WA: Bay P, 1983. 111–25.

———. *The Seeds of Time*. New York: Columbia UP, 1994.

———. *Signatures of the Visible*. New York: Routledge, 1992.

Johnson, Samuel. *Essays from the* Rambler, Adventurer, *and* Idler. Ed. W. J. Bate. New Haven, CT: Yale UP, 1968.

Jones, Leslie. "'Last Week We Had an Omen': The Mythological *X-Files*." Lavery, Hague, and Cartwright 77–98.

Joyce, James. *Ulysses: The Corrected Text*. 1922. Ed. Hans Walter Gabler with Wolfhard Steppe and Claus Melchior. New York: Random House, 1986.

Kafka, Franz. *The Castle*. 1926. Trans. Willa and Edwin Muir. New York: Schocken, 1988.

Kalinak, Kathryn. "'Disturbing the Guests with this Racket': Music and *Twin Peaks*." Lavery 82–92.

Kaplan, E. Ann. *Rocking around the Clock: Music Television, Postmodernism, and Consumer Culture*. New York: Methuen, 1987.

Kellner, Douglas. *Media Culture: Cultural Studies, Identities and Politics between the Modern and the Postmodern*. London: Routledge, 1995.

———. *Television and the Crisis of Democracy*. Boulder, CO: Westview P, 1990.

———. *"The X-Files* and the Aesthetics and Politics of Postmodern Pop." *Journal of Aesthetics and Art Criticism* 57.2 (1999): 161–75.

Kermode, Frank. *Continuities*. New York: Random House, 1968.

Knickelbine, Scott. *Welcome to Twin Peaks: A Complete Guide to Who's Who & What's What*. Lincolnwood, IL: Publications International, 1990.

Kristeva, Julia. "Word, Dialogue, and Novel." *Desire in Language: A Semiotic Apparoch to Literature and Art*. Trans. Thomas Gora, Alice Jardine, and Leon S. Roudiez. New York: Columbia UP, 1980. 64–91.

Lasch, Christopher. *The Minimal Self*. New York: Norton, 1984.

Lavery, David, ed. *Full of Secrets: Critical Approaches to* Twin Peaks. Detroit: Wayne State UP, 1995.

Lavery, David, Angela Hague, and Marla Cartwright, eds. *"Deny All Knowledge": Reading* The X-Files. Syracuse, NY: Syracuse UP, 1996.

Leach, William. *Country of Exiles: The Destruction of Place in American Life*. New York: Pantheon, 1999.

Ledwon, Lenora. *"Twin Peaks* and the Television Gothic." *Film/Literature Quarterly* 21.4 (1993): 260–70.

Lowry, Brian. *The Truth Is Out There: The Official Guide to* The X-Files. Vol. 1. New York: HarperPrism, 1995.

———. *Trust No One: The Official Third Season Guide to* The X-Files. New York: HarperPrism, 1996.

Lukács, Georg. *History and Class Consciousness: Studies in Marxist Dialectics*. Trans. Rodney Livingstone. Cambridge, MA: MIT P, 1971.

———. *Studies in European Realism*. Trans. anon. New York: Grosset and Dunlap, 1964.

Lynch, David, Mark Frost, and Richard Saul Wurman. *Welcome to Twin Peaks: Access Guide to the Town*. New York: Pocket Books-Simon and Schuster, 1991.

Lynch, Jennifer. *The Secret Diary of Laura Palmer*. New York: Pocket Books-Simon and Schuster, 1990.

Lyotard, Jean-François. *The Postmodern Condition: A Report on Knowledge*. Trans. Geoff Bennington and Brian Massumi. Minneapolis: U of Minnesota P, 1984.

MacDonald, J. Fred. *Television and the Red Menace: The Video Road to Vietnam*. New York: Praeger, 1985.

Macherey, Pierre. *A Theory of Literary Production*. Trans. Geoffrey Wall. London: Routledge and Kegan Paul, 1978.

Mandel, Ernest. *Late Capitalism*. Trans. Joris De Bres. London: NLB, 1975.

Markley, Robert. "Alien Assassinations: *The X-Files* and the Paranoid Structure of History." *Camera Obscura* 40–41 (May 1997): 77–104.

Marx, Karl, and Friedrich Engels. *The Marx-Engels Reader*. Ed. Robert C. Tucker. New York: W. W. Norton, 1978.

McCaffery, Larry, ed. *Storming the Reality Studio: A Casebook of Cyberpunk and Postmodern Fiction*. Durham, NC: Duke UP, 1991.

McHale, Brian. *Constructing Postmodernism*. London: Routledge, 1992.

———. *Postmodernist Fiction*. New York: Methuen, 1987.

McKendrick, Neil, John Brewer, and J. H. Plumb. *The Birth of a Consumer Society: The Commercialization of Eighteenth-Century England.* Bloomington: Indiana UP, 1982.

McNeil, Alex. *Total Television: The Comprehensive Guide to Programming from 1948 to the Present.* 4th ed. New York: Penguin, 1996.

Meehan, Eileen. "Not Your Parents' FBI: *The X-Files* and 'Jose Chung's From Outer Space.'" *The Postmodern Presence: Readings on Postmodernism in American Culture and Society.* Ed. Arthur Asa Berger. Walnut Creek, CA: AltaMira P, 1998. 125–56.

Meisler, Andy. *I Want to Believe: The Official Guide to* The X-Files. Vol. 3. New York: HarperPrism, 1998.

———. *Resist or Serve: The Official Guide to* The X-Files. Vol. 4. New York: HarperPrism, 1999.

———. *The End and the Beginning: The Official Guide to* The X-Files. Vol. 5. New York: HarperPrism, 2000.

Miller, Mark Crispin. "Big Brother Is You, Watching." *Boxed In: The Culture of TV.* Evanston, IL: Northwestern UP, 1988. 309–35.

———. "Deride and Conquer." *Watching Television: A Pantheon Guide to Popular Culture.* Ed. Todd Gitlin. New York: Pantheon, 1986. 183–246.

Moretti, Franco. *The Way of the World: The Bildungsroman in European Culture.* London: Verso, 1987.

Morson, Gary Saul, and Caryl Emerson. *Mikhail Bakhtin: Creation of a Prosaics.* Stanford, CA: Stanford UP, 1990.

Newcomb, Horace. "On the Dialogic Aspects of Mass Communication." *Critical Studies in Mass Communication* 1 (March 1984): 34–50.

O'Brien, Flann. *At Swim-Two-Birds.* 1939. New York: New American Library, 1976.

Orwell, George. *Nineteen Eighty-four.* 1949. New York: New American Library, 1961.

Polan, Dana. "Daffy Duck and Bertolt Brecht: Towards a Politics of Self-Reflexive Cinema?" *American Media and Mass Culture: Left Perspectives.* Ed. Donald Lazere. Berkeley: U of California P, 1987. 345–56.

Pollard, Scott. "Cooper, Details, and the Patriotic Mission of *Twin Peaks.*" *Film/Literature Quarterly* 21.4 (1993): 296–304.

Postman, Neil. *Amusing Ourselves to Death: Public Discourse in the Age of Show Business.* New York: Penguin, 1986.

———. *Building a Bridge to the 18th Century: How the Past Can Improve Our Future.* New York: Knopf, 1999.

Pynchon, Thomas. *Gravity's Rainbow.* 1973. New York: Penguin, 1987.

Rakoff, Ian. *Inside* The Prisoner: *Radical Television and Film in the 1960s.* London: Batsford, 1998.

Reeves, Jimmie L., et al. "Postmodernism and Television: Speaking of *Twin Peaks.*" Lavery 173–95.

Reeves, Jimmie L., Mark C. Rodgers, and Michael Epstein. "Rewriting Popularity: The Cult *Files.*" Lavery, Hague, and Cartwright 22–35.

Robbe-Grillet, Alain. *The Erasers.* Trans. Richard Howard. New York: Grove, 1964.

Rosenbaum, Jonathan. "Bad Ideas: The Art and Politics of *Twin Peaks.*" Lavery 22–29.

Ross, Andrew. "*Miami Vice*: Selling In." *Communication* 9 (1987): 305–34.

Rothenberg, Randall. *Where the Suckers Moon: The Life and Death of an Advertising Campaign.* New York: Vintage-Random House, 1995.

Schatz, Thomas. *The Genius of the System: Hollywood Filmmaking in the Studio Era.* New York: Henry Holt, 1996.

Sklar, Robert. *Movie-Made America: A Cultural History of American Movies.* New York: Vintage-Random House, 1994.

Slotkin, Richard. *Gunfighter Nation: The Myth of the Frontier in Twentieth-Century America.* 1992. Norman: U of Oklahoma P, 1998.

Spanos, William V. "The Detective and the Boundary: Some Notes on the Postmodern Literary Imagination." *boundary2* 1 (1972): 147–68.

———. "Postmodern Literature and Its Occasion: Retrieving the Preterite Middle." *Repetitions: The Postmodern Occasion in Literature and Culture.* Baton Rouge: Louisiana State UP, 1987. 189–276.

Stallabrass, Julian. *Gargantua: Manufactured Mass Culture.* London: Verso, 1996.

Stallybrass, Peter, and Allon White. *The Politics and Poetics of Transgression.* Ithaca, NY: Cornell UP, 1986.

Stam, Robert. *Subversive Pleasures: Bakhtin, Cultural Criticism, and Film.* Baltimore: Johns Hopkins UP, 1989.

Stevenson, Diane. "Family Romance, Family Violence, and the Fantastic in *Twin Peaks.*" Lavery 70–81.

Sturcken, Frank. *Live Television: The Golden Age of 1946–1958 in New York.* Jefferson, NC: McFarland, 1990.

Taylor, Charles. "Truth Decay: Sleuths after Reagan." http://www.bgsu.edu/ckile/popc290/truth/decay.html.

Thomas, Anne-Marie. "It Came from Outer Space: The Virus, Cultural Anxiety, and Speculative Fiction." Diss. Louisiana State U, 2002.

Thompson, E. P. *The Making of the English Working Class.* 1963. New York: Vintage-Random House, 1966.

Todorov, Tzvetan. *The Fantastic: A Structural Approach to a Literary Genre.* Trans. Richard Howard. Ithaca, NY: Cornell UP, 1977.

———. *Mikhail Bakhtin: The Dialogical Principle.* Trans. Wlad Godzich. Minneapolis: U of Minnesota P, 1985.

Twitchell, James. *Adcult USA.* New York: Columbia UP, 1996.

———. *Carnival Culture: The Trashing of Taste in America.* New York: Columbia UP, 1992.

Vargas Llosa, Mario. *Who Killed Palomino Molero?* 1986. Trans. Alfred McAdam. New York: Macmillan, 1988.

Wallace, David Foster. *A Supposedly Fun Thing I'll Never Do Again: Essays and Arguments.* Boston: Little Brown, 1997.

Wallach, Rick. "Socialist Allegory in Dennis Potter's *Lipstick on Your Collar.*" *The Passion of Dennis Potter: International Collected Essays.* Ed. Vernon W. Gras and John R. Cook. New York: St. Martin's, 2000. 41–51.

Watt, Ian. *The Rise of the Novel.* Berkeley: U of California P, 1957.

Weber, Max. *The Protestant Ethic and the Spirit of Capitalism.* 1904–1905. Trans. Talcott Parsons. 1930. London: Routledge, 1995.

Wilcox, Rhonda, and J. P. Williams. "'What Do You Think?'" Lavery, Hague, and Cartwright 99–120.

Williams, Raymond. *Marxism and Literature*. New York: Oxford UP, 1977.

———. *Television: Technology and Cultural Form*. 1974. New York: Schocken, 1975.

Woods, Paul A. *Weirdsville USA: The Obsessive Universe of David Lynch*. London: Plexus, 2000.

Zamyatin, Yevgeny. *We*. Trans. Mirra Ginsberg. New York: Avon, 1983.

Zavarzadeh, Mas'ud, and Donald Morton. *Theory, (Post)Modernity, Opposition: An "Other" Introduction to Literary and Cultural Theory*. Washington, D.C.: Maisonneuve P, 1991.

Zicree, Marc Scott. *The Twilight Zone Companion*. 2nd ed. Los Angeles: Silman-James P, 1992.

FILMS

Aladdin. Dir. Ron Clements and John Mukser. Disney, 1992.

The Amazing Colossal Man. Dir. Bert I. Gordon. American International, 1957.

The Attack of the 50 Foot Woman. Dir. Nathan Juran. Allied Artists, 1958.

The Birds. Dir. Alfred Hitchcock. Universal, 1963.

Blue Velvet. Dir. David Lynch. De Laurentiis, 1986.

Body and Soul. Dir. Robert Rossen. Enterprise, 1947.

Buffalo Bill and the Indians, or, Sitting Bull's History Lesson. Dir. Robert Altman. Dino de Laurentiis, 1976.

The Cabinet of Dr. Caligari. Dir. Robert Wiene. Decla-Bioscope, 1919.

Champion. Dir. Mark Robson. Stanley Kramer, 1949.

Detour. Dir. Edgar G. Ulmer. PRC, 1945.

Doctor No. Dir. Terence Young, United Artists, 1962.

Eraserhead. Dir. David Lynch. David Lynch, 1976.

Evil Dead. Dir. Sam Raimi. New Line Cinema, 1982.

Fire Walk with Me. Dir. David Lynch. New Line Cinema, 1992.

A Fistful of Dollars. Dir. Sergio Leone. United Artists, 1964.

Forbidden Planet. Dir. Fred M. Wilcox. MGM, 1956.

Freaks. Dir. Tod Browning. MGM, 1932.

The Hitch-Hiker. Dir. Ida Lupino. RKO, 1953.

The Incredible Shrinking Man. Dir. Jack Arnold. Universal International, 1957.

Invasion of the Body Snatchers. Dir. Don Siegel. Allied Artists, 1956.

It Came from Outer Space. Dir. Jack Arnold. Columbia, 1953.

It's a Wonderful Life. Dir. Frank Capra. RKO, 1946.

The Lady from Shanghai. Dir. Orson Welles. Columbia, 1948.

Looking for Mr. Goodbar. Dir. Ricahrd Brooks. Paramount, 1977.

The Manchurian Candidate. Dir. John Frankenheimer, United Artists, 1962.

Men in Black. Dir. Barry Sonnenfeld. Columbia, 1997.

Mullholland Drive. Dir. David Lynch. Universal, 2001.

Murder, My Sweet. Dir. Edward Dmytryk. RKO, 1944.

The Night Stalker. Dir. John Llewellyn Moxey. American Broadcasting Company, 1972.

The Night Strangler. Dir. Dan Curtis. American Broadcasting Company, 1973.

North by Northwest, Dir. Alfred Hitchcock. MGM, 1959.

Patterns. Dir. Fielder Cook. United Artists, 1956.

Psycho. Dir. Alfred Hitchcock. Paramount, 1960.

The Purple Rose of Cairo. Dir. Woody Allen. Orion, 1984.

Rashomon. Dir. Akira Kurosawa. RKO, 1951.

Requiem for a Heavyweight. Dir. Ralph Nelson. Columbia, 1962.

Rope. Dir. Alfred Hitchcock. Universal, 1948.

The Set Up. Dir. Robert Wise. RKO, 1949.

Seven Days in May. Dir. John Frankenheimer. Seven Arts, 1964.

Silence of the Lambs. Dir. Jonathan Demme. Orion, 1991.

Snow White and the Seven Dwarfs. Dir. David Hand. Disney, 1937.

Stigmata. Dir. Rupert Wainwright. MGM, 1999.

Sunset Boulevard. Dir. Billy Wilder. Paramount, 1950.

Vertigo. Dir. Alfred Hitchcock. Paramount, 1958.

Videodrome. Dir. David Cronenberg. Filmplan International, 1982.

Wild at Heart. Dir. David Lynch. Propaganda, 1990.

Will Success Spoil Rock Hunter? Dir. Frank Tashlin. Twentieth Century Fox, 1957.

The Wizard of Oz. Dir. Victor Fleming. MGM, 1939.

The Wrong Man. Dir. Alfred Hitchcock. Warner, 1957.

The X-Files: Fight the Future. Dir. Rob Bowman. Fox, 1998.

You Only Live Twice. Dir. Lewis Gilbert. United Artists, 1967.

TELEVISION SERIES

The A-Team. NBC, 1983–87.

The Adventures of Ozzie and Harriet. ABC, 1952–66.

Alfred Hitchcock Presents/The Alfred Hitchcock Hour. CBS, 1955–60, 1962–64. NBC, 1960–62, 1964–65.

All in the Family. CBS, 1971–78.

The Andy Griffith Show. CBS, 1960–68.

The Avengers. ABC, 1966–69. (Britain, 1961–69).

Batman. CBS, 1968–70.

Beavis and Butt-head. MTV, 1993–97.

The Beverly Hillbillies. CBS, 1962–71.

Cold Lazarus. BBC, 1995.

Cops. Fox, 1989–.

Dallas. CBS, 1978–91.

Dark Angel. Fox, 2000–.

The Dukes of Hazzard. CBS, 1979–85.

Dynasty. ABC, 1981–89.

Fernwood 2-Night. Syndicated, 1977.

The Flintstones. ABC, 1960–66.

Forever Fernwood. Syndicated, 1977–78.

The Honeymooners. CBS, 1952–59, 1961–70, embedded in *The Jackie Gleason Show.*

Howard Stern. E!, 1994–.

I Love Lucy. CBS, 1951–57. (Continued as *The Lucy-Desi Comedy Hour,* 1957–60).

I Spy. NBC, 1965–68.

The Invaders. ABC, 1967–68.

It's News to Me. CBS, 1951–54.

Jeopardy! NBC, 1964–75. Syndicated, 1984–.

Karaoke. BBC, 1995.

Kolchak: The Night Stalker. ABC, 1974–75.

Kraft Television Theater. NBC, 1947–58. ABC, 1953–55.

The Larry Sanders Show. HBO, 1992–.

Late Night with David Letterman. NBC, 1982–93.

The Late Show with David Letterman. CBS, 1993–.

Leave It to Beaver. CBS, 1957–1958. ABC, 1958–63.

Lights Out. NBC, 1949–52.

Lipstick on Your Collar. BBC, 1993.

The Lone Gunmen. Fox, 2001.

The Man from U.N.C.L.E. NBC, 1964–68.

Married ...With Children. Fox, 1987–97.

Mary Hartman, Mary Hartman. Syndicated, 1976–77.

Miami Vice. NBC, 1984–89.

Millennium. Fox, 1996–99.

Mission: Impossible. CBS, 1966–73.

Moonlighting. ABC, 1985–89.

Northern Exposure. CBS, 1990–95.

The Outer Limits. ABC, 1963–65.

Playhouse 90. CBS, 1956–60.

The Prisoner. CBS, 1968–69. (Britain, 1967–68).

Saturday Night Live. NBC, 1975–.

Secret Agent. CBS, 1965–66. (Britain, 1961, 1965–66, as *Danger Man*).

Seinfeld. NBC, 1990–98.

The Simpsons. Fox, 1990–.

The Singing Detective. BBC, 1986.

Soap. ABC, 1977–81.

The Sopranos. HBO, 1999–.

South Park. Comedy Central, 1997–.

Star Trek. NBC, 1966–69.

Talent Scouts. CBS, 1948–58, 1960, 1962–63, 1965–66.

Three's Company. ABC, 1977–84.

The Twilight Zone. CBS, 1959–64.

Twin Peaks. ABC, 1990–91.

The X-Files. Fox, 1993–2002.

Index

About the Author

M. KEITH BOOKER is Professor of English at the University of Kansas. He is the author of numerous articles and books on modern literature and literary theory, including *Dystopian Literature: A Theory and Research Guide* (1994), *The Modern British Novel of the Left* (1998), *The Modern American Novel of the Left* (1999), *Film and the American Left* (1999), *Ulysses, Capitalism, and Colonialism* (2000), *Monsters, Mushroom Clouds, and the Cold War* (2001), and *The Post-Utopian Imagination* (2002), all available from Greenwood Press.